VERTIGO

Vertigo
THE TEMPTATION OF IDENTITY

Andrea Cavalletti

TRANSLATED BY MAX MATUKHIN
FOREWORD BY DANIEL HELLER-ROAZEN

FORDHAM UNIVERSITY PRESS   NEW YORK   2022

This book was originally published in Italian as Andrea Cavalletti, *Vertigine: La tentazione dell'identità*, Copyright © 2019 Bollati Boringhieri.

The translation of this work has been funded by SEPS
SEGRETARIATO EUROPEO PER LE PUBBLICAZIONI SCIENTIFICHE

Via Val d'Aposa 7 - 40123 Bologna - Italy

seps@seps.it - www.seps.it

Copyright © 2022 Fordham University Press

All rights reserved. No part of this publication may be reproduced, stored in a retrieval system, or transmitted in any form or by any means—electronic, mechanical, photocopy, recording, or any other—except for brief quotations in printed reviews, without the prior permission of the publisher.

Fordham University Press has no responsibility for the persistence or accuracy of URLs for external or third-party Internet websites referred to in this publication and does not guarantee that any content on such websites is, or will remain, accurate or appropriate.

Fordham University Press also publishes its books in a variety of electronic formats. Some content that appears in print may not be available in electronic books.

Visit us online at www.fordhampress.com.

Library of Congress Cataloging-in-Publication Data available online at https://catalog.loc.gov.

Printed in the United States of America

24 23 22   5 4 3 2 1

First edition

Contents

FOREWORD BY DANIEL HELLER-ROAZEN vii

Incipit 1

1 Vertigo Effect 3
2 We Are Not Here 34
3 Habit, Mask 79
4 A Singular Rapture 106
5 Chasm 113
6 Surface 130

Explicit 147

NOTES 151

BIBLIOGRAPHY 177

INDEX 197

Foreword

A book of philosophy titled *Vertigo* arouses various expectations in a reader. Such a work might be a study of Hitchcock's 1958 film, an exploration of the incapacitating or intoxicating perception of "whirling motion," as dictionaries define the state, or an account of the significance of the film, or the ailment, for thinking. Anyone who reads Andrea Cavalletti's book will find that it constitutes a unique contribution to each of these subjects. But it is also more, being the witness to a critical and theoretical project of a range, force, and eloquence that defy easy comparison. This is the fourth of Cavalletti's books, which have been translated from Italian into several languages and are now in English at last beginning to receive the attention they deserve.

A word on the order and aims of Cavalletti's published work may be instructive. Cavalletti's first book, *La città biopolitica: Mitologie della sicurezza* (The biopolitical city: Mythologies of security, 2005) is an inquiry into the "relations between space and power" which explores the principles and presuppositions of urban studies, reconstructing the history of the distinctions between people and population, politics and police, from Hobbes to Ratzel, Genovesi, Schmitt, Deleuze, and Foucault.[1] Cavalletti's second monograph, *Classe* (2009), published in English as *Class* in 2019, constitutes a tightly focused yet consequential reading of a single, elliptical note to Benjamin's famous essay, "The Work of Art in the Age of Its Mechanical Reproducibility." Cavalletti approaches Benjamin's position by rereading his many sources, from Marx to Le Bon, Sorel to Lukács, even as he attends to Benjamin's successors, before reaching the contemporary moment, when "New Orleans is under water, and the National Guard marches against the enraged crowds." What is at issue at each step are the unprecedented "possibilities of connection" that are released when, in solidarity, the proletariat's "apparently compact mass . . . begins to loosen."[2] Cavalletti's subsequent book, *Suggestione: Potenza e limiti del fascino politico* (Suggestion: Power and limits of political fascination, 2011), takes its bearings from modern literature, rather than the social sciences or philosophy, while going further with the archeological projects conducted in *La città biopolitica* and *Classe*. Here the guiding thread is Thomas Mann's novella, "Mario and the Magician," which Cavalletti reads as an allegory of modern biopower, defined as "an immense spectacle of suggestion."[3]

Vertigo (2019) articulates a further step in Cavalletti's analysis of the subjective dimensions of technologies of power. It offers an exemplary illustration of the potential that an artwork can hold for thinking. In Cavalletti's *Vertigo*, a classic of Hollywood cinema functions as the point of departure for an exceptionally stimulating account of the "collaboration of security and violence" in "the modern meaning of politics."

Borrowing a geometrical figure from the famous opening credits of Hitchcock's film, one might say that the itinerary of Cavalletti's book is that of a curve emanating from a point, around which it continues to wind, even as it grows wider and wider, gaining an ever greater perspective on its source. The inception is the film's "most famous scene": a nocturnal chase and fall. "In the dark, a pair of hands grasps a ladder rung as a man hurriedly climbs up. Fleeing along the roofs of San Francisco, he jumps from a cornice, grabs onto some roof tiles, and continues his night-time escape, scaling a steep gable. Two men follow in his footsteps, in hot pursuit: the first, a policeman in uniform, is already on his heels and begins to shoot. The other, in plain clothes, jumps but misses a foothold and slips. Miraculously, he manages to hang onto a drainpipe and turns his gaze where he shouldn't, downward: all of a sudden he sees the chasm grow, the walls of the buildings grow taller as the street dividing them below seems to grow closer instead of receding, as if he were already falling."

In what one might call its first turn, the book revolves around the specifically cinematic invention that sustains this first moment of properly vertiginous perception. It is the ingenious filmic "mechanism" that Hitchcock devised to render the perceptual distortion of John Ferguson's overwhelming dizziness. Dolly and zoom are used simultaneously, while being set against each other, such that, even as the camera retreats in reality from the object, the lens appears to draw ever nearer to it. "Movement" and "countermovement," in other words, are combined, transposing to the film medium the "whirling movement" to which Flaubert had subjected an astonished Frédéric Moreau in one of the most memorable scenes of *Sentimental Education*. In Cavalletti's words: "The countermovement of the zoom does not simply impede a point or an object in the distance from receding, fleeing in perspective (while the dolly recedes), just as it does not merely limit itself, conversely, to bringing a distant object or surface (the ground) closer. Instead, it brings the very background of the visual toward which the object is falling closer while at the same time constraining it, via a sort of optical friction, to be subject to the effect of the tracking shot, which makes it precipitate. That which falls (along with the background) is thus the very center of the vision: the 'here' is dragged downward, while space as such barges into one's consciousness."

With a subsequent turn, the book draws the reader from the art of cinema into the domain of writing—and writing of several kinds. *Vertigo* appears as the cinematic revision not only of Boileau-Narcejac's 1954 novel, *Among the Dead*, of which it is an adaptation, but also as a response to a distinguished series of modern literary attempts—from Montaigne to Baudelaire, Rimbaud, and Poe—to probe the causes and effects of the peculiar intoxication incited by spinning movements. Yet Cavalletti also leads the reader further. *Vertigo* revisits early medical attempts to define the effects of "whirling motions," attempts that soon reveal themselves to be inextricably linked to philosophical ideas and theories.

A key role in this arc of the book's spiral is played by a treatise by Marcus Herz, an eighteenth-century physician known today largely as the friend of Lessing, Mendelssohn, and Kant. Cavalletti provocatively sets Herz's 1786 essay on vertigo (*Versuch über den Schwindel*) in proximity to the Kantian system of cognition. Beginning from the supposition that every individual consciousness possesses "a certain speed," Herz argues that a change in the timing of representation can be the immediate cause of a profound troubling of mental activity. If the velocity of representations diminishes or grows with respect to the usual average rate, then, as Jan Purkinje writes, presenting Herz's position, "the individual becomes confused concerning the very identity of his own self and the duration of his activity in real time, since the long or short moment is measurable only via the intensity of the transition from one representation to the next." With Herz, vertigo appears, in short, as a "temporal disorder"; but it is one that concerns less the time of objects than that of their representation. Evoking the Kantian terms that Herz knew well, Cavalletti draws a bold conclusion that the eighteenth-century author did not dare to formulate. Vertigo is for Herz nothing less than "a true affliction or impurity of the transcendental."

Continuously winding around what seems at first glance a mere disorder of perception, Cavalletti soon reaches a level of even greater philosophical consequence. The whirligig also draws transcendental phenomenology into its orbit, as space and time consciousness come to be moved—if not shaken—by its motions. Husserl's redoubtable attempt to surpass the solipsistic impasse first faced by Descartes appears as a sustained, if ever shifting, project to overcome a question that is dizzying in its very structure: how to set the transcendental ego in relation to an "alter ego," immediately and in its primary constitution, without the self's losing itself in the "analogical" structure of its relation to another consciousness. Cavalletti closely follows Husserl, from *Ideas* through *Cartesian Meditations* to the *Crisis of the European Sciences*, from his major published works to his diverse, posthumously edited writings, in his longstanding efforts to define the "I" in relation to an alterity and also the forms of its own alienation and "fracture" (*Spaltung*). The result of Cavalletti's inquiry is a new account of the phenomenological problematic and its reception and transformation among many of Husserl's readers. Heidegger, Lévinas, and Derrida, first of all, but also Ingarden, Fink, Patočka, and Stein all play roles in this portion of the book's argument.

If Cavalletti succeeds in defining the question of ego and "alter ego" in new terms, it is because he has perceived an extraordinary insight made by an author hardly known to the English-speaking public: the Franco-Rumanian writer Robert Klein, whose sudden death in 1967 interrupted an exceptionally fertile research project in early modern studies, art history, and philosophy about which Cavalletti is today one of the foremost experts.[4] In a 1961 essay, "Appropriation et aliénation" (Appropriation and alienation), Klein refers to Husserl's attempts to define the ego through the alter ego, following the principle that "to truly be 'I,' a person, I must . . . 'see myself through the eyes of another.'" Then Klein evokes a disturbance in the field of consciousness and self-consciousness to which Husserl hardly attended. This disturbance is, of course, vertigo, which Klein defines precisely as the temptation, felt by an *I*, to mistake its location (its *here*) for that of another. In a footnote to his essay, Klein explains his idea more fully: "The climber on the side of a cliff is no longer able to relate space to his *here* as center. The entirety of space bursts into the consciousness of the subject, who feels that his 'spatial center,' and therefore his 'here,' is elsewhere, below. It is the loss of an anchor-point in space, the disappearance of the spatial equivalent of the 'I': hence the temptation to throw oneself down (to reach that *here*) and the fear, which is not a fear of slipping, but of ceding to temptation."

Cavalletti draws out the extraordinary implications of Klein's original formulation, as well as their relations to the particular cinematic artifice that Hitchcock invented in *Vertigo*: "The void attracts because it is a 'here' all while being 'there,' because to be myself, my 'I,' must be there, from where the other sees me." Klein's terms correspond to Hitchcock's "mechanism," by which the "here" suddenly seems to consciousness to be "down there," as if beckoning to the viewer to draw closer.

That such a disturbance reorients, or rather fundamentally disorients, the consciousness of self and space, the ego and its indices, is all too evident. Yet Cavalletti demonstrates that the terms of Klein's account of vertigo also hold for the relation to alterity that defines the structure of Husserl's transcendental subjectivity: "Whereas the 'there' of the alter ego reveals itself analogically as a 'here,' the 'here' of my ego vertiginously confuses itself with a 'there'—and in the meantime precipitates, because being detached from myself in this exchange of roles, I must fall in order to continue holding onto myself. This is the paradox of vertigo. . . . On the brink of the precipice, I become another, or better yet, I see myself from a 'here' that is by now confused and ungrounded with another's eyes. To not fall, I would have to fall, to truly be 'here' (there) and at the same time 'down there' (here), I would have to forsake myself and become—since it is only from another's point of view that my 'here' is once again such—truly double, both ego and alter ego." Cavalletti's thesis is as startling as it is radical: "What is vertiginous is intersubjectivity and the very identity of the ego." More simply: "the structure of the subject . . . is vertiginous." This is why the self can scarcely grasp itself—if not by a "fall."

In its last turn, *Vertigo* draws out the consequences of Klein's speculative claim that, in vertigo, "the entirety of space bursts into the consciousness of the subject." How, Cavalletti asks, might such an "explosion" be conceived? How could one define the motion by which, in Henri Maldiney's closely related phenomenological terms, "there is no longer any *here*"? Before readers can anticipate an answer formulated in the terms of the study of cinema, literature, or philosophy, they will find that the curve of the argument has led further outward, into another discipline. Now Cavalletti evokes the history and theory of art and architecture, fields in which he was trained and to which he has often contributed, not least in his first book, *La città biopolitica*. Departing from Alois Riegl's distinction between "near vision" and "distant vision," or "haptic" and "optical" sight, Cavalletti recalls Wilhelm Worringer's related account of the difference between two equally "austere" renditions of surface: that in an ancient Greek frieze and that in a fifth-century relief in Ravenna. "The two are in fact at the opposite ends of an evolution," Worringer writes, arguing that the plane of the ancient Greek work suggests a "tactile meaning," while that in Ravenna points instead to a visual plane [*Sehebene*]. Whereas the figuration of the Greek relief arises from "absolute surface [*absolute Fläche*]," the late ancient Italian one derives from "absolute space."

In some of the most beautiful and beautifully surprising pages in *Vertigo*, Cavalletti shows how Worringer's notion of "absolute surface" was retrieved and transformed by the Italian art historian Sergio Bettini, whose writings Cavalletti has edited and introduced.[5] Bettini identifies the urban and architectural shape of the city of Venice with the construction of an "absolute surface," in which figuration is systematically minimized, while an infinitely variable plane of color remains. "Venice," Bettini wrote, "is born between air and water . . . it concretizes itself between these two limitless dimensions. . . . The entirety of Venice's form is color, which is to say surface. . . . No unifying number, no restful equilibrium . . . only effects of light . . . the light . . . the *locus* of moving splashes of color . . . where volume become lost, and the very scale of weights and substances, now unanchored, oscillates infinitely."

Such an "absolute surface" lies beyond, or perhaps before, the fundamental distinction between "here" and "there" on which the "vertigo effect" rests, from Hitchcock to Husserl and Klein: "Absolute surface revokes every relation between proximity and distance." On this plane, the oppositions between ego and alter ego, height and depth, and mask and face come undone, and the "temptation of identity" loses its force. This is perhaps the final point to which this book leads its readers. It resonates with the conclusions of Cavalletti's earlier "triptych on the archeology of contemporary power and counter-power,"[6] in Alberto Toscano's phrase, as well as with those of Cavalletti's most recent work, *L'Immemorabile: Il soggetto e i suoi doppi* (The immemorial: The subject and its doubles, 2020).[7] In each case, the meticulous analysis of a phenomenon of subjection leads not only to the reconstruction of a machinery whose effects are all too palpable but also, in accordance with to the etymology of word *analysis* itself, toward a loosening, if not a dissolution. In *Vertigo*, once the mechanisms of domination have been laid bare, the subject emerges as "nothing more than the dark side of artifice." At the end of this remarkable book, on the "absolute surface" that is no ground, what comes free is something and someone over which fear and its masters have no hold.

Daniel Heller-Roazen

In Rimbaud's famous phrase *Je fixais des vertiges,* the accent belongs on the word *fixer.*

—LEO SPITZER

Incipit

The machine has been operating by now for many centuries. It constitutes and forms subjectivity, gives birth to aspirations and fears, and alludes to an ever-desirable happiness, liberating its dynamics by obtaining adhesion to the pact of the state. Within this machine, as an expert in political economy wrote, "suffering" serves as a "stimulating impulse" if it is tied to the hope of its cessation. Every true "art of governing" is capable of tying this knot: what is in fact implicit here is that hope itself, in order for it to remain alive, must comprise and mask pain, that pleasure, in order to always remain desirable (surely an absurdity for genuine hedonism), must in fact be its own negation. The finality that must always remain the same is not merely the result of its opposite but produces it, as an everyday state, just as, in Vigilius Haufniensis's words, our "State" in the infelicitous series "of approximations to the next state." There is thus no hope that is not a realized fear, there is no security tension without an effective and "sui generis" exposure to risk. Moreover, Hobbes had already kept rationality and myth, the mask and the logical mechanism, the voice of the people and manifest fiction, and therefore the promise of peace as well as safety and the fantastical appearance of the Leviathan, in the most rigorous of conjunctions. A century later, between Naples and Vienna, between Antonio Genovesi and Joseph von Sonnenfels, this dynamism would finally be thematized. Since then, the threat of violent death has remained operative at the heart of all desires and, ambiguously exiled beyond the margins of the city, founded modern sovereignty. No longer merely feared but now barely veiled, it can take center stage, actualizing itself without troubling or belying the function of safety, all while appearing ever more real and threatening, in an endless spiral. And it can even conceal itself in its most shameless self-exhibition when the formula, as Alain writes, becomes "more or less the following: 'we die for our security' or, worse yet, 'We never think of anything other than dying for our security.'"[1]

There is a word that precisely describes the tendency to pursue that which one fears most or to carry out the action that one should avoid, to give in all while resisting or to call passivity action, and it is this word that an Italian student of Sonnenfels's used in the title of his 1790 pamphlet, "The Current Vertigo of Europe." Antonio De Giuliani thus recognized, even in the most powerful of states, the inevitable tendency toward crisis and decadence, and in "agitated sovereigns" and "restless ministers" the instruments of a "complicated machine"[2] capable of rendering every man a slave "thrust into a thousand vortices," who considers himself free all while being moved by impulses that conceal his destiny from him and render him the author of his own undoing.[3] At the height of the Enlightenment, he recognized the evil and the perilous tension inherent in the very rationality of the system, and therefore in the morality or pedagogy of governing the most important of social sciences and at the same time the principal cause of destructive confusion. But perhaps he could not imagine that almost a century later, and almost two centuries after Hobbes, the very possibility of a critique of values would in turn burst open before the one who called morality "the danger of dangers," to lay hold of mankind "like a vertigo."[4]

If hallucination acts upon us, it is because we, its prey, have given it life; and at times within us it escapes its latency and makes itself apparent in a sort of unexpected short-circuit as endured passivity, desire of desire, fear of fear. In the meantime, its mechanisms continue to operate and spread, displaying their petty deceit to those who in that instant believe they can discover and dominate it. Fictions outline reality, and their scene—the most famous one—is our story . . .

1
Vertigo Effect

1. It's the most famous scene. In the dark, a pair of hands grasps a ladder rung as a man hurriedly climbs up. Fleeing along the roofs of San Francisco, he jumps from a cornice, grabs onto some roof tiles, and continues his night-time escape, scaling a steep gable. Two men follow in his footsteps, in hot pursuit: the first, a policeman in uniform, is already on his heels and begins to shoot. The other, in plain clothes, jumps but misses a foothold and slips. Miraculously, he manages to hang onto a drainpipe and turns his gaze where he shouldn't, downward: all of a sudden, he sees the chasm grow, the walls of the buildings grow taller as the street dividing them below seems to grow closer instead of receding, as if he were already falling. His colleague, in the meantime, has abandoned the chase and come back to look for him: he offers him a hand and encourages him to grab on, stretching out to help, but loses his balance and falls into the void. The plainclothes detective is left there, hanging above the abyss, gripped by terror and vertigo. He leans his head back and finally half-closes his eyes, remembering perhaps a passage from Montaigne ("I could not suffer the sight of those boundless depths without a shiver of horror... Which shows how sight can deceive us"[1]) or maybe from Poe ("I tottered upon the brink—I averted my eyes—"[2]).

Then, the story unfolds as in a dream, in the way everyone knows. After the incident, John "Scottie" Ferguson (James Stewart) leaves the police force and spends his days in lazy convalescence. One day, however, he receives a call from a former classmate of his, the now rich Gavin Elster, who asks him to keep an eye on his wife, Madeleine (Kim Novak). For some time, in fact, the young woman has been behaving rather strangely, seduced by the image of an ancestor of hers who had committed suicide. "Do you remember... a

German film called Jacob Boehme we saw at the Ursulines back in the 'twenties? . . . Well, Madeleine's face looked like that German actor's. A bewildered, groping look; I might almost say a drunken look," observes the "poor little lawyer" Gévigne, the Elster of Pierre Boileau and Thomas Narcejac's detective novel, *D'entre les morts*,[3] from which Hitchcock drew the story for the film (and initially the title as well, which was later changed to evoke Marcel L'Herbier's similar work, *Le vertige*, 1926). "His pale eyes had a faraway look, to somewhere beyond life itself,"[4] wrote Georges Rodenbach of Hugues, the protagonist of his *Bruges-la-morte* (1892), which served as inspiration for Boileau and Narcejac. Before "the lustre of her melancholy eyes," one reads in Poe's *Morella* (1835) (which Éric Rohmer rightly compared with *Vertigo*), "my soul sickened and became giddy with the giddiness of one who gazes downward into some dreary and unfathomable abyss."[5]

Madeleine has lost her *compos sui*: "she no longer belongs to herself" or "Madeleine's no longer the same . . . And . . . and I can't help thinking sometimes . . . That the woman living with me isn't Madeleine."[6] As if in a state of hypnosis, in all she does, she imitates Carlotta Valdés (the Pauline Lagerlac of *D'entre les morts*), who took her own life. She wanders around the city, lingering in ancient, dreamy places, at the mercy of a lengthier dream of death. And so Scottie (or Flavières) accepts the mission, giving in to the fascination of the beautiful Madeleine . . . or of her spectral mistress. "It was no longer a question of watching her, but of helping her, protecting her. 'I'm blabbering,' thought Flavières. 'If I don't look out I shall find myself in love with her.'"[7] He therefore begins to follow the sleepwalker (but was she really a sleepwalker? "Flavières could intuit a few explanations: fascination, clairvoyance, personality disorders, but rejected them one after the other"[8]) and he manages to save her when she throws herself off the Quai de Courbevoie, or rather from the edge of the Golden Gate Bridge: "'You're not dead' . . . The eyes turned towards him, her thoughts seemed to come back from some other world. 'I don't know,' she said softly." How could she not be sure? "For you," she would go on to explain, "and for everyone else, in fact—life's the exact opposite of death . . . For me . . ."[9]

Then, once again, vertigo. Scottie and Madeleine set off together. He, a detective and psychologist, takes her (who lets herself be taken, of course) out of the city, to the Mission San Juan Bautista, where Carlotta had spent her youth. Here, Madeleine effortlessly remembers and relives the scenes of the dream with her half-entranced gaze, and he is able to show her that the world of dreams truly exists all around her, like her, and that she belongs to no one. Reality conquers the dream as Scottie embraces his beloved and the two kiss, professing their love. "No, it's too late," and all of a sudden Madeleine pulls herself free; he catches up with her, but she draws back again, asking to enter the church on her own, which he grants. She sets off slowly, but soon glances upward and flees toward the bell tower, to climb up to a place where Ferguson can't reach her. Scottie realizes and hurries after her (Antonioni, in the 1957 film, *Il grido*, had just filmed Irma's desperate rush to catch Aldo, already standing atop the factory tower), he impulsively makes an effort, tries to force himself but can't resist and gives in: as he's climbing, his gaze is fatally drawn down the stairwell and the perspective, once again, recedes. Sweating and trembling, he remains paralyzed by fear while his beloved, now at the top, lets herself go and falls. Madeleine has followed in Carlotta's footsteps—or at least so it seems and so he thinks.

Hitchcock follows the novel to the letter: "Reluctantly he followed, gripping the greasy rope which served as a banister rail. . . . Reaching a little landing, he saw through an aperture. . . . Already at this height he felt uncomfortable and, hurriedly turning away from the loophole, he went on up the stairs. . . . [T]he stairs swept round so as to leave an open shaft in the middle. . . . He was coming to another landing. . . . He knew very well what giddiness awaited him there. . . . He couldn't help looking."[10]

François Truffaut must have also known this page well, but for him the eye-opening moment came while looking at a screen. To remain faithful to the text, the director had in fact made use of all of his craft. A few years later, during the famous interview, Hitchcock would go on to swap roles, asking Truffaut point-blank (as he had already done concerning the famous glass of milk in *Suspicion*, 1941): "Did you notice the distortion when Stewart looks down the stairway? Do you know how we did that?" "Wasn't that a track-out combined with a forward zoom?" "That's it. When Joan Fontaine fainted at the inquest in *Rebecca*, I wanted to show how she felt that everything was moving far away from her before she toppled over. I always remember one night at the Chelsea Arts Ball at Albert Hall in London when I got terribly drunk and I had the sensation that everything was going far away from me. I tried to get that into *Rebecca*, but they couldn't do it. The viewpoint must be fixed, you see, while the perspective is changed as it stretches lengthwise. I thought about the problem for fifteen years. By the time we got to *Vertigo*, we solved it by using the dolly and zoom simultaneously."[11]

Even before then, Frédéric Moreau had witnessed ladies twirling in close proximity around him during a waltz at the masked ball hosted by Rosanette. And "this dizzy, whirling movement, growing ever faster and more regular, produced a sort of intoxication in his mind":[12] all of the women—Flaubert explains—passed before him, each one affecting him in a particular way, according to their different types of beauty. Intoxicating and marvelous, their whirligig was destined to continue, animated a century later by a new attraction.

The cinema is the last enchantment of the stage; it passes through halls like a peddler through a fair, parading in an atmosphere of sensational kitsch or of lies without end. And while it inscribes its own novelty in the great cycle of evolutions, schools and theatrical manners, "it takes on the air of reverting to their origins, which are puerile but universal."[13] Thanks to a sleight of hand, and an apparatus both ingenious and simple, Hitchcock manages to trick (using a dolly) artifice itself (in this instance, the zoom) and thus amalgamate the alcoholic evening at Albert Hall with the nighttime incident and acrophobia of James Stewart/John Ferguson, identifying the dizziness attributable to liquor—"vertigo or dizziness from intoxication," which as Erasmus Darwin admitted at the end of the eighteenth century, palpably augments one's pleasure—or to dancing—"vertigo occasioned by rocking or swinging," which through a supplementary "addition of pleasure" would produce weakness or somnolence[14]—with the paralysis of panic. As La Mettrie had written, "nothing excites vertigo more than fear!"[15]

Now, excitation implies, if not chronicity, then at least latency. "I have in me the engram of an immense fall," Gaston Bachelard once confessed. Perhaps it is an echo of this phrase that gave birth to Boileau and Narcejac's character, while the actor hanging up there, for his part, averts his gaze from the street only to lose himself in an abyss of insistent, bygone visions (Poe, Montaigne, Carlotta). His can be likened to "the vertigo of drunkards [which] continues . . . when the inebriate lies in his bed, in the dark, or with his eyes closed."[16] Hitchcock had encountered this populated obscurity, and it is in the night of San Francisco, and for its inhabitants, that the big screen comes alight.

2. In 1873, Maurice Krishaber published his famous study on *Névropathie cérébro-cardiaque*: the illness was new, but among its symptoms intoxication and dizziness were still united, following an ages-old medical tradition. According to the classic definition given by the medicine of fluids and humors, vertigo is a false imagination, in which all objects and even one's head seem to rotate and turn (*est falsa imaginatio, in quia omnia objecta et caput ipsum rotari ac circumagi videntur*), as Lazare Rivière transmits it.[17] Distinguishing the simple affliction ("which the Greeks called *dínos*") from its tenebrous counterpart (*skótoma* and *skotodinía*) and the idiopathic form from the sympathetic one, the master of the School of Montpellier specifies that vertigo—unlike phrenitis and melancholia—leaves the patient's reason intact all while afflicting the imagination. It is Lorenzo Bellini who would later go on to give the most important treatment of the phenomenon in modern medicine (*De urinis et pulsibus: De missione sanguinis, de febribus, de morbis capitis, et pectoris*, 1683). In his wake, the science of the Lumières would go on to

associate the idiopathic causes of vertigo—intoxication from alcohol (Bellini: *vertigo ab ebrietate*)—with external physical ones, and in particular the rotation of the body while dancing (Bellini: *vertigo per corporis rotatione circa se ipsum*), associated with a momentary confusion—produced, for example, by a whirling motion being suddenly brought to a halt—between the movement of the perceptive organ and the countermovement of perceived objects. If the fibers of the retina begin to undulate because of the liquor circulating in the veins, in other words because of the rarefaction of the blood (Bellini), the optical effect produced is similar to the impression made on those very same retinal fibers by objects that, while dancing, seem to spin in the opposite direction with respect to the body: "one will fall, dead drunk, for reasons that are easily deducible from what has been said regarding the rotation of the body," assures La Mettrie in the *Traité du Vertige*.[18]

Like La Mettrie, who often quotes him verbatim, Leibniz himself was already a reader and admirer of Bellini's. To explain that a simple substance can never be devoid of affections, and that even in a state of lethargy, in a swoon, or in a sleep without dreams, that is when the monads are "completely naked" (*toutes nües*), indistinct "little perceptions" nevertheless remain, he had evoked precisely the example of vertigo provoked by rotational movement. And he had compared dazedness with vertigo to assimilate vertigo to death: "when there are a vast number of little perceptions in which there is nothing distinct, we are stupefied [*quand il y a une grande multitude de petites perceptions, où il n'y a rien de distingué, on est étourdi*]; as happens when we continuously spin around in the same direction several times: this makes us dizzy, which can make us faint and prevent us from distinguishing anything at all [*qui peut nous faire évanouir et que ne nous laisse rien distinguer*]. And death can put animals into this state for a time [*peut donner cet état pour un temps aux animaux*]."[19]

Death is thus not the end of everything (and it does not, as we believe, come after the initial dizziness and the fall), but, in the world of indestructible monads, it is a sort of vertiginous daze, nothing more than an involution or a temporary diminution of life. Hence the famous polemic: incapable of recognizing this state, and confusing it like common folk with death itself, the Cartesians along with the Scholastics believed that the soul separated itself from the no longer living body, while certain ill-disposed minds even convinced themselves of its mortality.[20] In Leibniz, the theory of vertigo is the theory of the continuity of substance and, at the same time, of the inseparability of body and soul.

"For you . . . death is the opposite of life . . . but for me . . ." Despite her Leibnizian pose, Madeleine nevertheless identifies with Carlotta (or Pauline), once again confusing everything: "'You're not dead' . . . 'I don't know,' she murmured." Her uncertain appearance does not commune with death or nurture it, nor does it survive it. It is not a second life but, in the act of identification, a death (Carlotta) prior to death (Poe's Morella is not reborn in an identical daughter, but dies to her daughter, or rather to herself), or a daze that cannot merely be momentary. She is the cornerstone or agent of the anticipation, she is the one who holds the film in its typical esoteric suspense (*suspense ésotérique*),[21] both enchanting and deceiving: "for you . . . for me . . ." The death that penetrates and takes root in life is not, in fact, death *à la rigueur* but her very own vertigo, a death spell that captures the bare life of the monad.

3. After a long period of gestation, the effect is finally achieved, and economically as well, which makes Hitchcock doubly proud. A model of the stairwell (a particularly expressionist setting, reminiscent of the windmill in *Foreign Correspondent*, 1940) is placed horizontally, so that the camera can traverse it with a simple dolly while the zoom carries out its countermovement. The cinematic illusion achieves its desired effect, just as the impression of objects on the retina provokes a sense of dizziness or, as doctors claimed, the mnemic trace of sensations experienced during an old fall provokes vertigo in one who looks over the edge of a cliff. In the meantime, the scene from twenty-five years earlier ("one night at the Chelsea Arts Ball . . .") recalls La Mettrie's older recollection: "I remember having suffered such a fright on the tower of Antwerp that I could hardly keep myself from walking about in circles. To hold ourselves up we must have recourse to a great strength of spirit, especially if we focus our gaze on our point of support, which inevitably seems to give way, and we fall, despite ourselves, in an attempt to halt it."[22] Both images, along with the "vast number of little perceptions," find their fulfillment in Scottie Ferguson's daze, suspended on the verge of collapse. For him, that instant freezes and expands as the film slows down to that lazy, "contemplative" tempo so dear to Truffaut and, as Gilles Deleuze also observed, so rare in Hitchcock.[23]

In this time of a dazed life akin to death, Scottie now lives untied to anything (he has left his job; he is the quintessential bachelor: "I'm still available. Available Ferguson"), except for the obsessive memory of the man who fell trying to save him ("I have, this acrophobia. I wake up at night seeing that man fall from the roof and I try to reach out to him, it's just . . ."). He is aware of living in someone's stead ("Leriche took my place . . . He fell," Flavières confesses to Gévigne), he knows he cannot live without remembering it and, wandering about ("[I] wander about") in an almost crepuscular state, he becomes enthralled by a woman who is herself spellbound by the image of someone dead. "You can see how she's bewitched, her eyes seem to be intently watching something which moves": Madeleine, too, one could say, is afflicted by the same pathology, subject as she is—to use Bellini's Latin—to a *lapsus*. And indeed she will yield to it, and fall. And he who never ceases to live among the dead will continue, *en voulant l'arrêter*, to follow and love her. He worships the living image of Carlotta, but he loses her and then finds her again in the person that only the world of the living can offer him. He did not reach the top of the bell tower, having to give up and go back on unsteady legs; but the observation Georges Poulet made regarding Baudelaire concerns him as well: "descending the 'stairs of vertigo' is still vertiginous [*la descente de 'l'escalier de vertige' est encore un vertige*]."[24] His attraction to Madeleine thus transforms and coalesces into his impossible passion for Judy Barton (Boileau and Narcejac's Renée Sourange and Rodenbach's Jane). She is the former's shade—or her perfect counterproof,[25] brought to life in the somewhat slovenly clothing of a saleswoman, a provincial idol from some Midwestern county. After the death of his beloved, after the shock and lengthy torpidity, Scottie reopens his eyes, which land on Judy but (without realising just how right they are) see Madeleine. As Károly Kerényi has written regarding images created by the gods to trick mortals, "here one can speak of spectral similarity."[26] "To put it plainly, the man wants to go to bed with a woman who's dead; he's indulging in a form of necrophilia," as the director comments rather crudely.[27] But in reality, who is the dead woman? Is it Madeleine, who appears behind Judy (René), or Carlotta (Pauline), who appears behind Madeleine? Love's dominion is perhaps no longer animated by the image or idea of the person but rather by the mask (*persona*) that conceals the image itself.

4. "Take a philosopher . . ." Even before *Vertigo*, and before concluding the vertiginous scene of Mount Rushmore—with a beautiful temporal ellipsis—in a sleeping car (*North by Northwest*, 1959), Hitchcock had already had his fair share of fun. In the finale of *Jamaica Inn* (1939), for example, he had hoisted Charles Laughton up onto the main mast of a ship and had shot from his point of view the agitated crowd below, full of sailors and passengers, before letting the body of the suicidal man fall, ironically conjuring the effect that it was the camera itself, as Rohmer and Chabrol would later remark, that was plummeting toward the deck (shooting that film had in fact been an "an absurd thing to undertake," and the director was "truly discouraged"[28]). A year later, he had gotten rid of the wicked Krug in *Foreign Correspondent*, filming the fall of the maladroit criminal—the author of his own demise—from the tower of Westminster. Then, more recently, perhaps when he was already planning to make Brigitte Auber, the fake "Cat," slide down the roof only to be caught

by Cary Grant (*To Catch a Thief*, 1955), he had already suspended James Stewart from a window sill in *Rear Window*, only to immediately make him fall, earning the riotous convalescent and obstinate bachelor a second plaster cast (i.e., a *de facto* marriage to his beautiful, sophisticated girlfriend). The voyeur-photographer thereby becomes, in a certain sense, the direct and happy predecessor of the necrophiliac detective. But this noble lineage, it must be said, goes all the way back to Montaigne: "Take a philosopher, put him in a cage made from thin wires set wide apart, hang him from one of the towers of Notre Dame de Paris [*Qu'on loge un philosophe dans une cage de menus filets de fer clairsemés, qui soit suspendue au haut des tours de Notre-Dame de Paris*]. It is evident to his reason that he cannot fall; yet (unless he were trained as a steeplejack) when he looks down from that height he is bound to be terrified and beside himself."[29] What is vertigo? Perhaps it is not comparable, if we accept Klaus Heinrich's distinction,[30] with the abysmal "whirlpool" (*Sog*) or the famous undertow of the Maelström. But it is, at the very least, oblivion, apathy or the loss of "attention to life,"[31] depersonalization, and at the same time fear, or better yet anguish, in the sense given to it by Kierkegaard (whose cause "is just as much in one's own eye as in the abyss"[32]) and therefore also by Sartre. Without forgetting Jaspers and the seduction of absolute consciousness,[33] vertigo (*Schwindel*), with its unsettling nature, is already in Heidegger, one of the markers of philosophical thought—whose typical movement is precisely *schwindlig*, "circle and vortex" (*Zirkel und Wirbel*).[34] Even before that, though, it turns into the powerful figure of temptation or perversity, this time in Poe's sense (*The Imp of the Perverse*, 1845), and carries out that characteristic envelopment by which "an entire category of aberrations becomes comprehensible ... only in reference to the *type vertigineux*," to the coexistence of a certain physical malaise with a "moral anguish capable of transforming itself into delirium and madness."[35]

So what is vertigo? A whirlwind of answers, one could say, all suspended and whirling around their deficiency. All while knowing the *Versuch über den Schwindel* (first published in 1786 and then reedited in 1791) written by the friend and student of Kant's, Marcus Herz (the addressee of the famous letter dated February 21, 1772)—that is, the thesis that the excessive speed of representations throws the soul into a state of painful confusion—the renowned pathologist Johann Nepomuk von Raimann was forced to admit at the beginning of the nineteenth century that "the essence of vertigo remains unknown."[36] Unknowability would thus quite easily become the essence of vertigo: in fact, according to Krishaber, "the state of vertigo coincides with sensations of *emptiness* and *vagueness*: the patient seems devoid of thoughts; their memory is profoundly disturbed."[37] And emptiness itself can swiftly transform, in turn, into the heights of the imagination, reason's victorious antagonist. It is precisely the philosopher who had been placed up there to be pilloried who manages to appropriate Montaigne's lesson. Recalling a "familiar instance" in a famous page, Hume explains the effects of habit, which favors the imagination while impeding the faculty of judgment: "consider the case of a man, who, being hung out from a high tower in a cage of iron cannot forebear trembling, when he surveys the precipice below him.... His imagination runs away with its object, and excites a passion proportion'd to it. That passion returns back upon the imagination ... both his fancy and affections, thus mutually supporting each other, cause the whole to have a very great influence upon him."[38] For Kant, the cause of illusions that make us see as outside of us things that are exclusively within us and make us dizzy when we look down into a chasm from a safe viewing point, or generate in certain patients the capricious fear of voluntarily throwing themselves from a precipice, resides precisely in an imaginative paroxysm. Vertigo is therefore associated with nostalgia, with a tendency toward phantasmagoria or mimetic phenomena of sympathy.[39]

Sixty years later, the expression "mental vertigo" would go on to play no small part in the *néocritique* vocabulary. For Charles Renouvier—who would later adopt Gabriel Tarde's idea of universal imitation—it defines a mimetic phenomenon, that is, the actual causation of a movement contrary to one's will, one's natural inclinations, and one's lucid thought, on the basis of an imaginary representation capable of producing "a strong perturbation." If "vertigo in its plainest sense is what makes a man prone to throwing himself off a cliff despite the presence of a parapet, unless his will intervenes at the right moment,"[40] it is because—in an intensification, in a very Humean mutual amplification of imagination and passion—that which is most feared has the greatest likelihood of occurring. If vertigo afflicts us, it is because the *effort voulu* and the *sensation musculaire* are not immediately linked, as Maine de Biran posited, forgetting "an essential element separating them—the imagination that foresees the movement."[41] Nevertheless, both free and determined, active and passive, captured by the evocative force of ideas, the will (that is, the essence of a personality) still has reason on its side: it can therefore thwart vertigo by exercising doubt, suspending judgment in order to then base it on new and more solid motivations. If the vertiginous imagination can mislead it, the will must defend itself with rational thought and education, "to know how to doubt, to learn to doubt": "It is here that a new source of hope is to be found" and that free will—or, one could say, the teachings of Jules Lequier—confirms its supremacy for Renouvier.[42] Thus, Alain, who knew how to take inspiration from Renouvier—*ce bon kantien à la tête dure*[43]—all while rejecting his very conception of freedom, was able to recognize in vertigo an example of a

Biranian *effort* induced by the imagination, that is, in the very state of immobility, "by the foresight of or preparation for certain movements." When we cast a glance into the abyss, it attracts us, or in other words we experience "a great number of muscular sensations . . . which signal either contraction or relaxation" and "we begin both to fall and to hold ourselves back."[44] But this "nice example of fear," which for Alain serves to demonstrate the link between perception and movement, is still the model for the weakest and most diffuse of emotions or the "small fear that we always experience when we perform an action,"[45] and which we supposedly make use of to prepare our gestures: that tamed, hesitant trepidation or that natural panic of falling which we have dominated to keep ourselves in balance and place one foot before the other. One can easily see how in this case the habitual has replaced the voluntary, and that its statute is weak and its rule ever on the verge of collapsing, if he who is standing truly runs the risk of falling into a chasm, if the use of fear can itself be frightening while the most measured of gestures remains exposed to that which is irreparable or most likely.

Poe had indeed been less trusting: "because our reason violently deters us from the brink, *therefore*, do we the more impetuously approach it,"[46] and only a friendly hand or a miraculous jump backward could potentially save us from falling. Vertigo is both fear and at the same time voluptuousness, it is a terror that attracts, an evil that becomes as inevitable as it is fearsome, a halter that the imagination uses to bind and exploit reluctant reason.

Renouvier, the Kantian, does not cite Herz's treatise, *Versuch über den Schwindel*—which was not only widely known and held in high regard, by Joseph Frank ([*De vertigine*] *perbelle* [*scripsit*] Marcus Herz[47]) among others, but also, as has been noted, marked a turning point in the lengthy history of the concept of vertigo: Herz promoted it from an epiphenomenon and somatic disturbance, from a defect of the external organs, to a central problem of the sciences of the soul. What is more, according to the direct testimony of Ludwig Ernst Borowsky, Kant himself had barely deigned the book with a glance, although it had been dedicated to him by Herz, and declaring that he was "immune to vertigo" (*vom Schwindel frei*), he had it put away by a servant, never to open it again.[48] Such behavior, which according to Peter Fenves is attributable to an ever-increasing "ambivalence toward the Jew-Palestinians,"[49] seems all the more striking if one takes into account that Herz had appended to the book a letter in which he recalled how the idea for the study had come to him precisely during a conversation with Kant.[50]

What was the seminal idea? It seems to be identifiable with the notion of *Weile*, which Herz introduces in section 2 and which punctuates and orients the theoretically central part of the work. *Weile* means "moment," here in the sense of period, phase, or appropriate speed of consciousness. Developing an observation that Locke had made in passing without referring it back to the fundamental law of the soul,[51] Herz explains that *Weile* is the "time" that the soul requires after fully mastering one representation to regain its powers and undertake the effort of a subsequent one: it is the internal measure of the development of representations. It is a variable defined by peculiar laws: it differs in every individual and is relative to their state; it depends on the conditions of the soul and body, on the effort made by the former and the energy (measurable by the science of fluids and temperaments) at the disposal of the latter. But one must add that the effort also depends on the representations themselves: the *Weile* required for a sequence of ideas to be completely clear is dependent, in other words, on their relative nature as a whole, or rather on the proportion of monotony to variety in the sequence, on the relation between similarity and difference of its constituent parts, on their order or disorder, on the relation between their rarity, their novelty, or their habitual character. Completeness, harmony, and symmetry, for example, are forms of order capable of diminishing the required intellectual effort and demand a lesser *Weile*. Habit, for its part, helps to group together a series of representations as being similar, contemporaneous, or belonging to the same place, and facilitates the speed of concatenations. Herz observes that habitual developments are paths that we can follow even with our eyes closed, whereas unusual ones require a great deal of effort. Thus, a certain *Weile* is attributable to anyone in any given situation, which corresponds to the natural order of the soul and the economy of the body.

This is precisely what Herz must have discovered while reasoning and debating with Kant, namely that "every individual consciousness," according to Jan Evangelista Purkinje's paraphrase, "possesses a certain speed [*Mass von Geschwindigkeit*], on the basis of which it fills time with a concatenation of representations."[52] A series that may be simple and clear for one person may be too complicated for another, and when one's attention is subjected to an excess of activity, it weakens, while in the meantime the representation becomes vague and vertiginously "fading" (*schwindend*).[53]

One may perhaps recall the testimony of Salmon Maimon, who, having arrived in Berlin and become part of Mendelssohn's circle, met "a man with great knowledge and a generous heart"[54] who was ready to help him financially and place his own library at his disposal. "Herr [H.] . . . said that he was one of Kant's best students. . . . But he still didn't feel capable of judging the *Critique* or any work related to it."[55] Like Mephistopheles's student ("I feel as stupid, from all you've said,/As if a mill-wheel whirled in my head!"),[56] Herz had drawn from experience (*wie die Erfahrung lehrt*) a few elementary rudiments, which, however, implied, from the point of view of "philosophical medicine," a decisive theoretical leap. Vertigo thus extended beyond the realm of strictly physiological phenomena to reveal itself as "a possibility immanent to consciousness,"[57] a disturbance in the flow of ideas, a deviation from their natural course toward an unnatural condition (*widernatürlicher Zustand*), which produces in the mind an excess of liveliness, dragging it into a state of vertiginous confusion.[58] "If the speed of the resulting succession of representations diminishes or grows with respect to the usual average rate, the individual becomes confused concerning the very identity of his own self and the duration of his activity in real time, since the long or short moment [*Weile*] is measurable only via the intensity of the transition from one representation to the next": this is how Purkinje puts it, punctually restating Herz's theory while placing it under the promising title of "temporal vertigo [*Zeitschwindel*]."[59]

Herz had indeed introduced his *terminus technicus* within a conceptual vocabulary derived from Kant and empiricism, asserting not only that the *Weile* and "order" (*Ordnung*) of ideas are closely intertwined, but explaining thus the "affinity between representations of space and time." "Space and time are fundamentally nothing but types of order within the soul, according to which it can sensibly [*sinnlich*] imagine things as being either close or consecutive."[60] It is enough to read this direct reference to "forms of sensibility," which by now is certainly far from Locke's sensualism and in which one can hear echoes of Hume,[61] to understand what sort of pressure the idea of *Weile* exerts on the Kantian framework, and up to what point psychology can now penetrate into the realm of transcendental aesthetics. Of course, space and time are not merely empirical concepts here, and yet, as modalities of order, they are not immediately given and intuited but rather, being relative to *Weile*, are therefore, like it, subject to change and confusion.

We could say, in fact, that when the *Weile* is correct, space and time are perfectly commensurate to it, and are therefore pure forms. The acceleration (or deceleration) of *Weile*, however, undoes, so to speak, the Kantian *a priori*, producing an eccentricity of time and space which end up, in turn, in a state of vertiginous disorder. Time as *Weile* and empirical time are in that case sensibly separated, while space as such becomes sensible (*sinnlich*), its center shifts, moves, denying any proximity, upsetting and disorienting everything. Like every other thing, time too ceases to be the pure *a priori* form of change, seeing as it must undergo a change itself. The subsequent moment comes late or arrives early and becomes confused with the preceding one while the past takes the place of the present and absorbs the future. If vertigo is not exclusively a medical pathology, it is not an illusion caused by the power of the imagination (Kant),[62] or by the effects of habit on the latter (Hume), either. Vertigo is, rather, a true affliction or impurity of the transcendental. Herz was a doctor, and no doctor could have offered such an incisive explanation; he was also a philosopher, and there could be nothing more inadmissible for the doctrine of aprioristic forms than the idea of a space that, as such, oscillates and rotates and of a time that flows away from itself.

At this point, Kant's behavior becomes perhaps more understandable. Conversing with him, Herz had attempted a differentiation, thus discovering *Weile* and its relativity; in other words, he concretely experienced, while his ideas were taking shape and developing, that the habitual concatenation of one person could leave another confused and bewildered. Later, Kant avoided reading the book and responded with a conventional formula. The words addressed to Borowski explain the eloquent elusion. If the idea of *Weile* appears in the course of a dialogue, and if it is liable to provoke vertigo, then to be *vom Schwindel frei* means to elude said dialogue altogether. The obvious refusal of a relative *a priori* coincides here with the refusal of relation—a refusal that was as circumstantial as it was definitive. According to Karl August Böttiger's diary of his trip to Berlin in 1797, the dedication of the second edition of *Versuch über den Schwindel* would go unanswered.[63]

Another philosopher, however, was to prove an attentive reader of Herz: Johann-Christoph Hoffbauer. In his treatise on legal psychology, he observes—with an implicit but literal quotation—that as a result of an excessively quick succession of "lively representations" (*lebhafte Vorstellungen*), we lose awareness of our exact situation and are impelled to do the opposite of what we would like. In such a predicament, he adds, in spite of everything that could calm us down, we are dominated by the image of the peril we believe to be impending: the entire field of consciousness thus becomes invaded by fear and while we blindly try to escape it, that very same fear inhibits our ability to think, impeding us from avoiding the worst.[64]

5. A century after La Mettrie, when truly nothing seems to generate vertigo more than fear, the old scotodinia becomes a "condition of blind psychological overpowering" (*Zustand der blinden psychologischen Überwältigung*), which legal medicine naturally elevates to the paradigm of the unusual and imperious impulse, of the suggestion that breaks or deviates from the tendencies of habit to fatally collide with the power of the law. This opened the way for one last, particularly fantastical and rigorous, development. *The Imp of the Perverse*—another of Hitchcock's obvious sources (*Rope*, 1948)—would go on to add the final chapter to the study of crimes committed because of an irresistible attraction and cases of suppression or crises of responsibility: that of coercion not only or not so much to commit but to *confess* the gravest of

crimes against one's will (this would go on to be the subject of Theodor Reik's famous Viennese lectures, that is the psychoanalytic critique of punishment as impediment).

As an irresistible constraint and a fatal compulsion ("he felt uncomfortable . . . He couldn't help looking . . ."), that acts "like chains do on limbs or the walls of a cell on a prisoner,"[65] vertigo's political nature and sociological implications quickly become apparent. For, indeed, what could have possibly occurred in France between 1786 and 1792? Esquirol draws up his authoritative diagnosis: "all of society" has been "struck with vertigo" (*La société entière semblait être frappée de vertige*).[66] Almost a century later, in 1934, Simone Weil would go on to enact her effort of critical analysis to escape from "the contagion of folly and collective frenzy" promulgated by the modern social machine,[67] which is precisely "a machine for manufacturing irresponsibility, stupidity, corruption, slackness and, above all, vertigo."[68] Only a little later, Roger Caillois would go on to write, "one's being is dragged down to ruin as if persuaded by the vision of its own annihilation to not resist the powerful fascination that seduces one's being by terrorizing it," thus lending new luster to the psychological cliché and explaining, in a text that precedes at least "in its inspiration" the Second World War, that war is elevated to a supreme value precisely by the fear and repulsion that it provokes.[69] And war had in the meantime been declared from the famous balcony of Palazzo Venezia: certainly "the least fitting place for such ceremonies," according to the bitter irony of Salvatore Satta,[70] that is, the most coherent with the somnambular exaltation and three-year-long demise of the grotesque *condottiero*. Obeying the announcement, the metaphysics of the grotesque quickly left the proscenium to spread among the applauding crowd: "The fairy has willed it, and our fate hurls us on—I'm not worried. Come, let us go! Let us run! Let us set off!"[71]

It is well known that in the letters and writings of Marx and Engels, the term *Schwindel* appears often and not only in the sense of "deception." At times, it is associated with the "frenzy of universal brotherhood" (*allgemeiner Verbrüderungsschwindel*) of 1848,[72] at others with that of capital (for instance in the *Manifest der Kommunistischen Partei*), and especially with that of financial capital, which avoids the mediation of the production process.[73] During those same years, the liberal economist Charles Coquelin recognized in socialism the contagious vertigo by virtue of which the worst instincts were "brought out and given an immense outlet," and he called the inventor of the term, Pierre Leroux, a philosopher who was a friend of Heinrich Heine's, a "mystagogue and thaumaturge."[74] On the other hand, the idea, still alive in the studio of the neurologist Max Friedmann, concerning mass suggestion and variations in the stock market as a "well-arranged deception [*Schwindel*]" to the detriment of small shareholders,[75] would soon become widespread during the great crisis at the end of the nineteenth century, thanks predominantly to German anti-Semitic journalism. This ranged from the reports by Otto Glagau (*Der Börsen- und Gründungsschwindel in Berlin*, 1874–75) to the continuously updated pamphlet by Germanicus (alias Emil Richter, *Die Frankfurter Juden und die Aufsaugung des Volkswohlstandes*, 1880; *Der neueste Raub am deutschen Nationalwohlstand*, 1881). Imaginary vertigo thus produced true vertigo, spreading it well beyond the walls of the stock exchange: but for it to reach its apogee, it had to be dissimulated and presented as a false appearance precisely to those who could have opposed it. In other words, the time of the SPD had arrived. In 1923, a small party pamphlet, called *Der Judenschwindel*, written by Christoph Hinteregger and printed by the Wiener Volksbuchhandlung (which had historically been the publishing house of Karl Kautsky and Otto Bauer), warned the working masses: German nationalists were not true anti-Semites; they may have seemed so "judging by their words, but in reality they are the bodyguards of Jewish capital."[76] Similarly, Christian socialists supposedly hid *jüdische Elemente* among their ranks, and had even nominated an ex-minister (Viktor Kienböck) "of Jewish stock" (*Judenstämling*) for the presidency. Thus, when even racist vertigo was explained as a machination designed by the Jews themselves, or else justified by their own presence, the dice were already thrown: beginning with the party ("No Jew, no one of Jewish stock, no mason will be able to gain access to it: it remains the party of a race," the National Socialist Johann von Leers would go on to write in 1933[77]), and then proceeding with professions until, at the height of the collective hallucination, when the masses themselves would be indistinguishable from their own vertigo, there would no longer be any swindlers in sight.

In the nineteenth century, however, the political atmosphere could still dissipate into a more subtle moral theory, and the treatise of the neurologist could still take its place, via the same process, in the *encyclopédie critique en farce*. While preparing the second volume of *Bouvard et Pécuchet*, Flaubert didn't allow an observation made by Max Simon pass him by (*Du vertige nerveux et de son traitement*, 1858) — one that had originally been made by Joseph Frank (1832). It concerned the effects of beer, which could cause dizziness if produced in an economic manner, with little barley and too much hops: "Poorly made beer causes vertigo—Perhaps Paris's moral folly comes from there!"[78] In the burlesque register of the *sottisier*, as Roger Dragonetti has pointed out, the homonymy of *bière* (beer, bier) combines the meanings of drunkenness and burial as a flight into an abyss without end.[79]

Well before Frank, in 1700, Bernardo Ramazzini had written in the *De morbis artificum* that the beverage of the Northern countries does not merely inebriate those who partake of it too liberally, like the Ovidian waters of Lincestus, but produces in the workers who make it the same typical nausea and vertigo that afflict our distillers and winemakers.[80] Thus, for years and years, from obscure breweries to immense crowds, from speculators to revolutionaries, from learned economists to the *vile multitude*, "one probably won't find anyone," noted Étienne Trastour in 1858, "who hasn't suffered spells of dizziness; nor are there any doubts concerning the multiplicity of disorders that may accompany them."[81] Yes, the "human forms of vertigo are numerous,"[82] and its definitions are, to say the least, diverse or, better yet, looking back across the centuries, *almost* overlapping (for the same phenomenon), and perhaps this explains why, despite notable recent studies (such as that of Rebekka Ladewig), a reconstruction of the concept's genealogy is still lacking. The concept itself is so vague that in every case one can add or, depending on the circumstances, subtract something: "It is a pity," lamented a contemporary, "that the history of the concept of vertigo has been neglected as it is likely that under its wide umbrella typical cases of anxiety attack were included during the nineteenth century."[83] Indeed, reading the lengthy entry for *Vertige* in the classic *Dictionnaire encyclopédique des sciences médicales* by Amédée Dechambre (1886–89), one has the impression that Henri Leroux had been assigned a rather unenviable task, that is, a subject matter that was too fluid and dynamic, almost indescribable and impossible to delimit. At the height of its glory, at the dawn of psychiatry, "vertigo" was truly a *passe-partout* term: it indicated a vast pathological domain, whose origins dated all the way back to the Greeks and Avicenna, but which had been nurtured by a heritage of modern medical dissertations, by inquiring or enduring erudition, and which had been fundamentally renewed during the Enlightenment, under the pretext of ordering the vast quantity of data and theories transmitted by the tradition.

Among the most varied elements—divided into three species in 1678 by Johann Jakob Wepfer: "vertigo is gyrating, staggering and swaying [*gyrosa, titubans et vacillans*]"[84]—one counts continuous, periodic afflictions, which occur at night (Günther Christoph Schellhammer's *vertigo nocturna*, 1686) or are on the contrary cause by sunstroke.[85] Next come those provoked by nervous disorders, the visual ones described by Bellini, such as Johannes de Gorter's scotodinia (*Medicina dogmatica*, 1741). The latter, supported by the late eighteenth-century debate between the so-called vertiginous philosophers, Erasmus Darwin and William Charles Wells, concerning the psychophysics of balance and the inter-dependence between the rotation of objects and the movements of the eye (as a result of "a mistake we are in," William Porterfield observed in his *Treatise on the Eye*, everything continues to spin despite the eye and object's now being still),[86] would go on to consign the mysterious vertigo of the ancients to the analyses of nineteenth-century neurologists and ophthalmologists (e.g. Abadie's *vertige ampioculaire,* or else Cuignet's *vertige oculo-cérébral*). One can also enumerate the auricular forms of vertigo—the famous syndrome of Prosper Menière or the discovery, made by Marie-Jean-Pierre Flourens (1824–28), of the relation between balance and lesions of the vestibular system, and its impressive history, which was "not simple,"[87] dominated today by neuroscience, but which made it to the Nobel awarded to Robert Bárány (1914) via Purkinje, Ernst Mach (*Grundlinien der Lehre von den Bewegungsempfindungen,* 1875), and Joseph Breur's "static sense." Next comes cardiac vertigo (the "essential" one according to Ramskill, which is hereditary and owed to the pathological dilation of the organ), Van Helmont's gastric vertigo, Armand Trousseau's dyspeptic vertigo, the one caused by arthrosis (Guéneau de Mussy), and fits of the "falling illness" (the typical "aura" is the first symptom of a convulsive seizure, as Jules Falret assured),[88] at times so brief as to not even impede a violinist from continuing to perform or a priest from continuing to officiate a service.[89] To this incomplete list one must then add intellectual vertigo, the hyperbolic one of the *comique absolu*, the contagious, affinitive one suffered by those who witness vertigo, that is (as Joseph Frank suggested, citing Boerhaave) those who witness the succession of or the excessively rapid changes in appearance of an epileptic's expressions ("Boerhaave saw such a quick reciprocation whereby he was seen to be grasped by vertigo [*tam celeri reciprocatione factum vidit Boerhaave ut in vertiginem raperet videnter*]"[90]); and finally that paralyzing epidemic which spread throughout Switzerland and France and was diagnosed between 1884 and 1886 by Georges-Gabriel Haltenhoff and by Félix Gerlier,[91] and which, like every self-respecting vertigo, "does not resemble any ordinary vertigo" (*ne ressemble à aucun des vertiges ordinaires*).[92]

The phenomenon reveals itself to everyone under an entirely new light, and there is not a single person who does not attribute to himself some completely new discovery and does not underline its singularity. It is precisely this singularity that Max Simon upholds in his attempt to subtract vertigo from the category of symptoms of pathological anatomy (and especially cerebral inflammations) to instead define it positively as a "pure neurosis [*névrose pure*],"[93] and thus endow it with a specific and consistent symptomatology, a clear and persuasive etiology, and a clear and articulate therapy. It was therefore not a case of identifying and combatting the effects of gout, arthritis, or tetanus, or the consequences of a passion, a moral influence, or excessively strong emotions, but of alleviating a true "abnormal activity of the nervous system."[94] Attempting to "isolate in the studio that which is distinct in nature,"[95] Simon, who unlike Herz was not a philosopher, was aiming squarely at the "very soul of his patients."[96] However, he still had to refer to the old nosological understanding of vertigo as an affliction of the *sensorium commune* and thus deal with the dense and cumbersome legacy of Boerhaave or Barthez's clinics, with the hygienic tradition of Samuel-Auguste Tissot and Johann Peter Frank, and with Joseph Frank's theory of internal pathology, all while attempting to avoid the pitfalls of both anatomic exposition and of the doctrine of irritation. Thus he could finally seek refuge in direct experience and in an autonomous anamnesis, studying first of all the very hypnagogic vertigo from which he himself suffered, much like his son, the alienist Paul-Max, to whom he had accurately described it.[97] The nascent theory demanded a new form of practice, and the operating theater of the Salpêtrière would soon form its apprentices, as ever more numerous throngs of magnetizers fixed their gazes on those of their patients and skillfully moving and placing their hands were able to provoke "a kind of vertigo."[98] Suggestive imitation and repetition would become the accelerators of experience, producing its initial accumulation and forming the basis for a new diagnostic tradition or custom.

For their part, Charcot and Freud himself would still go on to study the relation to the symptoms of agoraphobia described by Westphal (1872) or by Henri Legrand du Saulle (1877), which Bellini and La Mettrie had already uncovered. Even the particularly psychological, nineteenth-century notion of imitative contagion, whether admitted or denied, was much of a novelty. It was rejected by Gerlier who nevertheless, returning to Charcot's studies on the visual field, had noted in victims of paralyzing vertigo the distinctive sign of *facies hysterica* (a slight lowering of the upper eyelid over the corneal limbus). But already a century earlier, proceeding along the path originally trodden by the "subtle Bellini" and by his studies of ocular pathologies, La Mettrie had traced the phenomenon back to "false imagination" and added, with good reason, to his treatise the *Description d'une Catalepsie Hysterique*. A copy of this study must have certainly been present in Charcot's library and must have, therefore, ended up, along with his "rich collection of books and notes on vertigo," on the desk of his student, Edmond Weill who in 1886 published his *thèse d'agrégation*, fittingly entitled "Des vertiges." Evoking Charcot's authority and citing his contemporaries of the British-American school (such as Thomas Grainger Stewart), Weill proposed a measured definition that renewed and refined the classic definition of Frank and Claude-Marie-Stanislaus Sandras. The term "vertigo" could, according to Weill, be reserved for "that state in which the patient has a sense of his own body's instability, which to him seems animated by oscillations as well as linear and circular movements, as if he were drowning or oscillating on the surface of the sea . . . and in which, nevertheless, whatever the illusory sensations might be, the patient retains complete consciousness and can always report what he has experienced."[99]

One day, Sir William Gowers would go on to authoritatively locate the illness (along with fainting fits, vagal syncopes, migraines, and certain sleeping disorders) in the "border zone" of epilepsy. If the most acute and painful forms of encephalic vertigo give the awful sensation that the brain is rotating on its own axis and almost culminate in epileptic seizures, it can also begin with the truly Mephistophelian impression of a millstone spinning in one's head, in other words, of objects that move and float, or with the sudden awakening of one who is plummeting in a dream.[100] In Charcot's Paris, however, news of this liminal zone had not yet arrived, and Leroux could therefore easily reprove Weill, thus challenging the prestige of the Salpêtrière and claiming that the *"petit mal"* (Max Simon would have perhaps protested) was nothing more than dizziness accompanied by a loss of one's senses (Paul-Max Simon, the former's son, would go on to carefully distinguish between an incomplete vertiginous attack and one that produces actual convulsions). Opinions at the time were strongly divergent, and that of Charcot was so authoritative as to have more far-reaching implications than one could have imagined: a new theory of the psyche, a complex understanding of consciousness was coming to life.

6. As is well known, Freud received a scholarship to the Salpêtrière in 1885; about seven years later, he would go on to treat, without any recourse to hypnosis, the hysterical vertigo of Miss Lucy R. and Katharina. In the meantime, in 1888, Louis le Prince, a student of Daguerre's, was filming in Leeds his *Man Walking around a Corner* and *Roundhay Garden Scene*. And what is cinema if not a new form of enchantment capable of taking advantage of the "impressions" noted by Bellini much better than the old magic of panoramas, silhouettes, and rotating drums (phenakistoscopes or zoetropes)? If setting Plateau's disc in motion could unexpectedly animate its images, and if the figurines drawn on the inside of William G. Horner's cylinder could enchant anyone who saw them fly past through one of its slits with their movement, it is with the optical theater of Charles-Émile Reynaud and later with Charles F. Jenkins's *phantoscope*—in other words, thanks to the merging of this Victorian system with the older mechanism of the magic lantern—that a prodigious reversal could take place. Iconic memory would henceforth be evoked by mobile images on a cylinder that a ray of light projects onto the exterior through film or via a mirror reflection. Thanks to the speed calibrated according to the interval (or *Weile*) of the presumed "retinal persistence" (a sort of physiological "retention"), the phantoscope could already reproduce, with the same dynamic diversity, a perfectly recognizable image. Horner's "wheel of life" was therefore an apparatus capable of governing

movement and, by extension, vertigo. It still made use of the principle of speed, excluding the subject from the center of rotation, and thus preserving and holding back those who would otherwise have suffered from dizziness. If those cylindrical walls punctuated by calculated slits had not excluded the subject from its rotating circle, the gaze would have been overwhelmed (like Frédéric by the waltzing women or Flavières by the angular spiral staircase) by a thanatotropic panorama that spins on its own axis and undulates, in other words, by a "a vast number of little perceptions in which there is nothing distinct." Instead, the nineteenth century invents and disseminates these devices which, reaching and maintaining for a certain period the correct rotational velocity, produce with unexpected mastery a miraculous clarity in the realm of shadows and confusion. Cinema, which finally transforms the old cylinder into a film reel and liberates the eye from the slit by conquering for itself a free field of view, thus perfects the illusion of not being a naked monad by expanding it and making it more long-lasting, concealing torpor with torpor. It is for this reason that Marcel Duchamp would one day be able to easily awaken vertigo and constrain the mechanism to turn back on itself (*Anémic Cinéma*, 1926), or return to its proto-origins, by setting in motion on the screen Plateau's very discs with their strange and barely readable spiraling phrases, which retain the gaze at the speed of their rotation and bring the audience of frustrated readers back into the center of the rotation.

Yes, "we are stupefied" at the cinema as well. Jean Epstein, among many others, expressed it clearly: "the cinema's spectator, for whom nearly every distraction is eliminated and whose attention is directed toward a sole center—the screen—finds that hypnosis and poetry are generated at the same time."[101] If cinema could not be reduced to merely an *opéra fantastique* or an absurd *trompe-l'oeil*—in other words to all of the "art that flourished with singular abundance in the films of Méliès, in German expressionism, in Scandinavian mysticism, in French surrealism"[102]—if it did not have to put in so much effort after all, it was because it could produce a marvel whose essential automatism was truly novel. "The Delirium of a Machine,"[103] a delirium of images, of the laws of the theater and of Aristotelian logic itself, a disorganization of the commensurability of space and time, an instance of anarchy, a derationalization triggered by a rationally built automaton, cinema replaces life with a vertiginous mirage and, at the same time, being able to "put animals into this state for a time," replaces death with a dream of life. It restores and keeps alive, one could say, a life that is but the obverse of death. In cinema, it is well known that everything is, by definition, an illusion, and the very success of its realism decrees that every trick is necessary. The cinema is not a circus or a theater, but it is also a circus, because there is no effect that is not a somersault for this art, and it is a theater, because there is no trick that does not end in a dramatic conflict. It is as unlike a laboratory as it is unlike a church, but it is obviously one (for it is the scene of experiments and a *locus* of secrets that belong more to alchemy than to an industry) and therefore also the other (with its officiants, its own cult, its rituals, its luminous altar, punishments, and excommunications). It is the circus of all effects and illusions, their stage, their temple but also their severe tribunal. It is for this reason that Jacques Rivette was able to unleash from his pulpit at the *Cahiers du cinéma* his famous anathema against the "abjection," both stylistic and moral, of Gillo Pontecorvo, or rather against the framing that in *Kapò* (1959) focuses on the face and then the hand of Teresa (Emmanuelle Riva), who has committed suicide on the barbed wire fence: "The man who decides, at that moment, to do a forward tracking shot to frame the corpse from below, taking care to precisely include the raised hand in a corner of the final shot, deserves utmost contempt."[104]

If the unrivaled magician, Orson the Magnificent, the prestidigitator of *F for Fake* (1973), could already enchant his audience at the Mercury Wonder Show (1943) with his astonishing repertoire of tricks ("Born in Flames," "The Strange Aquarium," "The Fourth Dimension," "Audubon's Dream," "The Hindu Mango Mystery," "Fruit Under a Spell," and "The Haunted Aviary with Invisible Pigeons and Transparent Doves"), a poor director is rather like an arrogant prestidigitator who crowns his misdeed with a musical crescendo and, when he shouldn't even be using them, confuses decorative with illustrative value like some inept painter. Then the effect, in ruins, complains about its rights, until the blame of a severe critic restores them.

In his most-cited essay, Walter Benjamin explains that a cinematographic set is radically different from a theatrical spectacle because in the latter there will always be a perspective that reveals the mechanisms behind the staging, whereas in the former, and for the first time ever, the camera lens excludes them entirely from sight. The epitome of artifice (extreme technification) reestablishes a nature that is no longer artificial in the least and is finally emancipated of all technology. But the return to this uncontaminated world cannot but constitute a new encounter with the knowledge of good and evil. It is along this risky path that cinema plies its trade, and a technique that draws on nature by concealing itself from view calls for and challenges moral judgement. Once again, here too, where everything is a trick, tricks become serious. This has already been repeated on more than one occasion: "Morality is a question of tracking shots [La morale est affaire de travellings]," said Luc Moullet[105]; "Tracking shots are a matter of morality [Les travellings sont affaire de morale]," echoed Jean-Luc Godard,[106] with a formula that became canonical in criticism and which Serge Daney considered to be "one of those truisms one cannot deny [*un de ces truismes sur lesquels on ne reviendrait pas*]."[107] And yet one must return to this phrase, or to Moullet's, because in both cases, in one way or another, morality effectively loses its mask of severity, unveiling its shady dealings with deception. Not only emphasis (e.g., Pontecorvo's rhetoric) but even sobriety is, in this instance, an enchantment. Dialectically, however, only pure enchantment will ever truly be sober, like a technique finally turned back on itself. The dolly can move forward slowly or quickly, toward a face, a detail, or else a gesture, reflecting the values of a freakshow morality. But it can also be combined with a zoom, drawing away while the counter-zoom/dolly-zoom/compensated-zoom approaches, encounters, and disarms it. It is well known that a follower of Hitchcock's often tried to ironically lift the veil on the mechanism, for example, by making the microphone hanging from its "giraffe" appear (at the very edge of the shot), as if by mistake. This minor intruder who plays with the spectator could potentially be capable of destroying the naturalness of the image, of reconverting cinema into theater. But like the good Lord, the devil sometimes hides in the details. What remains foreign to this artificial and didactic reproduction of the *lapsus* is the vertigo effect. Here, two opposing senses of *Schwindel* unite and negate each other: "deceit" and "temptation," "trick" and "illness." In this act of encroachment, the technique grasps itself—a pure and disenchanted technique, deprived of any illustrative quality, without emphasis, lacking any moral tone.

7. The figures painted on Horner's wheel are the ancestors of those impressed on film by light. And these, which don't simply move but also live and love, reveal that the other ones were also, originally, alive. As Johann Peter Frank, and Max Simon along with him, recalled, in German cities in the Middle Ages, prostitutes who were arrested were brought onto the market square and enclosed in narrow wooden cages that were then vertiginously spun until the poor victims collapsed, unconscious. In early nineteenth-century England, in the belief that provoking vertigo unto circulatory collapse was the best way "to correct erroneous ideas," Joseph Mason Cox would inflict on his patients the therapy of the *circulating swing* (1811). It was "a sort of pirouette produced by a rotating machine invented by [Erasmus] Darwin,"[108] immediately adopted in its various versions in Great Britain by William Saunders Hallaran (at the Cork Lunatic Asylum, which had a machine capable of a hundred revolutions per minute), "by Hufeland and Horn in Berlin, Odier in Geneva, Martin in Lyon."[109] Regarding the latter we have a noteworthy witness's account: "Esquirol remembers," writes Max Simon, "that a doctor in Lyon had tried to treat various forms of madness with Darwin's machine, which only differs in appearance from the medieval wooden cages: the effect was identical,

and the mental state of the patients did not ameliorate in the slightest. They were finally forced to give up a form of treatment whose utter uselessness could have easily been foreseen, had they thought about it a little less senselessly."[110] In 1828, George Man Burrows noted that the rotatory machine, which was quite widespread in public English mental asylums, had already fallen into disuse in many places.[111] It would seem that progress does indeed exist. We could therefore enter without fear into a modern-day "Vertigo Ambulatory, as its 'creator' calls it," or more prudently just trust the newspaper reports: "Rooms after rooms are filled with special apparatuses with unpronounceable names: a mask that allows one to record ocular movements in the dark, platforms that move in various directions to test the patient's sense of balance, a chair that rotates about its own axis and a camera that records ocular movements when the patient responds to a series of stimuli on a screen. And another apparatus, similar to the ones used in nightclubs, to subject the patient to stroboscopic images while he is standing in the dark. All of these apparatuses . . . aim to 'stress' the patient and provoke vertigo in order to investigate its causes."[112]

In the early 1820s, during his *Heautognosie* experiments, the courageous Purkinje endured an entire hour on Darwin's rotating chair; a century later, Raymond Dodge, taking up the study carried out earlier by Coleman Griffith on disorientation and the habituation to vertigo in pilots, sat down in Robert Bárány's new rotating chair to be subjected to a training of a hundred and fourteen consecutive rotations at a uniform speed to be repeated over six days.[113] For many years, Friedrich W. Murnau's tenacious disciple had kept in the reserves of his mind the *petite perception* experienced at the Chelsea Arts Ball. In 1957, when the vertigo effect is finally perfected, sympathetic and idiopathic causes, vertiginous dances, and intoxicated swinging, dizziness, dazes, and fear all unite and disappear in Scottie Ferguson's gaze. Of course, for punitive or curative purposes, the atrocious apparatus also reappears from century to century as one of history's *idées fixes*. And Hitchcock, himself so distant from neorealism, had been able to extract from fiction a perfectly documentary piece of evidence and, with the help of Bernard Hermann's score, had just inflicted a slight dizziness on his audience in *The Wrong Man* (1956), making the image of Henry Fonda behind the bars of his cell sway and spin. Thus, right before *Vertigo*, the ball and the old Albert Hall hallucination were already making a disquieting appearance at the climax of the action: the camera "suddenly gets dizzy" and "dancingly gyrates before Fonda's face."[114] It is also true that a similar and more sophisticated "vertigo-inducing movement" would go on to introduce the most famous scene in *Psycho* (1960) and that, even earlier, Novak and Stewart kiss in the room of the Empire Hotel while standing on a rotating platform.[115] Just like this scene (as Rohmer immediately noted), all of the images, the space, and time of *Vertigo* rotate in a winding spiral that never ends. And yet, since 1958, the camera's film rolls at the right speed, and the dolly moves together with the parts inside the lens, and in that ever-repeated moment every spectator can say, "everything was going far away from me" (or, in Daney's case, distant things were receding while close ones grew even closer). He would go on to say it without suffering in the least, maybe without even imagining that his armchair is nothing other than the asylum's rotating seat, *l'espèce de fauteuil* on which the patient was once placed before being subjected to the cure. It took Hitchcock's genius and humor (which Saul Bass's title sequences, with their echoes of Duchamp, bring out) to reproduce that terrible centrifuge and even render it comfortable.

One can therefore recognize the close affinity between the social machine (*machine sociale*) "manufacturing irresponsibility ... and, above all, vertigo," as Simone Weil put it, and the "delirium of a machine [*délire d'une machine*]." And even before that one can recognize behind the powerful mechanism for impressing the masses the rotating cage or pillory that debilitated the prisoner, terrorizing and agitating the crowds with the thousand grimaces of her tormented face. Having survived the darkest of the German Middle Ages, this machine reappeared at the height of modernity and began to hallucinate, lending an ambiguous, seductive beauty (that light beauty of inebriation) to that same rigid fixity imposed by panic.

Perhaps we should recall, in speaking of the seventh art and of the vertigo effect, that while the Lumière brothers were giving their first shows, Bernard Berenson introduced the twin concepts of "tactile values" and "ideated sensations," as if in a last, brilliant reformulation of the eighteenth-century aesthetics of energy. For Berenson, who refers back to one of Bergson's passages on tactile and visual images, art "belongs to the realm of ideated sensations and not of actuality"[116]; in other words, it is a technique capable of transmitting, via visual representation, the presence or tactile force of bodies. And if these "tactile values" produce satisfaction and pleasure, it is because they operate a transfer of the sensible from the domain of actuality to that of fiction.

Cinema would therefore be a felicitous delirium of the old mechanism, which in changing forms has not stopped turning, but it has transferred the effect of its rotation from the actual to the imaginary. More than an uncontested dominion over visual images, it would be a technique capable of producing in every image the tactile value of dizziness which every image would be capable of provoking in us, offering in exchange the pleasure of a fictitious vertigo.

But everything happens in the meanwhile, and in order to stop the rotation in a world without time, one must not miss a cue or tarry (*weilen*) for too long: "The rapid and angular succession approaches the perfect circle of impossible simultaneous action," Epstein wrote in 1921, adding that if everything is perhaps a matter of practice ("It is at least possible that the speed with which we think might increase over the course of a lifetime or over successive generations"), not everyone thinks at the same speed: "the slowness that bothers us in Italian films, where gestures drag out across the screen like slugs, testifies to Italians' slowness of thought," and it is the same slowness that exasperates the reader of the *Illuminations* who, setting aside Rimbaud, switches to Marinetti.[117]

Perhaps this, then, is the famous "identification" that cinema, a "form of time," produces in us. By dominating the effect (or "the sensorial writing of the film [*l'écriture sensorielle du film*]," as Cohen-Séat called it), that is the meter, the rhythm, the effects' music, and abbreviating into the instants on screen the long days of editing during which "the weaving of the most delicate living and organic tissue of the film takes place"[118]—does the seventh art not consist, after all, precisely in *this* abbreviation?—the director must be able to avoid the temporal disjunction of the *Weile*, to conquer thus our center and make the luminous rectangle coincide without our visual field, the space of the film with our space, to inhibit vertigo only to then potentially reproduce it as a "behavior,"[119] and convey it.

Herz's voice can be heard in Epstein's, and a lengthy thought process ("I thought about the problem for fifteen years") finds its fulfillment on screen in the "moment" (*Weile*) when the zoom intersects the dolly. And we can now affirm: the vertigo effect is not a vertiginous form of deceit—it does not merely tend toward empathic contagion, like the famous camera mounted on a trapeze by Ewald André Dupont and all of the movements or caleidoscopic images of his *Variété* (1925)—rather it is vertigo *qua* deceit, or *Schwindel* as such, pure artifice. It halts the rotating chair because it coincides with the technique in itself, which is devoid of violence. For this very same reason, one can say of having watched a poor, badly made film: it was torture.

8. In 1892, while translating the *Leçons du mardi* (*The Tuesday Lessons*), Freud made a note next to a passage by Charcot on the "true cause" of hysterical fits, vertigo, and agoraphobia in a young patient: "Here I must contradict him. The most frequent cause . . . resides not in heredity, but in anomalies related to one's sexual life."[120]

The innovative principle makes its first conspicuous appearance here, against the "neuropathic family" of illnesses passed on from father to son. The causes will turn out to be libidinal and the symptoms will be the words of a hidden language that resounds in phobias, convulsive movements, and dizzy spells; in the paralyses of hysteria as well as in transfers and symbolisms; in subtle unmaskings and resemblances; in peculiar movements, substitutions and inversions. Michel Foucault would go on to say that "Freud has peopled the imaginary world with Desire, just as classical metaphysics had peopled the physical world with divine will and intellect: a theology of signification in which the truth anticipates its own formulation and constitutes it in its entirety."[121] This is the linguistic linchpin of analytic truth understood as the historical truth of the soul, or rather the literal adherence to a text written in ancient and at first incomprehensible characters. And it is a new order of truth that emerges, in turn, from Freud's early practice, in the coherent form of a metaphor: "We [Breuer and I] had often compared the symptomatology of hysteria with a pictographic script which has become intelligible after the discovery of a few bilingual inscriptions. In that alphabet vomiting means disgust."[122] Sexual causality can therefore legitimately replace Charcot's hereditary one, offering itself as a precise translation of the ailment's symptoms. The hysterical hieroglyphics finally become decipherable, and it is on the basis of their own transposition that vertigo itself reveals its "true" meaning. Thus, already in his *Studies on Hysteria* (in an important note on the pages devoted to Lucy R.), Freud, as if guided by some "lucky conjecture," explains the case of "a woman suffering from . . . agoraphobia, attacks of fear of death, etc." by the "precipitating factor" of the menstruation she had as a girl on the eve of the first ball to which she had ever been invited.[123] Other such examples, however, mostly belong to the 1920s. "The Psychogenesis of a Case of Homosexuality in a Woman" (1920) reveals the bilingualism of the verb *niederkommen*, which can be understood both as "to fall" and "to give birth." In this double signification, the secret language can resound, so to speak, in unison with the overt one. And thus the suicide attempt (a jump "down" onto the tracks of the metro), that the young patient justified as being in response to the death of her friend, revealed to the analyst "two other motives besides the one she gave: it was the fulfillment of a punishment (self-punishment), and the fulfillment of a wish. As the latter it meant the attainment of the very wish which, when frustrated, had driven her into homosexuality—namely, the wish to have a child by her father, for now she 'fell' [or 'gave birth'] through her father's fault."[124] A year later, regarding the refined symbolism contrived by a woman who for a long time was pursued by the same nightmare, Freud would write: "At the end of this dream, which is clearly charged with anxiety, the dreamer falls out of bed. This is a fresh representation of childbirth. Analytic investigation of the fear of heights, of the dread of an instinct to throw oneself out of the window, has doubtlessly led you all to the same conclusion."[125] Finally, in 1925, he would go on to dedicate a note in *Inhibitions, Symptoms and Anxiety* to situations of true danger in which a supplementary instinct is added to a truly motivated fear: "In that case the instinctual demand before whose satisfaction the ego recoils is a masochistic one: the instinct of destruction directed against the subject himself. Perhaps an addition of this kind explains cases in which reactions of anxiety are exaggerated, inexpedient or paralysing. Phobias of heights (windows, towers, precipices and so on) may have some such origin. Their hidden feminine significance is closely connected with masochism."[126] If interpretation can thus uncover a sequence of secondary significations, which unite masochism and death with sexuality (menstruation, childbirth), it is because the truth of the symptom partakes of bilingualism: just as vomiting signifies disgust, so falling means giving birth. If "vertigo" is but a single word, we are faced with two languages: one overt, the other covert.

But perhaps "vertigo" is not just any word, or is not merely a word. It may be said to be an affliction of language itself which, fixed in a grammar and at the same time suspended above an abyss ("The language of symbols, as you know, knows no grammar") is systematically anticipated by its own truth and, to reach the latter, it must fatally slide and fall into the secret vocabulary of libido. Indeed, if in these writings of the 1920s the symptoms of dizziness and of loss of balance become intelligible, if they become translatable, it is because language (not only the words of psychosis, neurosis, or hysteria) possesses a double structure and a vertiginous nature, which can emerge in the simplest act of forgetfulness.

This is in fact what happened in the two famous examples at the outset of *The Psychopathology of Everyday Life* (1901). In the first, Freud goes back to a passage in his *The Psychical Mechanism of Forgetfulness* (1898), reconstructing through psychoanalysis the process that one day, while he was speaking of the Duomo in Orvieto with a fellow traveler, led him to forget the name of Signorelli and replace it with the much less well-known one of Boltraffio. With this strange substitution—whose complex mnemic stemma he had already described in 1898—the conversation was in fact fatally drawn toward "the sensitive topic . . . of 'death and sexuality'" which Freud had tried to spare both himself and the foreigner.[127] In the second example, a young academic quotes in an impassioned speech on anti-Semitism a famous line from the *Aeneid*, but with an obvious lacuna (which he then tries to remedy with a substitution). The omitted word (*aliquis*, later broken up by the young man into *a-liquis*) leads through a series of associations ("relics," "liquidation," "fluidity," "Simon of Trent"[128]) to the revelation of an unconfessed but pressing fear—that of an unwanted pregnancy.

If in his writings from the 1920s, the symptom of vertigo translates into "parturition" or "death and sexuality," here, in an inverse but complementary way, it is the themes of "death and sexuality" (in the first case, the confusion of the names Signorelli/Boltraffio) and "giving birth" (in the case of the young academic and the lacunary quotation of Virgil) that produce an authentic linguistic vertigo, drawing speech toward what it otherwise wouldn't utter. In *Inhibitions, Symptoms and Anxiety*, a very specific relation ties—in terms of translation or analytic rationality—symptom to libido: and the names of the second language can decipher and unveil the entire pictography. In *The Psychopathology of Everyday Life*, where anxious attraction comes to afflict language itself, the words, the names of the first language can be substituted by others and are treated "in a manner analogous to the ideograms of a phrase that must be transformed into a rebus."[129]

That which escapes words calls for them, just as symbolism corresponds to that which is repressed. And if bilingualism exists, and can explain a fall or a fear of heights, if, once again, a translation is given, it is because a vertiginous relation exists between the two languages—one apparent, the other concealed. Or better yet, because a head-spinning distance separates the word from itself, making it declare itself in the course of a ruinous fall. This *lapsus* is the Freudian slip (*freudsche [sprachliche] Fehlleistung*), which has gone unnoticed and crept into the medium of written, oral, and gestural language: it is the collapse or breakdown of speech which escapes and flees from itself only to then stumble back on itself.

Foucault observed that "Freudian analysis only takes up one of the possible senses via divinatory shortcuts or the lengthy paths of probability: the expressive act in itself is never reconstituted in terms of its necessity."[130] It is precisely because there is no grammar of the imagination (which remains irreducible to the play of signification), that divination can only go so far, where it cannot but end, and the paths of probability will end up being similarly ill-fated. Thus, Freud was able to explain via self-analysis his own forgettings and substitutions; he resolved the rebus by reconstructing its outline and translated the vertigo that affected him in Monaco in November 1912, via the terms of the secret language, into the latent anxiety experienced during those days as a result of a quarrel with Carl Gustav Jung and Sándor Ferenczi's illness. But the term *Fehlleistung* (*lapsus*) itself does not in this case substitute another and it is not translatable into a second language; it is instead perfectly transparent and indicates the vertigo that afflicts language itself when traditional psychiatry's most vague and indefinable of illnesses is finally tied to its proper signification. Here, condensed into one word, perhaps the necessity of the expressive act finally appears; certainly, only to simultaneously evade analysis, but demonstrating nevertheless that desire (unlike its divine equivalent) is in itself vertiginous.

9. Freud's discovery—or, one might say, his intelligence—gives everyone dizziness; it places one before a chasm. And it can be dealt with in two opposing but complementary ways. The first consists in reinstating the old rule, consigning the method that unites Signorelli and Boltraffio and its mind-boggling connections to the category of aberrations and, in the case of *aliquis*, replacing the "arbitrary" interpretation with a "pedestrian (but true)" one. It is a matter of filling in the void or eliminating the gap by reducing the omission to a mere "banalization" of Virgil's text, to an imperfect but nevertheless effective quotation. What this reestablishes is a matter-of-fact truth which, however, demands the rigorousness of a philologist to explain with precision this simplification of a "strongly irregular syntactic construction." For indeed on what grounds did the analytic interpretation stake its pretensions? "Cristopher bore Christ; Christ bore the whole world; Say, where did Christopher then put his foot?"[131] Freud once directed this "old joking question" at the theory of suggestion, which pretended to explain the world without being able to explain itself. The question would continue to echo, however, and another voice would go on to observe: your Christopher stands not on the firm ground of libido but vacillates on a slippery form of symbolism, and despite the odd combinations and the shaky world of psychoanalysis, an authentic science still persists and resists, respecting the rigorous adhesion of language to its material tenor. Such was the response of the Italian philologist.[132]

The second strategy, by contrast, requires an actor's demeanor. As far as it is concerned, the *lapsus* is no longer a fall from one language into another, nor is it the intersection of bilingualism. It is in and of itself a word, a word of a language consisting exclusively of signifiers. There is therefore no precipice, if the symptom is itself "structured like a Language, because the symptom is a Language from which the Word must be liberated."[133] There is no vertigo if the Lacanian "structure" replaces the grammarless fluctuating symbolism, while the speech of the symptoms is liberated—notable paradox—by a "signifying chain" which, by including or drawing to itself the *lapsus*, prevents the fall. No dizziness is possible if there is no lacuna, if "it speaks even when it is silent,"[134] and "it is clear that every parapraxis is a successful discourse—one might call it a nicely turned 'phrase'—and that in the *lapsus* it is the muzzling effect or gag that which hinges on the Word, and exactly from the right angle for its word to be sufficient to the wise [*pour qu'un bon entendeur y trouve son salut*]."[135]

The first strategy confronts risk by keeping to a path without difficulties, leveling to the ground the superabundance of the theoretical construction.

"Pedestrian (but true)," it claims to rid itself of the precariousness that Freud's argumentation (which is rightly the privileged target of criticism) skirts at every moment, exhibiting it as a limit and an inevitable risk. The second strategy, by contrast, achieves its result by touching the bottom of the abyss, or rather dragging the surface down to it in order to discover (like in Poe's seminar on *The Purloined Letter*) that death and language coincide.

Thus, neither one nor the other, nor even the strategy of negation (nothing speaks, all is silent), nor that of overcoming by excess (it speaks even if it is silent) manages to refute vertigo: "if we fix our gaze on our point of support . . . we fall, despite ourselves, in the attempt to grab hold of it."

In 1914, however, in a reflected image that was also a sort of counteraction, something could be made out. In the brief essay "Sensations of Giddiness at the End of the Psycho-Analytic Session" ("Szédülés érzete az analízis-óra végén"), Sándor Ferenczi noted that when they were about to leave, certain patients were struck by dizziness. Given its liminal nature, this symptom could not be explained by the symbolism of the unconscious. He did not accept a translation because upon further examination it concerned bilingualism itself. When the doctor ended the therapy, the patient, immersed in a flow of free associations, had to all of a sudden interrupt the transfer—as if suddenly braking, a young man with obsessive mania explained—to find himself in a psychic state to which he was no longer accustomed. Thus, the agreeable situation was all of a sudden replaced for him by the (very materialistic) principle of reality: he was merely a patient among others, and "it is the paid doctor, and not the helpful father that stands before him." The disillusionment, the difficulty of bearing and adapting to the new situation resulted in a momentary loss of balance. "Naturally at the moment of this disillusionment that part of the *belief in the analysis* that did not as yet rest on honest conviction but only on a filial trust disappears very easily, and the patient is again suddenly more inclined to regard the analytic explanations as a 'swindle,'" that is, both vertiginous and deceiving, given that in Hungarian *szédület* has the same double meaning as *Schwindel*.[136]

It is with this sensation of precariousness experienced at the end of a session, and with the delicate "mechanism" that finds itself displayed in it, that Ferenczi compares the vertigo of hysterical conversion. As a psychic tension that penetrates the corporeal sphere, dizziness is not merely a symptom like any other, since it belongs to the relation between reality and interpretation; it positions itself between the manifest language and the secret one and therefore has a special role that is closely related to the dynamic of analysis. And yet nevertheless, or perhaps as a result of this privilege, it still remains a symptom that despite everything has not yet been considered in and of itself. But perhaps this merely means that in vertigo one finds condensed the imaginative status of a dream that calls itself psychoanalysis, whose elementary symbolism is reducible to a series of pseudonyms (Dora for Ida Bauer, K. for Hans Zellenka, B. for Merano). This means that the role played by the imagination must not be included in the compendium of cases (keeping, as Freud asks, to what Freud recounts or what the patients supposedly recounted) but must be considered at the level of fiction, or, in other words, of their own narrative construction (to which the patient obviously contributes no less than the therapist). It is only at the level of this construction (which, according to the old law of suggestion, is always double, always ambivalent), that is, only within the dynamic of analysis or in the genesis of the case-study, that the dreams become knowable or exist as expressions of the imagination. And the grammar that Freud did not recognize—according to Foucault—is nothing other than the analysis itself, or the structure of the "clinical case-study" which makes of every dream a dream framed by an agrammatical symbolism whereby "fire," in contrast, stands in for something that is wet and signifies desire and sexuality. Only according to the Freudian grammar of the imagination can the leg that poor Ida Bauer dragged along as the result of a pelvic appendicitis become the (agrammatical) symbol of the misstep that Dora made with K.

In 1954, while simultaneously reading Freud, Binswanger, and Husserl, Foucault discovered a meaning of dreams that oneiric images obscured. Contesting the primacy of Freudian semantics, he affirmed that the "presence of meaning in a dream is not its own meaning" and that "a dream betrays its meaning while enacting it,"[137] thus unknowingly taking up and transforming the distant echo of the young Benjamin: "The language of dreams is not in their words, but below them. Words in dreams are the arbitrary products of meaning [*Zufallsprodukte des Sinns*], which lies in the wordless continuity of a flux. In oneiric language, meaning is hidden in the same way that a figure is hidden in a rebus. It is even possible that the origin of the rebus must be sought in this direction, in an oneiric stenograph, so to speak."[138]

The relation between the ideogram and the rebus does not correspond, as in the *The Psychopathology of Everyday Life*, to the semantics of the libido: meaning flows beneath the oneiric language and the relation between the meaning and the language of the dream is dictated only by "chance" (*Zufall*). Thus, analytic interpretations truly totter once they are exposed to the vertigo of contingency—and this is precisely their truth.

2
We Are Not Here

10. In 1961, Robert Klein published an essay entitled "Appropriation et aliénation" in Enrico Castelli's *Archivio di filosofia*; it was the first chapter of a rich and unfortunately prematurely interrupted research project concerning the limits and difficulties of transcendental ethics. Dedicated to the "Fourth" and "Fifth Cartesian Meditation" and at the same time felicitously inspired by the reading of Gerd Brand's study of Husserl's so-called "Group C" manuscripts,[1] the essay takes as its starting point a reflection on the Husserlian notion of *habitus*.

As is commonly known, in §29 of the *Studies in the Phenomenology of Constitution* and in §32 of the *Cartesian Meditations*, Husserl conceives the constitution of the "I" as a rigorous connection between identity and the permanence of the subject in terms of the "original constitution" (*Urstiftung*) of properties, of *habitus* or of the "sphere of that which is my own" (*Eigenheitssphäre*). One could also say that the secular theme of *compos sui* reappears, adapted to the new figure of the pure *ego*, the center of a constitutive consciousness, whose "performances [*Leistungen*] constitute meaning and being,"[2] and which, in its flux, remains faithful to itself. Turning to its current theme, which is given in the "presentation," the ego is in fact "extended" toward the future, but already before then it keeps an eye on its previous thought, even without thematizing it. Without this "retention" of the past (which is "not actually a perceiving grasping, but it is a grasping"[3]), the consequentiality of the *cogito* (or the relatedness of the *Leistungen*) could not in fact exist. Instead, thanks to this retention, that which has passed remains (despite not being present, that is, implicitly) in my possession and therefore determines me: it is a "stance" taken with reference to the preceding ones and to which the following ones will, in turn, refer back; it is a conviction of mine, both consequent and foundational. If every action of the constitutive consciousness is thus an appropriation, the multiplicity of these actions or acquisitions forms an *"identical substrate of Ego-properties"* and the Ego "constitutes itself as 'fixed and permanent' [*stehend und bleibend*] personal Ego."[4] The pure ego, the pole of consciousness's flux, appropriates, in other words, the world while forming itself as a concrete subject (or monad), acquiring both passively and actively forms of *habitus*, which then become empirically observable as dispositions and determinations of character. This amphiboly of possession, which keeps the subject under the tutelage of its property, has attracted a variety of interpretations. With a sensibility inherited from Ravaisson and Maine de Biran among others, Jean Wahl observed in his lectures on Husserl (which were influenced by Brand's work) that the use of the term *habituality* testifies to "the need to find a middle term between activity and passivity."[5] For his part, Wilhelm Szilasi has underscored that "Husserl rightly labels as *habitus* the totality of that which is retained by the stream of my thought, or in other words the entirety of what I possess [*die gesamte Habe*]. The fact that these possessions [*Habe*] accumulated over the course of an entire lifetime also constitute my *habitus* of thought, my characteristics, my manners, is aptly conveyed by the term's double meaning."[6]

The notion of *habitus-Habe* therefore both conceals and betrays its Greek origin: now fully subjected to the dominion of the Cartesian subject, *héxis*, which Aristotle had conceived as an intermediary disposition in between potency and act, or rather as the pure operativity and permanence (via the repetition of actions) of *dýnamis*, becomes fully integrated into the "essential law of the I's identity." At the height of its modern interpretation—after Samuel Butler, the Hegelian "second nature," the connection with *effort* and the internal sense conceived by Maine de Biran (in the wake of Cabanis and Condillac) in terms of active and passive habits, muffled sensations, and acute perceptions, and after Félix Ravaisson's brilliant treatment of it—habituality thus constitutes the Husserlian ego as a subject accountable for the resolutions, convictions and actions that it attributes to him. Confirming them, certainly, but not only: even when it seems inconsistent, unfaithful to itself, the "concrete subject" cannot in fact erase the choices it has already made; if it changes opinion or disavows its own position, it nevertheless continues, according to §29 of *Studies in the Phenomenology of Constitution*, to be "the same, though in a changing stream of lived experience."[7] And if it can abandon its old convictions to become another—even someone whose behavior is as different as possible—if it can therefore retrace its own steps and change, it is, according to §32 of the *Cartesian Meditations*, only because it remains the very same *I*.

The notion of *héxis* is therefore consigned and reduced to the possessive principle of identity: the Husserlian argument ties having to being, transforming one into the other, restricting the temporal horizon of possibility to the relation between determination and freedom, between pure choice and constraint, that is to the permanent properties of the personal subject, the center of all appropriations. Wherever retention is the rule, wherever the flow of time is tied to a subjective focal point, freedom and potency can only exist under the sign of possession, of the identical ego that is "numerically one" and ever and only equal to itself.

The true development of this notion coincides with its radical critique—that is, with the brilliant return to the Kierkegaardian idea of a possibility that is bound to itself. It was Heidegger—a careful reader, as we know from Frédéric de Towarnicki, of "Ravaisson's excellent essay on habit"[8]—who definitively eliminated the idea of freedom from the traditional view, which understood it, against any notion of forced sequentiality or mechanical determination, as "beginning with oneself" or a form of pure spontaneity. For Heidegger, freedom does not derive from an "indefinite 'velleity,'" just as it does not depend on an "empty '*habitus*'"[9]: it is instead the "original *bond*" that ties *Dasein* to itself as a *being-in-the-world*, that arranges it "for-the-sake-of-itself" and ties it to its "world" as the totality of its effective bonds. In freedom, which is the internal possibility of every will, what reveals itself, in other words, is the very transcendence of *Dasein*. It is not therefore "unimportant here to what extent something defined as free is, in fact, free or to what extent it is aware of its freedom. . . . Only a free being can be unfree."[10] One could furthermore observe that the notion of voluntary servitude is also thus removed from the ontic domain of habit to which La Boétie had attributed it and situated in a sphere that precedes action: here, where effective obligation originates in the original bond to oneself, the intertwining of freedom and determination can finally be revindicated as such. It can and *must*, however, under the sign of the *se ipse*, of the still inviolate tie that in grasping truth breaks its wings (Rachel Bespaloff) and disposes it to every sort of bond. "Selfhood," writes Heidegger, "is the free ability to be bound for and to oneself."[11]

One could add that in France, while man was being "condemned to be free [*condamné à être libre*]" via a revisitation and secularization of Kierkegaard (Wahl),[12] an eminent student of Husserl's and Heidegger's was distancing himself from both, contesting the notion of immanent transcendence and the conception of the self as an identification with and enchainment to itself (*identification et enchaînement à soi*). From the early 1940s (in the studies that became *Existence and Existents*) to the middle of the 1970s (*Otherwise Than Being*), Emmanuel Levinas conceived with admirable coherence the "there is" (*il y a*) as the "anonymous rustling,"[13] the "horror, trembling, and vertigo"[14] of pure existence which subjectivity must suffer in a relation of radical passivity, without being able to constitute it as existent. That which breaks the chain of habit or the bond of the self is thus not a freedom that claims to be original or a beginning that considers itself of its own will, but "all the weight that alterity weighs supported by a subjectivity that does not found it."[15] Existence is revealed as a foundation-less compulsion which, preceding (rather than mediating) the opposition between activity and passivity, opens to unassumable alterity or diachrony and both imposes on itself and flees from philosophic meditation, pushing it to the verge of the abyss and holding it there: "It is as though thought becomes dizzy pouring over the emptiness of the verb to exist."[16]

Klein, for whom Heidegger's thrownness (*Geworfenheit*) is "revealing of being just as vertigo is revealing of space,"[17] never cites Levinas. Instead, he carries out a critique of "faithfulness to oneself" that does not merely take aim at the reference to "an external (and therefore 'instituted') norm," but also touches on and highlights the paradoxical structure of *habitus*, demonstrating how it is impossible to define a choice that may or may not conform to what one retains via recollection, which remains "before one's eyes" but cannot be thematized. Of course, the "demythologization of morality" undertaken by Klein proceeds rigorously in Husserl's footsteps, and one could ask whether it could thus free itself from the fundamental egological constriction or if it remains impaled—as a "reflection on the morality of a particular individual or collective subject"—on the unitary stream of consciousness, that is to say, held back by older and still solid Cartesian boundaries. Even a reading that grasps, as Robert Klein put it, in an "intimate contradiction" the "specific trait of pure consciousness" seemingly continues to respect the Husserlian unity of the stream, whose "source bears the title *I-myself* [*diese Quelle hat den Titel 'Ich-selbst'*]."[18] But in investigating this contradiction from the point of view of habitualities or "transcendental genesis," Klein, with his characteristic genius, recognizes at the very heart of appropriation or *habitus* the need for an objectification that would constitute a paradoxical shift to an intersubjective point of view or, in other words, to the dimension of the inappropriable. Thought radically, and pushed to its ultimate consequences, transcendental morality appears like "Wittgenstein's ladder, which must be climbed to then be gotten rid of."[19] It is only then, or from up there, that the subject—even the one whom Ricoeur would go on to call "oneself as . . . other"[20]—gives in to "the exceptional circumstance of vertigo."

11. Klein's problem is the relation between coercion and freedom. He had already approached it from a different angle in 1953, in his dissertation, which was supervised by Étienne Souriau and entitled "Ars et Technè dans la

tradition de Platon à Giordano Bruno." The central role is given here to the theory of Aristotelian origin, which is based on a well-known passage in the *Nicomachean Ethics* (6, 4, 1140a), which challenges the principle of *mímesis* by associating art as production with art as faculty, or rather renders *téchne* and *héxis* historically compatible within *poíesis*. According to Klein, the long story of this difficult relation—and therefore the analysis of its solutions, including those of the Renaissance and baroque period—developed along two fundamental lines: the first conceives of artistic mastery under the aegis of the rule or true reason (*recta ratio*); the second understands artistic mastery as a power of transgression and places the accent on the freedom and ingenuity (*ingenium*) of the subjective spirit, which is in every case superior to its product. In this case, art appears as a "property of the subject," a disposition, a *habitus* capable of constituting and modifying itself, oscillating "between potency and act as between power and knowledge, faculty and routine, the individualized quality and the objective acquisition," between the extremes (perhaps similar but not reducible to those of *parole* and *langue*) of the unrepeatable gesture and the codified and transmissible operation, precisely between determination and—one could gloss—freedom.

Ten years later, at the end of *Le rire*, a dense essay dedicated above all to Georges Bataille, Klein reaffirms that the appearance-reality dichotomy "within which people have wished to confine art for years" conceals instead the true aesthetic polarity, which is instead between the real situation and the situation that is freely created by consciousness or via an intersubjective agreement concerning its meaning. Art thus reveals its affinity with laughter; it is the *genus proximum* of this special act of freedom which escapes from the real situation (experienced with embarrassment), installing in its place, and with the complicity of the other, a ludic dimension: "The joy of art, which has the same nature as the joy of laughter, is the concrete experience of the fact that the word is not merely what it is, but that we can alter its appearance according to the meaning that we confer on it."[21] Both in the artwork and the joke, fiction and the imagination play an unrealizing role, transforming—via an authentic transition to the intersubjective point of view (*passage au point de vue intersubjectif*)—the actual situation into a potential spectacle and thus routine into freedom. One can observe that by bringing together the themes of *habitus*, alterity, and *poíesis* (habit itself can in fact be an object of ludic exhibition), Klein tries to stretch the limits of the aesthetic *epoché*, or of the "aesthetic destitution of the world's reality [*ästhetische Enthobenheit von der Weltwirklichkeit*]" defined by Husserl.[22] The coherence with the ideas of 1953 is indeed evident and is confirmed both by later re-elaborations of his work on technique (the unpublished so-called "Thèse Bédarida" of 1957 or the "Thèse Chastel" on mannerism from 1962, recently published by Jérémie Koering under the title *L'esthétique de la technè*) and by other essays that appeared in the "Archive of Philosophy": certainly in "L'art et l'attention au technique," which forcefully takes up the idea (seemingly of vague Schopenhauerian origin, "significant spectacle" [*bedeutsames Schauspiel*]: *The World as Will and Representation*, §52) of the work as "spectacle for a consciousness," or of *téchne* which "necessarily stretches between the two opposing extremes of perpetual invention . . . and total codification."[23] But even in the first text given to Castelli, that is, the admirable essay on Rimbaud and the *Saison en enfer*,[24] where the literary existence of the poet only appears "through Verlaine's eyes," "truth is *essentially* linked to artifice" and fiction reveals itself as the domain of *justesse*, a criterion of subjective choice as such and on the basis of which something can be declared valid as true.[25]

Despite *Le rire*'s having been published posthumously by André Chastel, at least in one of its versions,[26] the 1953 thesis is still unpublished. But Klein never stopped going back and developing that work, weaving the dominant theme of *habitus* into his studies of art history, of the history of ideas, of literature and philosophy, shining a light on it from new points of view until it came to be synonymous with his work as a scholar. The frame (in the technical, literary sense) of this adventure is phenomenological, and he expounds it in his philosophical essays in the period between 1961 and 1965 (in "Appropriation et aliénation," where some of the conclusive passages of the so-called "Thèse Souriau" make a reappearance, and in "Les limites de la morale transcendantale").

12. To use Husserl's terminology, if I am determined by my possessions, by my permanence and identity, I am free precisely insofar as I am already determined even in my most authentic possibilities: I can only be thus (on the basis of my acquisitions, of what I have become and of the objective situation of the person that is "I"), and yet I am still compelled to respect my possibilities, I *must* be as I truly am. "I carry within me, in my actual, present life, my painful, false facticity—but I also carry within me the idea of my true being, of my having to be."[27]

For historical reasons, the phenomenological tradition was primarily received and developed in Italy beginning in the late 1930s and during the postwar period (from the second half of the 1950s, when the reading of *The Crisis of European Sciences* triggered a more definite and active interest in Husserl), first of all by Enzo Paci, in the context of an ethics of values, of risk and destiny understood as mission and work (one may also of course think of the encounter with the current of existentialism influenced by idealism and Giovanni Gentile, or with Benedetto Croce's school and therefore the career and role of

Ernesto de Martino). The "I" itself appeared then as a duty; truth was an "intentional direction" (and at the same time the truth of intentionality) which included art, and above all literature, while factitious "painfulness" (*Schmerzhaftigkeit*) conferred a concrete sense to *praxis*, to every will as well as personal and social duty (as Paci wrote in his introduction to Brand's work).[28]

Accepting Castelli's invitation, Klein intervenes in a field where no one laughs, one that is full of commitment, severity, and even a touch of mournfulness, to present a decidedly different reading. He begins with the criticism of mythical morality, which considers itself established, and with its false analogies with jurisprudence, nature, and religion; he then notes that a morality without myth could only derive from the structure of consciousness. Reaching thus the properly Husserlian dimension of "transcendental morality," he concludes by recognizing that even it could not undergo a complete demythicization or be based on it, since a demythicized ethics could not affirm itself without in turn becoming mythical. No longer the rule of duty, transcendental morality thus becomes "both necessary and impossible."[29]

While he invites his readers to ask "whether the need for freedom always consists in conforming to it rather than in escaping its predeterminations," Klein does not recognize the existence of an internal imperative set in place "by the 'idea of my true being,'" and even unsettles the very dogma of the essential unity of the "true 'I.'"[30] He does not turn to the "ought to be" as an "inaugural valorization" (de Martino), but to those singular moments or phenomena that suddenly interrupt the foreseeable sequence of choices and decisions or of consciousness's acquisitions, and do not allow themselves to be integrated into the flux of appropriation, originating instead in the painfulness (*Schmerzhaftigkeit*) of not being able to be what one is. This is the experience of remorse described by Vladimir Jankélévitch in *The Bad Conscience* (1939): "The fault committed," Klein observes, "'is here,' present 'in person,' in my conscience and in my past, as an inappropriable piece of reality: no identity is conceivable between myself and him who has committed the fault."[31] And the crisis which, as Leibniz put it, does not let us distinguish anything (*ne nous laisse rien distinguer*), functions in precisely this manner. "It can occur that suddenly becoming conscious (*une prise de conscience*) of a reality separates it from the sphere of what is my own [*Eigensphäre*], from its relation to the center, 'I': in the exceptional case of vertigo provoked by heights, this awakening can go so far as to determine my perception of space."[32]

As a special alteration of consciousness, as an internal avoidance of its own grasp (it was Ricoeur who had translated Husserl's *Besinnung* in *Krisis* as *prise de conscience*), which removes the intentional nature of the very act that constitutes it as such, vertigo is, more than simply a pathology, a consciousness of the inappropriable which propels the 'I' beyond its own sphere. It is truly an impurity of the transcendental (and Klein is truly Herz's Husserlian successor), whose origins go back to *héxis*, or rather to its paradoxical nature. If everything is indeed consciousness, if every conscious act constitutes its object as such and every constitution is a different appropriation of the world, if everything I grasp and possess produces a *habitus*, this totality should in theory extend to the *habitus* itself: the unavoidable conscience of the *habitus* would thus imply "a having of my having, and so on *ad infinitum*."[33] It is to this primary difficulty, whose origin, as is known, goes all the way back to Aristotle ("it is impossible to have a having (*héxis, habitus*), because if it were possible to have the having of what one has, one could go on infinitely"[34]) that Klein offers a brilliant solution. Being both having and the impossibility of having, constituting in the moment the concrete ego, unable to escape consciousness and yet remaining at the same time unassumable and inactual, the *habitus* demands a whirling passage through alterity. To truly be "I," a person, I must therefore "see myself through the eyes of another." The *prise de conscience* of the *habitus*, which is inevitable, coincides with its being totally called into question, with the feeling that, well before any fiction, the "I" is an other (constituted by and constituting the other consciousness), though I cannot but continue to be me. *Héxis*, vertigo, and intersubjectivity thus seem to be integral and fundamentally intertwined. And it is perhaps by virtue of their connection that, just as in remorse the past becomes unrecognizable, so we can experience vis-à-vis another a perilous attraction or an ambivalent repulsion and discover in ourselves a predisposition or adopt a habit that is openly vertiginous.

In any case, the Husserlian construction is subjected to a novel and powerful stimulus. And henceforth the phenomenologist too must confront that "sensation of instability" which, for its part, psychology had continued to study as the "fundamental element"[35] of a disorder that in the meantime was spreading from the narrowest of precipices to vast open spaces in the guise of agoraphobia or "the fear of not being able to keep one's balance in the absence of objects nearby to potentially hold on to."[36] "The climber on the side of a cliff," Klein writes, in an important footnote to his essay, "is no longer able to relate space to his *here* as center. The entirety of space bursts into the consciousness of the subject, who feels that his 'spatial center,' and therefore his *here*, is elsewhere, below. It is the loss of an anchor point in space, the disappearance of the spatial equivalent of the 'I': hence the temptation to throw oneself down (to reach that *here*) and the fear, which is not a fear of slipping, but of ceding to temptation."[37] "We are tempted to throw ourselves into the void," reads an alternate version of the same passage, "to fill in this space whose suddenly perceived reality displaces us from our central position and renders the place in which we find ourselves contingent."[38]

The void attracts because it is a "here" while being "there," because to be myself, my "I," I must be there, from where the other sees me. Husserl's alter ego comes to mind, who while being "there," before me, is a "here," an "I-center." One may think of the mechanism invented by Hitchcock: the countermovement of the zoom does not simply impede a point or an object in the distance from receding, fleeing in perspective (while the dolly recedes), just as it does not merely limit itself, conversely, to bringing a distant object or surface (the ground) closer. Instead, it brings the very background of the visual toward which the object is falling closer while at the same time constraining it, via a sort of optical friction, to be subject to the effect of the tracking shot, which makes it precipitate. That which falls (along with the background) is thus the very center of the vision: the "here" is dragged downward, while space as such barges into one's consciousness. If a simple zoom, in other words, makes objects recede or draw nearer to the center of observation ("the viewpoint must be fixed, you see, while the perspective is changed as it stretches lengthwise"[39]), the counter-zoom both brings closer and distances. It thus shifts the center itself (the Husserlian *Nullpunkt* or zero point of space) to an eccentric and unstable position. The "here" is down there, it beckons to us from down there and the intensity of the beckoning is not dependent on distance: to fall would in fact mean to grasp one's own *habitus*, to refind oneself, to respond to that which must be responded to, to give in to the old disposition, to carry out all the way to the very end one's "ought." There will probably be someone irresponsible who will not let himself be attracted, because of a lack of personality (or a lack of masochism, perhaps the Freudian would say), or an essential unfaithfulness that renders him morally untrustworthy. Because of a disturbance of the "I," because of an excess of passivity, and in any case as a result of having missed the fatal moment, he will hold back from vertigo itself, which in turn will become habitual, paradoxically impeding him from falling. It will thus be the duty of the next individual to solve the ambiguity and—we will see if a policeman exists—sacrifice himself. Will he experience, having just come to the rescue, the fatal attraction? Of him we know only that he is in uniform. And a being perfectly determined by his clothing (*habitus*) and by present circumstances is a dead one.

13. "Nothing excites vertigo more than fear!" For Bachelard, the fear of falling is a primitive fear (*peur primitive*).[40] But if fear induces vertigo, it is because vertigo is fear *in itself* and with respect to itself, the fear, that is, of giving in to a temptation that is in turn vertiginous. "Far from being born of

peril, it generates it," warned Caillois.[41] And almost in unison, Bachelard (glossing Thomas de Quincey) noted that "the darkness of the abyss is not the cause of fear" but, on the contrary, "the abyss is *deduced* from the fall. . . . *My fall creates the abyss*, whereas the abyss is far from being the cause of my fall."[42] The fall as origin and producer of the chasm is a form or acute manifestation of the fundamental and latent vertigo that encounters itself and emerges as such: it frightens and gives in to itself.

The state of convalescence—Scottie's barely alleviated and habitual dizziness—consists instead in a singular compromise. It is the simultaneously calm and restless condition of one who has crossed the threshold of determinations and now lives down there, where the other has fallen, and therefore still with them. The profound vertigo that was once awakened has now become a prevailing habit for him. Scottie now lives among the dead, in a state into which "death can put animals . . . for a time [*la mort peut donner pour un temps aux animaux*]." And the key concept of the phenomenology of religion, according to which "the border between life and death is that which distinguishes two modes of being, not that which opposes existence to nothingness,"[43] has become for him the ordering principle of his everyday rituality. He drags himself through the long days of a life he cannot make his own, as an incomplete bachelor, as a man without relations and without a center, indolent and indeterminate, beyond everything but prey to everything.

He therefore sees Madeleine and surrenders to her charm. But Madeleine is not Madeleine. She is actually Judy, Elster's accomplice, who by attracting Scottie lays a trap for him: she welcomes him, presenting herself in Madeleine's stead, entering into his world, into that lazy rhythm, or into that place which is at the same time an atmosphere. With her, as with the mysterious gesture of the fairy "some years ago, at the *Théâtre des Variétés*," anxiety makes its entry, slow but inexorable, and "vertigo circulates in the air; we breathe vertigo; it is vertigo that fills the lungs and renews the blood in the ventricles."[44] And he follows her into that world, when she lays flowers at Carlotta's grave in the small cemetery filmed by Hitchcock with a soft focus effect and that strange greenish aura that returns toward the end to illuminate the famous hotel scene, or Madeleine's last appearance. That will be a posthumous and artificial apparition, both evanescent and definitive. For a while now she had disappeared: Scottie had believed in her life before and in her death afterwards ("he had seen the body"[45]). He had suffered the effects, and been hospitalized for a long time, reduced to an almost catatonic state of depression. In short, Elster's plan had worked out perfectly. If not that the love of death cannot be extinguished by death. And thus, one day, while once again roaming about, in front of the shop window of Podestà Baldocchi, Madeleine's florist, Scottie accidentally notices Judy among a group of saleswomen leaving a store. He does not know who she is, nor does it matter: although a brunette and vulgar in her clothes, gestures, and features ("Renée was an ageing woman . . . she had neither Madeleine's distinction nor her charm";[46] Rodenbach writes that "Jane's face had taken on a certain hardness, as well as a weariness"[47]), for him the woman dressed in green—a jade framed by the florist's two green cars—evokes Madeleine. And he seeks her out. Madeleine thus returns for him, as the specter projected by the neon sign of the hotel, she returns in the room belonging to Judy, who now accepts to become (no longer according to Elster's plan, but for the sake of the man she loves) the dream and mask of a dead woman and dressed and made up as Madeleine, she *truly* becomes her for the first time. But she thus also simultaneously becomes Carlotta, and the ethereal, greenish or "linden green" haze of the cemetery finally glows for her, Judy, who advancing slowly, solemnly, both apprehensively and passionately, can surrender herself, docilely, to the embrace of the necrophile.[48] And while the camera rotates (framing the two actors standing on a rotating platform) and space and time (the images of the Mission San Juan in a 360-degree panorama) whirl around them, the less than ordinary alcove becomes for her a sepulcher looking out onto the street: "The roar and clatter or the town seemed to come, filtered, from far away. One might have been transported to some other country on the margin of this life of ours, as if existence had changed all of a sudden." This is the description of the atmosphere in the cemetery of Passy.[49] But it is the same muffled atmosphere that now invades the hotel room, the one in which Scottie remained immersed throughout his wanderings, Madeleine's aura, to which Flavières was the first to surrender: "He could smell her perfume. A complicated smell, which had affinities with rich earth and dead flowers. Where had he come across it before? The previous day, of course, in the deserted part of the Cimetière de Passy. . . . He liked it. It reminded him of his grandparents' house near Saumur, built on the side of a steep rocky hill,"[50] or else it reminded him of the ravines, the rocky caverns and "forbidden world of galleries and passages" that the house gave access to.[51] Then, as if by enchantment, the city appeared in the reflected mossy light, and the most crowded of streets became a sepulchral passageway. "Just as in adults such is the experience of vertigo, so for that matter is that of the labyrinth, with its subterranean space and its exit through death."[52] And thus the steep streets of San Francisco, down which the car slowly descended, were like the Boulevard Saint-Germain in Paris: "And there on the sunny boulevard under the budding trees, Flavières experienced once again the fearful attraction of the shades, and he understood why, at the first glance, Madeleine had touched him."[53] Later on, she will go on to say, even closer to the mark: "For you—and for everyone else, in fact—life's the exact opposite of death... For me..."[54] We know these words; but she knows they come from him and so must be addressed precisely to him, while others, the "all of you," living or dead, remain estranged from those intimate passageways where sepulchral solitude is explored and lived. She should have said: "For *me*, for everyone... but for *you*..." Instead, meeting him and repeating back to him the words of his own dream, she retains Scottie down there and fabricates an enchantment whereby he, no longer alone, is like her ("Every other is a self like myself. He is like that double which the sick man feels always at his side"[55]) and is close to her ("Myself and the other are like two *nearly* concentric circles"[56]) in a world that is finally shared, and in which the dead (Carlotta, and so therefore also the fallen colleague) play their part. Madeleine—the strange and powerful somnambulist—has attracted and reunited, on this street inundated with people and light, in that swarm of confusing sensations, the sick patient and the frightened child; and he has of course given in to the temptation, begun to follow her and can now no longer stop. He cannot move away if not to once again turn toward her, Madeleine, alias Renée (Judy), whom Flavières explicitly calls Eurydice, "Eurydice resurrected." "You frighten me... but I need you.... Perhaps I need to be frightened... to despise my petty existence..."[57] That ambiguous existence is now presented to him by the same gaze (the "groping look") that frightens and captivates him. Nothing in fact excites vertigo more than fear, but only fear can awaken vertigo from its ordinary (and ignominious) form. In the greenish light, the encounter and transfiguration of a solar dream and a mossy night, for both one and the other, for Scottie as for Judy, "something rather complicated" happens.

14. Vertigo is a trick, an intrigue that seems perfect. Judy cannot be recognized because she does not disguise herself as Elster's wife but as Madeleine, or as Carlotta. Madeleine is the mask of the dead woman (Carlotta): that is why Judy does not merely imitate a model but *becomes* the imitation, turning into Madeleine, or into a pure mask. Now, if Judy becomes Madeleine, it is Carlotta who plays a role, imitating and recalling yet another image: becoming Madeleine, playing and evoking Carlotta, Judy is actually conjuring up, in Scottie's eyes, the unfortunate colleague or double. Madeleine's dream is Scottie's nightmare. It is in fact only for him (for his vertigo), or better yet only *through* Scottie, that Madeleine can be Carlotta as Judy will later be able to become Madeleine. It is therefore Scottie who in this farce—a "spectacle for a consciousness"—truly becomes another and remains and lives among the dead. It is Scottie's "here" that, in the encounter with Madeleine, becomes a "there," is drawn

"down there," where the other has fallen. Thus the role play sketched out by Elster grafts itself onto Scottie's vertigo: it recalls and maintains it so as to extend and complicate it in an indefinite convalescence (the stay in the clinic after Madeleine's disappearance, a new and perfect solitude of depersonalization).

The game plays itself out in an instant. Perhaps when Madeleine (seemingly) falls from the tower (she finally joins Carlotta, and so Scottie must lose himself—join the dead—in a vertigo without end), that is when Scottie believes in the suicide of his beloved, ignorant of the fact that the woman who escaped from his grasp is in fact Judy (Renée), the mistress of the diabolical Elster, and of the fact that the latter had waited for her at the top of the bell tower, ready to push his true wife off the edge. Or earlier still: everything has already happened when, while climbing up the stairs, Scottie cannot resist and looks down once and then again and, petrified by that vision, loses his beloved, who reaches the top of the tower through the trapdoor before falling. "Did you notice the distortion . . . ?" Hitchcock asks Truffaut in his famous interview. "He had to sit down. He felt he was going to faint. Then, without standing up, he lowered himself from step to step. . . . He didn't even think of going to her assistance. She was dead. And he was dead with her."[58]

It was not an entirely gratuitous effect; rather, it compensated for or concealed Hitchcock's worries. "One of the things that bothers me is a flaw in the story," one reads in the interview with Truffaut: "The husband was planning to throw his wife down from the top of the tower. But how could he know that James Stewart wouldn't make it up those stairs? Because he became dizzy? How could he be sure of that!"[59] Actually, he could be. If Boileau and Narcejac's novel does not present even the smallest of incongruences (Madeleine has even witnessed and laughed at her friend's dizziness on the terrace of the Galeries Lafayette: she has been able to test Flavières's limits, and so Gévigne can therefore calibrate his plan up to the last essential detail), it is because right from the beginning, the criminal knows that the other man would have stopped. Or better yet, he knows ("I remember now," said Gévigne, "you never had a head for heights"[60]) that his former classmate's malaise precedes and follows the detective's *habitus*, that vertigo bursts into habituality (interrupting the career of the lawyer who once had the ambition of becoming head of the police) because the latter does not contradict but rather confirms the continuity of the illness. It is therefore on the basis not of certainty but of possibility, of the concrete eventuality that Flavières *might* still suffer from acrophobia ("'Anyone's nerves can give way,' said Gévigne"[61]) that the murderer constructs his plan. He bets on Flavières, and when the latter accepts the case, he receives a confirmation of his intuition. It may not exactly be proof, but it is already something (a first weakness) and is enough to set the game in motion. It is not, in fact, a matter of transforming an intuition into a definite certainty, but rather of carrying out an exercise, of proceeding by degrees and experimental attempts, of moving from the possibility of vertigo to its actual realization. The whole farce—not only the bell tower scene, but every action that precedes it as well as every glance and word—is thus nurtured and confirmed little by little by the passion for Madeleine and by its evolution, as the initial intuition becomes, for Gévigne, an empirical certainty and for Flavières, who undergoes the trials, a true *dressage*. Every stage derives from the preceding one and prepares the subsequent one; every acquired proof awaits the confirmation of the ensuing one. Why? Because here the game is precisely a *habitus*: every action is an action that defines the "I," "both passively, because it is accomplished by everything my constituted personality has acquired, and in an active form, insofar as it contributes to defining me with respect to my future actions."[62] The story, or rather, the dramatization of Madeleine, begets a certain disposition—a certain weakness, in Janet's sense, or a more typical "mix of 'tension' and psychological 'destitution'"[63]—and guides the gradual constitution of the ego, which in its dazed flux becomes ever more stable and structured. According to a paradox that is merely apparent, the success of the criminal plan is assured by the resistance of the detective personality which, like a force that facilitates an opposing one, blocks Scottie/Flavières and imprisons him: "She was dead. And he was dead with her." Gévigne's idea was perhaps elementary, and maybe even ingenuous, but he was capable of obtaining a confirmation and producing the consequences of that initial intuition. If anything, it is Hitchcock who is unable to follow him, mistaking for a lack of logic the very point that holds the whole structure together, and without which it would crumble. Vertigo is not simply a fear of falling but rather the temptation, the attraction exerted by a "there" that is a "here," that is, by an alter ego: being subject to it, Flavières could therefore potentially follow Madeleine to the summit of the tower, the most dangerous of places for him. But it is also and most importantly true that, bewitched by Madeleine, Flavières drags himself along in his vertiginous state. What is the vertiginous state? As the neurologist Lasègue explained, it is the *fear of vertigo*, from which one may suffer even without dizzy spells:[64] if vertigo is merely an eventuality, the fear of it is not; even if one cannot be certain of a paroxysm, one can easily wager on the fear of a paroxysm.

But it is precisely because Scottie/Flavières does not free himself of his "vertiginous habit" (since he remains a policeman—not having acquired the vocation of roofers, as Montaigne said, or Cary Grant's feline agility in *To Catch a Thief*) that he is capable, at a certain point, of recognizing an incongruence and discovering the criminal plan. And just as for the patient on the couch who must interrupt the transfer, a new vertigo corresponds for him to the surfacing of the old *habitus*, which breaks the torpor of the more pleasant (but contemptible) suspended existence. Something indeterminable therefore remains in Scottie, just as it remains in someone who after him (having suffered one day—"Oh yes, I remember . . ." at a ball—the "vast number of little perceptions [*grande multitude de petites perceptions*]") will be so fascinated by Gévigne's scheme as to make a film out of it. Both one and the other will at a certain point lose their docility. Neither of the two—and in this sense, one can say, as Daney does, that Scottie/Stewart is Hitchcock's skinny alter ego[65]—will succeed in truly surrendering to the spectacle, and the crisis will reappear for both as a logical vertigo (or as a disturbance caused by a failure in the criminal plan). The crisis that breaks the flow of habit has become habitual, and now, reappearing once again, will not let itself be reduced. To overcome it, so that a slow routine may reestablish itself, would require making a habit of that very same vertiginous habit. But here the inebriation of infinite regression is set free. Here, logic gives way to the imagination; here, the imagination, as Hitchcock knew well, shows itself to be more powerful than logic. One and the other, the director and the policeman, are the victims of this imaginative state; the former, suffering from this disturbance, must create his film; the latter must return, go back down the stairs, to then once again love Madeleine in Judy, and uncover the deception.

Hugues had experienced "a strong disappointment" when he dressed Jane in the dead woman's clothes: "Through wanting to unite the two women, their resemblance had diminished."[66] But now there are three women, and the three are but one: in the hotel room, Scottie (Flavières) notices Madeleine's necklace (one of Carlotta's jewels), which Judy has kept. It is she who takes it out of the jewelry box right before his eyes; perhaps because of a fatal moment of distraction (it would seem thus), or out of love, and in the name of the words uttered under the tower of San Juan ("If you lose me, you'll know that I loved you and wanted to go on loving you"). For his sake (because of his reply back then: "I won't lose you") she has accepted to once again become Madeleine, and she can now do so entirely. Putting on the necklace, Judy abandons all hesitation, she completely and finally renounces herself. Now she can truly offer herself as a pure mask. Now the perfect fiction could be attained, through an act of love or free complicity, which by evading the real situation (experienced with embarrassment) would install a fiction in its place. "The joy of art . . . is concretely experiencing that the world is not exclusively what it is. [*La joie de l'art . . . est l'expérience concrète que le monde n'est uniquement ce qu'il est.*]"[67] But once a policeman, always a policeman . . . And Judy's gesture remains an unheeded invitation; for him it is nothing but an error, or rather a definitive *lapsus* (slip) ("That was the slip. I remembered the necklace. You shouldn't keep souvenirs of a killing. You shouldn't have been that sentimental"). For Scottie, that detail is not a laissez-passer to go beyond death but the proof that destroys the mask, revealing the identity of its bearer. By a sort of counter-vertigo whereby the sight of Judy/Madeleine evokes Carlotta's portrait, he precipitates from his dream-like existence toward himself (toward the detective that, after all, he has always been), unmasking Judy and immediately recognizing Elster's wife (down there, below the bell tower, disguised as Madeleine). One could argue that everything occurs because of a disjunction in *Weile*; Judy's quicker (or slower?) thought process: let's get this lengthy torment over with, play the game of masks with me, because if we love each other we are nothing but masks; his slower (or quicker?) thought process: you've exposed yourself, believing you had tricked me. And because she is both right and wrong, he falls, or rather he loses Madeleine and Judy. And with him, she who had remained (hiding herself) in a suspended state *must fall*, down there, in that place which has now been revealed as *her* "here," joining the victim whom she had concealed with her disguise. The spectacle staged by Gavin Elster-Gévigne is turned into an identification process, that is, in essence, into the examination of a corpse.

Judy will go on to fall from the tower, but she already died in the hotel room. She, who had once put on a show for Scottie, tricking him in the guise of Madeleine, and who but a few hours earlier could still let herself be admired. Everyone remembers the shop scene, and Truffaut and Hitchcock agreed: by dressing her (as Madeleine), Scottie was in fact undressing Judy. But one must point out that the doubleness of the action resides in the fact that Madeleine, finally clothed, was none other than Judy, stripped and unmasked: the erotic object coincides here with the object of the investigation. Now she can only attempt to restore the fiction, to once again transform reality into deception, imploring with that necklace around her neck a complicity that it renders impossible. All she can do is look for something to grab hold of and so she finds the necklace, puts it on before the mirror, and already she finds herself precipitating ("if we fix our gaze on our point of support . . .").

As far as Hitchcock is concerned, we all know: the fact that he, an overlooked director and an illogical and daring screenwriter, could not get over Flavières's presumed frivolity, actually explains his passion for Boileau and Narcejac's novel: his "here" had also ended up "down there," in the story's apparent flaw. He too had been unable to resist and, launching himself, had transformed the book into a film or, in other words, technically, the fatal attraction into pure effect.

Scottie's *habitus* thus communicates with the fascination or *habitus* of the director, who transforms a limping scenario into a perfection of visual play. A new act of freedom responds to Judy's offer, transforming the fictions of destiny and identity into a second, purer form of fiction, by inserting between the extremes of spontaneity and determination, instead of the perfidious machination invented by Gévigne, the artifice of a game of tracking shots and zooms. "One must therefore return to the idea that artistic exhibition or the production of artistic objects is at least in part a spectacle for a consciousness, and therefore its finality is linked to the effect that it produces."[68]

We can then say, recalling Epstein, that in cinema vertigo is imparted simultaneously with poetry: the trick (or joke) devised by Hitchcock restores its hallucinating nature in the form of an amusing spectacle; he drags consciousness itself onto the screen and transforms it into the greatest poetic invention of the twentieth century.

15. In one of the most felicitous and original developments of the tradition once outlined by Eugène Minkowski and at the same time as a sort of counterpoint to the *Cartesian Meditations*, Kimura Bin studied the problems of individuation and intersubjectivity in the experiential field of schizoid delirium from a "'quasi-spatial' or topological" point of view. According to this specialist in phenomenological psychopathology, the schizophrenic process can be explained as a disturbance of alterity's appearance, which no longer appears as external to the "I," but infiltrates and penetrates into its sphere.

> When the patient is conscious of himself, of himself as such, others are experienced as "non-I" which unforeseeably arise from the depths of the constitution of the self, that is, as an "alterity of the *for-itself*" of the patient. In cases of schizophrenic delirium, the other is difficult to situate as a "here," situated in the exterior space of everyday existence, outside of the interior space of the "I." For the schizophrenic, the other is instead a presence that "takes on the forms of an alienation of the self" and that actuates the constitution of "his own 'I' in a foreign dimension," because of a transposition of the topological field, according to the rigorous formula of a patient. The becoming conscious of the self does not come about via a process of purely subjective individualization, of selfness (*Selbstheit*), but develops on the basis of the *a priori* of internal alterity.[69]

Klein traced his own interpretive path through the *Cartesian Meditations* in a different way. For him, acrophobia does not derive from an impossible anchorage. It is not a delirious individualization, distracted by a topological alterity, which is itself in turn reduced within the subjective space. Instead, much like the phenomenon of remorse, it *exceeds* the flux of appropriations and does not allow itself to be absorbed into it. It does not concern the alterity of the for-itself (as Kimura defines it, in existential terms) but rather—according to an essential nuance—the "paradox of the nonappropriated 'within' my consciousness."[70] And if the schizophrenic process originates in the failed placement of the other in the external space, and therefore in his unforeseen inclusion in one's own, vertigo, by contrast, consists in the dislocation of the "I"'s center, which, so to speak, slips beyond simple having (*Habe, habitus*), acceding to the ulterior dimension of the intersubjective world. The vertiginous crisis appears in this sense comparable with the sentiment of shame, analyzed by Klein in a lengthy and significant unpublished article on responsibility (or rather, on the foundations of assumed responsibility [*sur le fondement de la responsabilité assumée*]).[71] Much more radical than remorse, which is born of an external action and its results (in these pages, he does not yet cite Jankélévitch), shame is here a conscious realization, a *prise de conscience* of the situation in which I find myself or an authentic discovery of "that which I am [*ce que je suis*]." As Levinas had already affirmed in *De l'évasion*,[72] it bares the "unpardonable presence of the 'I' to itself." Perhaps unaware of this essay, so well-known nowadays but which for a long time remained little noticed, Klein aligns himself more closely with the Husserlian scheme of consciousness and intentionality. In the meantime, the third part of *Being and Nothingness* could only offer him an implicit background: he admits, in fact, that shame can be induced by the gaze of another, whose presence "forces the subject to see himself with the eyes of another,"[73] and adds that one can protect oneself from this gaze—which makes character, "the *persona*, mask, role or personality" knowable through *"emploi*, as one says in the world of the theater,"[74] in its empirical functions and duties—by identifying oneself in advance with "public opinion."[75] But he goes on to point out that in such a way one only obtains a precarious and deceptive form of safety, which is nothing but a prelude to complete catastrophe. Shame does not, in fact, derive from the world in which others observe us, but from the primacy of the "inner judge": it is, above all, a revelation of the subject for the subject. "The gaze of the other is, before everything, the instrument that provokes this reflection" ("*through whom I gain my objectness*," Sartre had written in a different context[76]), it does not exceed it, but serves it.[77] The apparent doubleness of the "I" as both the object and subject of shame thus reveals itself, in the unity of reflection, as "*the unity of . . . an 'I' in a situation that is a problem*—to be accepted, resolved or eluded, depending on the case."[78] And in instances where the assumption of responsibility is not a direct intentionality but rather a prolongation of the reflexive act, shame manifests itself as an entirely unique *Besinnung*: it is "the only realization of consciousness that presents the self as inevitably bound to its own situation as an open problem; and it is for this reason, incidentally, that it makes it advance."[79]

In the case of vertigo, by contrast, it is interiority itself that has been conquered: the gaze of the other captures me from an outside that impedes the movement of reflexive consciousness. "At a level above the *Eigensphäre*, consciousness ... is not in fact appropriative; it has the strange faculty of seeing itself no longer simply 'from without,' as happens when one reflects on oneself, but more specifically through the eyes of another, whether that be a specific other or a formal and general other. Accessing intersubjectivity decentralizes the world of consciousness; an interlocutor in a dialogue, remorse for a past error, the void (or any other horrible or unbearable presence) that 'draws' into vertigo, are forms of 'here' all while being forms of 'there.'"[80] Similar but also essentially different from that of the schizophrenic, according to Kimura, the *prise de conscience* of vertigo is not born of "the *a priori* of interior alterity" that brings about an ever-excessive effort of individualization but interrupts instead the foreseeable succession of choices and decisions, imposing thus a change of dimension: as a manifestation of the inappropriable "within" consciousness (in the *habitus* itself), it shakes up the framework of individual property all while demonstrating that, beyond the ever-changing border of actual possession, consciousness is merely a consciousness among many. Vertigo is thus also radically different from that "sort of scission of the 'I'" which takes place in the phenomenological reduction and by virtue of which the "neutral" or "transcendental observer" of himself "places himself above himself, watches himself, and sees himself also as the previously world-immersed ego."[81] The "there" that now exerts an attraction is a "here," a center of space, or of the alter ego; it is the foreign point of view through which the "I" must pass to see itself as such and fully be itself. Consequently, those who suffer from dizziness experience the essential temptation and will thereafter have to fear the other's gaze and will always have to appeal to it, remaining captured by it precisely when they are trying to "advance" or liberate themselves from their situation: "You frighten me ... but I need you ... to despise my petty existence."

16. Klein does not cite the famous passages on vertigo from *Being and Nothingness* and does not explicitly address the theory of the person present to consciousness only "in so far as the person is an object for the other."[82] Despite the seeming affinity, the notion of eccentricity remains irreconcilable with the Sartrean idea of the other's gaze that "makes me be beyond my being in this world."[83] For Sartre, the other, *qua* gaze, is "a transcended transcendence."[84] For Klein, decentralization is not a mode of being, but of having;

habitus is not transcendental in Heidegger's sense; nor can it be transcended, strictly speaking, despite lacking actuality. And, furthermore, if for Sartre it is from the moment in which the other sees me that "the self comes to haunt the unreflective consciousness,"[85] Klein explains that the ability to see oneself from without is a faculty of consciousness itself. He thus invokes Merleau-Ponty, observing that the transition toward intersubjectivity already occurs in linguistic communication and in the phenomenon of mute signification. And subsequently in the passage that follows, when he affirms that the interlocutor in a dialogue is "a *here* all while being a *there*," he overtly lets his sources transpire. These are made up of an amalgam of voices. If the first clearly recognizable one is that of Husserl,[86] it is precisely in its predominant theme—the experience of alterity, or monadological intersubjectivity—that one can distinguish a tone typical of Merleau-Ponty, especially of the latter's lecture in Bruxelles, "On the Phenomenology of Language" (published for the first time in 1952 and then reprinted in *Signes* in 1960).

At the outset of the "Fifth Cartesian Meditation," in an attempt to define the intersubjective sphere, Husserl rejects, as is well known, the possibility that phenomenology might be stigmatized as a form of "transcendental solipsism." Against such accusations, he offers a simple statement of fact: "In any case then, within myself, within the limits of my transcendentally reduced pure conscious life, I experience the world (including others).[87] In translating the adverbial locution *Jedenfalls* (in any case), Gabrielle Pfeiffer and Emmanuel Levinas resorted to a paraphrase: "We can consider already established the fact that I have within me [On peut considérer d'ores et déjà comme établi, le fait que j'ai en moi]."[88] The rendition is faithful: the reference to concrete evidence will in fact go on to punctuate the entire phrase and will return, with few variations ("we encounter first of all . . .") in a prominent passage, that is when Husserl affirms that the appropriating, constituting subject does not merely encounter in the other a "body" (*Körper*), but a "living body" (*Leibkörper*) from which a constant, autonomous "original foundation" (*Urstiftung*), which belongs to the other and only to the other, originates contemporaneously. This factual datum thus introduces the decisive argument: if phenomenology cannot be reduced to a mere solipsism, it is because it cannot contemplate empathic identification. For Husserl, the constitution and appropriation of the subject are exclusive: one intentional center or *habitus* delimits another, and if that which belongs to another's being were directly accessible to me, then it would be a part of my own being and, fundamentally, he and I would be the same person.[89] By contrast, in the intersubjective dimension, it is indirect intentionality that is operative in the form "appresentation" (or analogical perception) and, consequently, the "pairing" (*Paarung*) of distinct intentional centers.

The famous passage on which Klein bases himself openly states that in the sphere of primordial appropriation my "animate bodily organism" (*körperlicher Leib*), in its relation to itself, "has the central 'Here' as its mode of givenness; every other body, and accordingly the 'other's' body, has the mode 'There.'"[90] Thus "I can change my position in such a manner that I convert any There into a Here."[91] Therefore when I experience the other, I perceive him neither as a mere "body" (*Körper*) nor "simply as my duplicate, I do not apperceive him as being part of my original sphere . . . or of the spatial phenomena that belong to me because they are related to my 'here,' but . . . as belonging to those phenomena that could just as well occur to me if I went and were 'there.'" I experience the "there" of that body which does not appear to be just any body, but a living one, as the center, the "here," of another's "I," which cannot be mine but which, for the same reason, would be mine if I found myself in the other's place. Their manner of appearance is not thus immediately associable "with the manner of appearance actually belonging at the time to my living body (in the mode Here); rather it awakens reproductively *another*, an immediately similar appearance. . . . It brings to mind the way my body would look 'if I were there.'"[92]

The encounter with an alter ego, with a being constituting itself, whose *Urstiftung* is active during this very encounter, is presented in the form of an "as if" (*als ob*): it is an appresentation, an analogical coupling and an assimilation, in other words, an adaptation to my sphere.[93] The impossibility of a coincidence or identification between primordial centers thus founds and at the same time limits the possibility of an "empathy" (*Einfühlung*) of psychic contents: it is only in an indirect manner, that is on the basis of my behavior in similar circumstances, that another's demeanor is offered to my comprehension.[94]

If the experience of the other is therefore a fact, it is also "self-evident" (*selbstverständlich*) that it leaves the dominion and centrality of the ego intact: "it is now self-understood that what is appresented by the 'body' over there, in my primordial 'environment,' does not belong to my psychic sphere or, all the more so, to my sphere of ownness [*Eigenheitssphäre*]. I, as a living [*leiblich*] being, am the center of a primordial 'world' oriented around me. Consequently, my entire primordial ownness, proper to me as a monad, has the content of the Here and not . . . of some There. Each of these contents excludes the other; they cannot be the same thing."[95] As a sort of primary spatialization, the "situation" of the ego precedes and founds the separation of psychophysical beings which is, for its part, "spatial, owing to the spatial character of our Objective living bodies."[96]

One could observe that Husserl has read Feuerbach: "Here I am—this is the first sign of a real, living being . . . the 'here' is the first boundary and separation"[97]—or at least he made himself the spokesperson for this fundamental caesura when (against Theodor Lipps) he excluded any immediate fusion from empathy and founded the community of monads (of concrete individuals) on the inviolability of having. Klein reads Husserl and conforms to his views. But at the same time he also seems to depart from Husserl when he writes that intersubjectivity—as an overcoming of the "sphere of what is one's own" (*Eigensphäre*)—"decentralizes the world of consciousness." For Husserl, the "there" of the alter ego is a "here," and it could become my "here" if I were to move to where the other is currently. Klein adds that my "here" can end up "there," despite my being suspended and paralyzed, only to vertiginously attract me to it.

17. In commenting on the "Fifth Cartesian Meditation," Merleau-Ponty observed that the transition to intersubjectivity introduces a clear contradiction within the horizon of consciousness: if "to be conscious is to constitute," then to be conscious of another would equate to "constituting him as constituting, and as constituting in respect to the very act through which I constitute him."[98] It is around this problem, "which we encounter from the very outset" and which resurfaces in various passages of the "Fifth Cartesian Meditation,"[99] that Husserl develops the theory of mediated intentionality (of appresentation) and of *Paarung*. "This difficulty of principle," Merleau-Ponty observes, "which is introduced as a limit in the first pages . . . is nowhere eliminated. Husserl *disregards* it: seeing as I have an idea of the other, it follows that in some way the difficulty mentioned *has in fact been overcome*."[100]

A privileged source for Klein and his conception of vertigo, the interpretation of this critical moment of the *Cartesian Meditations* marks a decisive moment in the genesis of Merleau-Ponty's thought. Solving the problem required, in fact, that profound transformation of the notions of body and consciousness which—already initiated in *The Structure of Behavior* (1942, written in 1938) with the double abandonment of the psychological conception of the body and the criticist conception of consciousness—is later fully fleshed out in *Phenomenology of Perception* (1945) and leads all the way to the posthumous pages of *The Visible and the Invisible* (1964), that is to the overcoming of the problem of the alter ego in the name of anonymous visibility or of the universal and individual flesh (*chair*), which irradiates everywhere. In the pages written in 1942, perception is "the act which makes us know existences."[101] He nevertheless adds in an essay from 1945 that it is an act that is complicated by a number of difficulties that are not resolvable by the discovery of behavior, since they go back to the fundamental contradiction that exists between the natural and social transcendental on the one hand and the solipsistic dimension of consciousness on the other hand, or, in other words, the ambiguous nature of the world, which surrounds and envelops me but only from my own point of view. The perception of the other brings up once again the problem of an independent presence that is simultaneously a "de-presentation" and "throws me outside of myself." What thus resurfaces, in a different key, is the problematic theme of "de-presentation" (*Ent-Gegenwärtigung*) or of "alienation" (*Ent-Fremdung*), which Husserl resolved in the sense of auto-temporalization.

The amphibology of transcendence is in fact thought by Merleau-Ponty as a personal reinterpretation—which also passes through *Being and Time* and Heidegger's *Kant and the Problem of Metaphysics*—of the Husserlian problematic of temporality: "It is true that the other person will never exist for us as we exist for ourselves; he is always a lesser brother, and we never feel in him as we do in ourselves the thrust of time-creation. But two temporalities are not mutually exclusive as are two consciousnesses, because each one arrives at self-knowledge only by projecting itself into the present where both can be joined together. . . . The solution of all problems of transcendence is to be sought in the thickness of the pre-objective present, in which we find our bodily being, our social being, and the pre-existence of the world."[102] It is along this path that ontology's dominion over corporeality, over the body that is both one's own and common, mine and anonymous, that ties me to others without my needing to decide anything, reveals itself and becomes usable. It is in fact only in the pre-objective present that I attain my secret, and "it is in the very depths of myself that this strange articulation with the other is fashioned."[103] The original is thus revealed as dialogical and since it precedes and is implied in speech, it reveals itself in every word. As a result, language too, as a cultural object, plays an essential role in the perception of the other: "When I speak or understand, I experience the presence of others in myself or of myself in others which is the stumbling-block of the theory of intersubjectivity. . . . I finally understand what is meant by Husserl's enigmatic statement: 'Transcendental subjectivity is intersubjectivity.'"[104]

The "initial difficulty" of the "Fifth Cartesian Meditation" is therefore overcome *de facto*. Constituting consciousness yields to perceptive consciousness, just as the object of intention yields to the subject of behavior as being in the world or existence. And a form of dominion is now lost: "The other's *cogito* strips my own *cogito* of all value, and causes me to lose the assurance which I enjoyed in my solitude of having access to the only being conceivable for me, being, that is, as it is aimed at and constituted by me."[105] For Merleau-Ponty (who shares with Max Scheler a critical view of analogical reasoning), in appresentation, the appropriating ego does not maintain its canonical primacy or its sovereign autonomy. To be sure, if the presence of the other is a fact, it is in any case a fact for me. But it is also true that the "I" suffers a blow and falters. Certainly, there remains a shadow of the "singular philosophical solitude" engendered by the Husserlian *epoché*: "There is here a solipsism rooted in living experience and quite insurmountable."[106] I do not identify myself with the other, I am not my own "lesser brother" and will never entirely be in their place. But it is this very impossibility of merging with the other that shakes consciousness to its very core, making the center of intentionality oscillate between the "here" of the ego and the "there" of the other.

The sense of this dialogic decentralization of consciousness is defined, returned to, and refined first in *The Structure of Behavior*, then in *Phenomenology of Perception* and in the pages of *Signs*: the appropriating ego slips, is dragged, pulled, attracted, and captured by the other that addresses it. In phrases and expressions similar to the ones later used by Klein, the encounter with alterity allows its vertiginous nature to transpire. When a form of behavior, as the 1942 work argues, "is addressed to me, as may happen in dialogue, and seizes upon my thoughts in order to respond to them . . . I am then drawn into a *coexistence* of which I am not the unique constituent."[107] As a result, "my perspective of the world," reads his response in *Phenomenology of Perception*, "slips spontaneously towards that of the other" and "round about the perceived body a vortex forms, towards which my world is drawn . . . to this extent, it is no longer merely mine."[108] Finally, I can only overcome the initial difficulty, as one reads in the lecture "On the Phenomenology of Language":

> Because he within me who perceives others . . . is able to live that contradiction as the very definition of the presence of others. . . . It happens that my gaze stumbles against certain spectacles (those of other human and, by extension, animal bodies) and is thwarted by them. . . . Everything happens as if the functions of intentionality and the intentional object were paradoxically interchanged. The spectacle invites me to become its adequate spectator, as if my spirit were attracted down there and moved into the spectacle that it was offering to itself. I am grasped by a second myself outside me. . . . Now speech is evidently an eminent case of these "ways of behaving" [*conduites*] which reverse my ordinary relationship to objects and give certain ones of them the value of subjects.[109]

As one already finds written in *The Structure of Behavior*, "the 'I think' can be as if hallucinated by its objects."[110] What still needs clarifying is the nature of this hallucination, which Klein calls "vertiginous." It afflicts the "what if" dimension, or the very core of the Husserlian interpretation of empathy, and it also corresponds to the view of a spectator, who certainly is no longer the "neutral" one of the phenomenological *epoché*. It is not merely an affection or condition of the subject, but concerns and highlights its very constitution.

18. "The movement that gives me a world of my own gives me to that world."[111] Klein reads Husserl through Brand: "Every step that constitutes me as a person, every *habitus*, appears at the same time as a step towards alienation.... I am always, at every instant, what I possess, and the appropriation is reciprocal.... Brand has said, following in Husserl's footsteps, that the movement of the 'I' consists in making oneself foreign to oneself."[112] He would, however, go on to lend a particular nuance to this idea and to §32 of the *Cartesian Meditations*.

Let us reread Husserl's original: the "I" centered around itself is not an empty pole of identity, but—according to the argument also expounded in *Studies in the Phenomenology of Constitution*—for every action that emanates from it, it obtains a "stable ownness" (*bleibende Eigenheit*). I make a decision, and this act of decision passes and disappears, but I can always go back to it since "I remain the same 'I' who is thus and so decided."[113] I may change my mind or retract a decision of mine, but for that very reason, once again, I will never cease to be the one who had a certain conviction or made a certain decision. Regarding *habitus* and its irreversibility, one may borrow the words of Vladimir Jankélévitch: "We can *cancel* and even *annihilate* what we willed, but not *annihilate* [*nihisiler*] the fact of having willed."[114] *Habitus* is long-lasting, enduring (precisely *bleibend*), it marks—as Ricoeur aptly put it—"the inflection of being to having, from the me to the mine, through a sort of inertia in duration."[115] In other words, it ties the ego to *its own* stream of consciousness, it confers to it a style, it renders it the object of an empirical self-consciousness, revealing to it (more or less truthfully) its own character.

Describing in terms similar to the ones used by Ricoeur an "'I' weighed down by all of *its own* domain [*moi alourdi par tout son domaine 'propre'*],"[116] Klein nevertheless notes that the series of choices and decisions that consigns me to what it gives me, which ties me to the past while disclosing the possibilities of the future, does not proceed as an inexorable concatenation but is subject to that which is unpredictable and, in turn, remains indeterminable. As acrophobia or the remorse described by Jankélévitch attest, consciousness can all of a sudden be torn out of the sphere of that which is one's own (*Eigensphäre*) and exposed to the inappropriable or to the intersubjective dimension. The sensation of *habitus*'s contingency is vertiginous, and it is, "for every human consciousness, the most intolerable of malaises."[117] But when the sphere of appropriation is shaken and decentralized, the turn toward alterity is immediate, as vertigo and alterity coincide and both are tied to the paradox of *habitus*: I am, as a concrete "I," as a substrate of habitualities, as an "I" that persists, "attracted down there," "grasped by a second myself outside of me." The Merleau-Pontian interpretation of alterity (the paradoxical exchange of intentionalities) thus perfectly coincides with the Kleinian interpretation of *habitus* (and its paradox): if being conscious of one's alter ego means "constituting it as a constituent with respect to the very act whereby I constitute it," being directly, currently conscious of my *habitus* means constituting myself as the constituent of the act whereby I constitute myself. But precisely this superimposition also introduces a novel element. Whereas the attraction of another's gaze afflicts the very stability of the subject and of its having, the relation to the other is neither empathic, mediated (in Husserl's sense), nor purely dialogic but, first of all, dramatically vertiginous. The ego will not just be dragged into the dimension that precedes my every action and where bodies coexist: a gesture or a gaze will produce instead a fatal magnetism; the slight divergence that separates my sphere from another's will become an abyss. And if, to use Merleau-Ponty's famous example, seeing another raise their arm to block the sun's rays, I will distractedly do or tend to do the same, it is because every center flees from itself and collapses, and the simplest of gestures calls out to me from down there where the other fell. Every relation with the alter ego is fraught with the temptation of rejoining oneself.

It would therefore seem that the pairing (*Paarung*) of subjects itself is inevitably linked to an intolerable feeling, that the very burden of property threatens their stability and exposes them to temptation, that the "fact" of interpersonality is on the whole indissociable from an unexpected other fact, which is just as paradoxical and quite difficult to reduce. To overcome it, phenomenology would perhaps need to devise a solution worthy of the one invented by Hitchcock. If "thought and technical effort are heading in the same direction,"[118] the "performance" (*Leistung*) of the speculative subject—or its habituality—should therefore produce a new vertigo effect, assembling the conceptual elements available in the Husserlian armory. Provided that it is not instead cinema that is experiencing true philosophical vertigo.

Certainly, perhaps better than anyone else, Husserl saw in the imagination, which can develop the possibilities of its object and exhaust them, the source and at the same time the technique of thought. But regarding the inchoative aspect of phenomenology,[119] Pascal's old thought experiment is still instructive, in which, to use his famous words, he finds in himself what he sees in Montaigne, and according to which philosophy cannot dry up its own fount: "Put the world's greatest philosopher on a plank that is wider than need be: if there is a precipice below, although his reason may convince him that he is safe, his imagination will prevail."[120]

19. Ernest-Charles Lasègue was a philosopher and a student of Victor Cousin's before following the advice of his friends Claude Bernard and Bénédict Morel and the teachings of Jean-Pierre Falret and Armand Trousseau to become a famous neurologist (Benjamin Ball would go on to compare him to Esquirol and Pinel), especially for his studies on persecution delirium, hysteric anorexia, *delirium tremens*, and the discovery, shared with Jules Falret, of the *folie à deux* or communicated folly (1877). His classes were attended by the young Baudelaire in 1839, when the latter still frequented courses at the Collège Saint-Louis as an auditor. And the poet would go on to remember his onetime teacher, though this time as an alienist specializing in "madmen and hysterics," himself afflicted by the strangest of infirmities, unbearable neuralgia, vomiting, and vertigo: "even when I was crouched on the floor," he wrote to Ancelle on January 18, "I kept falling over, head first."[121] Reading Lasègue's *Études médicales* (1884), one recognizes not so much a refusal of theoretical inclinations in favor of clinical observation as a faithfulness to Georg Ernst Stahl's motto, which he had cited in his doctoral thesis in medicine: "not how much theory, but how much falsehood harms" (*non quantum theoria, sed quantum falsa nocet*).[122] What is not false, in these pages, is a characteristic philosophical tonality, capable of highlighting the insufficiency of a psychology directed exclusively toward one's own resources,[123] allowing one to potentially catch a glimpse, albeit certainly a premature and nebulous one, of the phenomenological horizon. It is, in fact, specifically the definition of vertigo that raises the problem of the intersubjective relation—the theme, dear to Lasègue, of the limits imposed by "the innate dispositions of every personality,"[124] both those of the patient and of the doctor—not only with respect to symptomatology but also to semiotics itself: it considers and questions the presumed objectivity of the sign, which therapeutic interest can barely grasp in its flickering from within an alterity that is fundamentally unreachable. Indeed, the patient cannot but be conscious of his illness, which he alone knows: "A necessary collaborator of the doctor's," explains the communiqué to the Académie de Médecine on "Vertige mental" (1876), "he expresses [*énonce*] sensations which only he can be the judge of."[125] Consequently, "vertigo is a subjective sign . . . concerning which the patient is more competent than the doctor, since the former can reason about his own vertigo, whereas the latter can only reason by analogy."[126] And if psychopathology is deceiving itself in assigning "to expressed ideas an importance that in reality belongs to the mental conditions that produced them," true medical research or phenomenology of vertigo focuses "before all else on the mental process and only then on its products."[127] It takes as its unavoidable point of departure the fact that the patient, domi-

nated by the illness that afflicts him, is perfectly conscious of his own apprehension,[128] while the doctor can only approach it by means of generic comparisons. Now, if it is obvious that Lasègue's theory of mental therapy (*théorie de la thérapeutique mentale*) remains very distant from Husserl's undertaking, and is equally so from the Freudian theory of transference (*Übertragung*) (about as much as his few observations concerning sentiments that are "transfused"[129]), the phenomenon of vertigo nevertheless seems to teach psychiatric research that by imposing a relation or a complicity (a sort of *Paarung ante litteram*) between two innate and radically irreducible personalities, it proclaims itself to be the experience of something that remains inexperienceable or, in Husserlian terms, defines itself as the original consciousness of nonoriginality. In order to be able to cure in a nonapproximative way, one would have to at least suffer from the illness, thus defying the paradox of a current knowledge of dizziness. From a different point of view (but one that is coherent in its extravagance), a century before "know thyself" (*gnóthi seautón*) made its appearance in *First Philosophy*,[130] or in the solemn ending of the *Cartesian Meditations*, Purkinje could thus experience the meaning of the Delphic motto, bringing about in himself the symptoms of vertigo, and reflecting on subjective signs from the empiric vicinity of his self-knowledge (*Heautognosie*).

Employed by Husserl in the thirties, the formula "intersubjective sphere of what is one's own" (*intersubjektive Eigenheitssphäre*) combines in a manifest oxymoron the famous and subtle analyses of the "Fifth Cartesian Meditation," reinstating the problematic of alterity within the full spectrum of its enigmatic reverberations. The other is an alter ego, "the ego indicated as one moment by this expression being I myself in my ownness [*Ich-selbst in meiner Eigenheit*]."[131] If the centrality of the egological pole remains inviolate in intersubjective experience, the latter can occur—as is written, with only slight variations compared with the postulate of the *Studies in the Phenomenology of Constitution*, in a manuscript from September, 1931—"only through the possibility of empathy and already by virtue of a potentiality of mine [*ausschliesslich durch die Möglichkeit der Einfühlung und zwar als meine Vermöglichkeit*]."[132] What therefore remains to be understood is in what way "can my ego, within his peculiar ownness, constitute under the name, 'experience of something other,' precisely something other [*mein Ego innerhalb seiner Eigenheit unter dem Titel 'Fremderfahrung' eben 'Fremdes' konstituieren kann*]."[133] Indeed, to encounter another means to know a being that belongs to my experiential field like "a transcendence that is much more momentous than that of an inanimate thing,"[134] or better yet remaining "irreducible to *my* ego, precisely because it is an ego, it has the form of the ego."[135] But, indeed, what is this experience that is both mine and not mine, that is both obvious and strange, this original experience of the nonoriginal, this paradoxical constitution of a constituent labeled using the technical term *appresentation (Appräsentation)*?

Its possibility, Husserl responds, lies in the very life of the ego, which in its reflection and remembrance is both original and not, both reflecting and reflected. The reflecting, functional, current, anonymous and phenomenologically emergent "I" differs, in fact, from the "I" that is held back by retention and therefore positioned or thematized in the reflexive act or in memory. Just as with remembrance—Husserl explains with an "instructive comparison"—"my memorial past, as a modification of my living present, 'transcends' my present, the appresented other being 'transcends' my own being (in the pure and most fundamental sense: what is included in my primordial ownness [*primordiale Eigenheitliche*]). . . . Just as, in my living present, in the domain of 'internal perception,' my past becomes constituted . . . so in my primordial sphere, by means of appresentations occurring in it and motivated by its contents, an ego other than mine can become constituted."[136] If auto-objectification in memory is therefore the paradigm for experiencing the other, it implies nevertheless another center (capable of its *own* appresentation) and cannot, like the former, be reabsorbed into the original sphere of what is one's own. The possibility of intersubjective experience lies in its being "similar" (*ähnlich*) and only "similar" to remembrance.

The lengthy reflection on the problem of intersubjectivity began sometime around 1905, when Husserl, in the process of systematically constructing his theory of empathy (*Einfühlung*), surveyed other contemporary versions, and first of all that of Theodor Lipps. After an initial rejection, he once again took up the problem of analogical reasoning to offer an original and positive elaboration of it (in the sense of lived analogy), that would be articulated around the imagination and, indeed, around memory. The publication of his posthumous writings (especially Husserl's *Zur Phänomenologie der Intersubjektivität*, vols. 1 and 2, and *Randbemerkungen Husserls zu Heideggers Sein und Zeit und Kant und das Problem der Metaphysik*) documents this theoretical work in detail. But the testimonials are certainly not limited to autograph works. To cite the most famous example, in the dissertation *On the Problem of Empathy* (from 1916, but published a year later), his student and future assistant Edith Stein— who would later go on to focus (perhaps already in working on *Einführung in die Philosophie* and later in *Beiträge zur philosophischen Begründung der Psychologie und der Geisteswissenschaften*, 1922) on her point of disagreement with her teacher: "the necessity of a *Leib* for *Einfühlung*"[137]—defines empathy in synthetic and faithful terms via a comparison with other actions of pure consciousness (memory, waiting, imagination). When the subject, Stein notes, looks back in time, "the present 'I' and the past 'I' face each other as subject and object. They do not coincide, though there is a consciousness of their being identical."[138] Conversely, "the subject of the empathized experience . . . is not the subject empathizing, but another. . . . These two subjects are separate and are not joined . . . by a consciousness of their being identical or by a continuity of experience."[139] But a note written by Husserl between 1914 and 1915 anticipated even more precisely the pages of the "Fifth Cartesian Meditation": I can perceive the other, they read, render him present even if his lived past does not coincide with mine, because I can render my own past present without its coinciding with my living present. But what is essential, Husserl points out, is that the experience of the other does not possess the characteristics of memory. This is the rendering present of an admirable "I" because it is capable, in the present, of transposing itself into the past and being conscious of its own identity in that very doubling. It is here that the role played by memory in the positive definition of analogy gains its due prominence: I cannot perceive the other if not by intuitively transferring their *Leib* into my "here," my zero-point of orientation; in other words, "I do not possess a representation of the other if I do not represent *myself*, with my body, in the other's situation." A clarification is in order, however: "Naturally, the 'myself' here is not yet differentiated in the sense of 'I' and 'you.' Nevertheless, the following is clear: *just as I am present in my past or even in a fiction, so I am also present in the psychic life of others whom I render present in me through empathy*. Now, this being-present is not tied to the need for identification as memory is . . . the essence of memory, the essence of the flux of consciousness demands identification, and necessarily carries it with itself."[140] Thus, the framework is laid out. As a key passage of *The Crisis of the European Sciences* (§54b) will go on to explain, "self-temporalization through depresentation (*Ent-Gegenwärtigung*), so to speak (through recollection), has its analogue in my self-alienation (*Ent-Fremdung*) (empathy as a depresentation of a higher level—depresentation of my primal presence (*Urpräsenz*) into a merely presentified (*vergegenwärtigte*) primal presence).[141] If, therefore, the centrality of the ego is maintained, if the "I" does not identify with the other, if the foreign "is therefore conceivable only as an analogue of my peculiar ownness [*ist . . . nur denkbar als Analogon von Eigenheitlichem*],"[142] it is because "analogizing empathy" (*analogisierende Einfühlung*)—and therefore the familiarity of every gesture, or every behavior, of every likeness, whether of the parts or of the unitary structure of my *Leibkörper* with that of another—is, in turn, a tacitly circular structure, which is only analogous to memory.

On the other hand, the ego's possibility of self-identification (in its doubling, that is in the difference between past and present) still lies in the intact centrality of the "here." By affirming that I do not possess a representation of the other if I do not represent *myself*, with my body, in the other's situation, Husserl once again defines the "I" as the being that differs from itself without transferring itself "there." The "here," it would seem, is the center of identification in memory: the adherence to the centrality of the "here," and the difference from the "there," is such that it distinguishes memory from empathy, and it is on the basis of this distinction that the ego can imagine itself in someone else's place without conflating itself with the other. No memory or imaginative fiction could therefore overcome the boundary of the "here."

We know, however, in its many versions—in the examples repeated in both male and female versions, ranging from the *Analyses Concerning Passive and Active Synthesis* and the *Logical Investigations* II to *The Crisis of the European Sciences* and *Experience and Judgement* and via Hans-Georg Gadamer's testimony[143]—Husserl's paradigmatic alienating experience when, as a young student in Berlin, he once mistook a wax mannequin for a living person: "I *remember* the scene at the waxworks in Berlin: How startled I was when that all-too-amiable 'lady' on the staircase beckoned to me. . . . *At present*, while I am telling this, I have a clear memory."[144] The "as if" of apperception enters into a crisis here, since a deluded perceptive consciousness prevails over the imaginative one that recognizes it: "We indeed 'know' that it is a semblance, but we cannot help ourselves—we see a human being."[145] Certainly, Husserl uses this example to introduce his analysis of "fantasy" (*Phantasie*), understood—as Marc Richir rightly underscores—as vision or, in a stronger sense, as an apparition that is autonomous from the image object (*Bildobjekt*) and therefore distinct from hallucination.[146] And yet here one is not dealing with a faint consciousness of the apparition that lingers while fantasizing, when the presence of the real world in the background is only barely perceptible, but rather with an ambiguity that precedes it and does not allow one to isolate fantasy from memory or imagination. It concerns and alters—as §21b of *Experience and Judgement* explains, developing and radicalizing the assumption of the *Logical Investigations*[147]—not only the mode of consciousness but, crucially, that of belief and of being. It is precisely when the perceptual conflict is resolved, when the mannequin appears, excluding the woman, that it becomes clear that she will no longer be the same as before the discovery of the illusion or, rather, the appearance of doubt, as if nothing had happened (his perception [*Wahrnehmung*] is no longer the same as before, as one reads in the same paragraph of the *Logical Investigations*).[148] At this point, the way in which living individuals manifest themselves to consciousness (the *Modus der Leibhaftigkeit*) has "become different": no longer simple and univocal but "uncertain" (*fraglich*), "ambiguous" (*zweifelhaft*), "controversial" (*strittig*). And this uncertainty conditions the past, extending to remembrance and producing a memory that is itself double, both woman and mannequin together.[149] The contrasting possibilities possess the same, equally contestable value; and whether one or the other prevails, or in other words becomes a "probability" (*Wahrscheinlichkeit*), depends on the more or less favorable conditions, on the "weight" of their respective "claims to existence."[150]

Husserl adds that the possibility of its own dissolution is part of the essence of doubt, and consciousness, however undecided, can always make a decision (for example, by approaching the object, touching it, and discovering that it is made of wood instead of human flesh [*Leib*]), and thus arrive at a "negation" (*Verneinung*) or an "affirmation" (*Bejahung*). But it would seem that precisely this *possibility* casts a shadow of its own on any "yes" or "no"—one that is full of ambiguity.[151] Indeed, what remains truly uncertain when the object is subjected to the attraction of certainty and, at the same time, of conflicting intentions,[152] is how far the misunderstanding extends. And what seems perhaps less contestable—as far as we are concerned—is that it has now irremediably touched on the theme of intersubjectivity. If at least for an instant, even within a context of pure fiction (the waxworks on Friedrichstrasse), the alterity of the other is no longer quite certain, if an inanimate body has been able to reproduce, from its "there," the "here" of the alter ego and to gesture to us from "a transcendence well beyond" that of objects, one may indeed ask whether these have ever been thus and therefore who or what the ego and the others we refer to are, who or what is truly "present in the psychic life of another that I render present within me," and whether or not those memories have ever been ours, and therefore who or what ever made those choices, to whom or to what does the past belong as a "first objectification" or first time "in itself." One may wonder whether the Husserlian notion of an analogy between *Einfühlung* and memory was not essentially a response to the need to find in the latter a certainty, an original normality proven wrong or placed in doubt by perceptive experience and if, in a game of masks, alterity and memory did not have the function of coalescing and mutually confirming each other. Precisely when an obvious *analogon* can pass for living and guide the imaginative consciousness ("a very distinct memory" means "as much as reason tries to convince it," uncertainty will nevertheless prevail) so much as to obscure the alterity of the other, one could also be led to ask whether the search for perfect mimesis has not been replaced by the reproduction and exhibition of analogy as such. "Aesthetic effects are not country fair effects" (*Ästhetische Effekte sind nicht Jahrmarktseffekte*), Husserl explained; and in fact the two seem inimical: wherever "reality and semblance play hide-and-seek with each another," what is produced is "the most extreme antithesis [*äusserster Gegensatz*] to aesthetic pleasure, which is grounded on the peaceful and clear consciousness of imaging."[153] Hans Blumenberg therefore seems to be right when he suggests that the condemnation of the waxworks, or of artifice incapable of stabilizing the imaginative consciousness, is linked to Husserl's embarrassment before a youthful yielding to poor taste.[154]

And yet these very circus tricks, mimicries, and analogies may deserve greater respect and even lead us to suspect that "aesthetic effects" themselves are not exclusively and strictly speaking "aesthetic." If no memory or imaginative fiction can overcome the boundaries of the "here," the "here" itself can nevertheless end up down there and gesture toward me, from the distance of a mannequin, to surprise and attract me with all of my memories, to confuse reality with seeming. Vertigo is not imaginary, it is a fall or slip (*lapsus*) of the imagination.

20. Whereas Husserl's manuscripts from the 1930s (collected in *Texte aus dem Nachlass*, vol. 3) revolve around the relation between the "scission of the 'I'" (*Ichspaltung*) and the dimension of alterity, those belonging to Group C, presented and studied for the first time in Brand's book, investigate instead the temporal nature of egological immanence.

Reflection (or memory) produces, as we have seen, an alienation inherent in and limited to self-experience, a "scission of the 'I'" that can never be abolished because it animates the synthesis of identification as a temporal process. Consciousness—as is already explained in *The Phenomenology of Internal Time-Consciousness*—precedes retention instead of deriving from it. It is originally unreflexive self-consciousness and therefore remains immune—as the "Second Cartesian Meditation" specifies—to infinite regression: it is a form of pure conscious living which, in the admirable being-for-itself-of-the-ego, takes on the form of intentionally-bringing-oneself-back-to-oneself,[155] and it can, according to an assertion in the *Studies in the Phenomenology of Constitution*, catch itself in reflection, which posits the identical both as an objectified and a nonobjectified ego, rendering manifest—as Brand's effective synthesis states—"the difference and the coinciding of the 'I,' the bridged gap, the original rendering explicit of a 'now' and a 'some time ago' . . . of time and temporality."[156]

In this sense, I can therefore say: I and the other (*Ich und Andere*). The alterity that temporarily animates the process of identification can, over the course of interpersonal development, disclose itself in duality, in compresence, a pairing (*Paarung*) of egological poles in the simultaneity (*Zeitliches zugleich*) of a "now" that is mine and therefore both distinguishes me from and unites me with the other. The "commonality" (*Gemeinschaft*) with oneself in which the ego finds itself within a temporal flux that is both difference and coincidence (*Deckung*) renders the "community" (*Gemeinschaft*) of monads possible. In this sense, once again, time is "truly the secret of subjectivity"[157]: and it will remain so, an inviolate enigma, as long as the transcendence of the other will only be analogous or irreducible to the internal difference of the "I."

Now, the relation of similarity between empathy and memory is essentially articulated around the factual unicity of the living body (*Leibkörper*), to which the scission of the "I" is traced back and on which the flow of time is based. In a variation on the same theme, a manuscript dated August 1931 reads: "The unicity of this 'I' which reigns in the living body, in the living body (this unicity) is a fact [*Faktum*] that does not leave any space for other possibilities. A second 'I' in my primordiality would mean a second life that would belong to me in a primordial manner, a second reign established according to a psychophysical modality, either in my body (*Leib*) or in another. But as much as I may affirm that I have all of a sudden become another, that I have experienced a rift in my personality, and as much as a personality may split, all of these scissions occur as scissions of the same identical egological pole, which persists in them."[158]

Indeed, there cannot be two in a single living body, just as there cannot be two living persons in a single body (*Körper*) or in the same place. Identity is a form of unicity guaranteed by the exclusive manner in which a being occupies its own space or adheres, so to speak, to its own body. The "here" of my body (*Leib*) is in other terms such because it coincides, first and foremost, with the body (*Körper*): it is the zero point of kinesthesia or the center of the only *Körper* that for me is a *Leib*, to which I adhere so closely as to not be able to move it by grasping it in its entirety, and which is also "the only Object 'in' which I '*rule and govern*' immediately [*das einzige, 'in' dem ich unmittelbar 'schalte und walte'*], governing particularly in each of its 'organs.'"[159] The "here," the center, is thus "in": the body is animated via "intertwining" (*Verflechtung*) while it spatializes the "lived body" (*Leib*), pressing it to itself as the origin (or immediacy) of property. And when Husserl writes (as at the end of §53) that for me a single body (*Körper*) is "there" and for the other it is "here," he confirms that precisely this physical body founds the unicity of the ego, that every intertwining is an "embodiment" (*verkörpern*) of the "I," that the living being is literally in the hands of the organism it governs.

In fact, the possibility of "imaginative fantasy" (*Hinein-phantasieren*) corresponds to this concrete impossibility: I can only imagine (precisely via analogy) being in someone's place, there, in that place where I cannot effectively bring myself if the other, their corporeal body (*Leib*), does not leave it. I can also believe that I am another, or two people at once, or that I have multiple personalities, since I remain the one who cannot lift himself by his own hair. One can thus say, borrowing Levinas's words, that the adherence of the body to the "I" "*is of value in and of itself.* It is an adherence *one cannot escape,*"[160] adding, in a coherent manner, that the "I" does not escape from the body if the latter adheres to itself, or if it separates itself as *Leib* only to reunite with the *Körper,* if indeed the physical body clings to the living being like a mask that cannot be removed (or as a "true," unique person, one might gloss).

Nor is that it. The experience of alterity is not limited to an act of thought. On the contrary, analogical understanding is based on perception, and the likeness that connects memory with interpersonality is based on the immediate, originally experienced resemblance between my *Körper* and the other body. As §50 of the *Cartesian Meditations* reads, "it is clear from the very beginning that only a similarity connecting within my primordial sphere, that body [*Körper*] over there with my body can serve as the motivational basis for the '*analogizing*' *apprehension* of that body as another living body [*Leib*]."[161] Already Ricoeur defined this passage as "the most important one of the entire 'Fifth Meditation.'"[162] A contemporary scholar such as Richir has concentrated instead on the annotations collected in volume 1 of *Zur Phänomenologie der Intersubjektivität: Texte aus dem Nachlass*, which are devoted to the same notion of internal apprehension, which, as Richir specifies and insists, "is not a representation in the form of an image."[163] If it aimed at an "imaginal object" (*Bildobjekt*), it would in fact miss the living organicity of the body (*Leiblichkeit*) and "there would be no difference between the other's body and that of a statue." By contrast, the "apprehension that understands from within" (*einverstehende Auffassung*) has no need for images and all the more so for specular images: "it is the *immediate* apprehension of a non-present present caused by an external perception."[164] Now, there is one text in particular, "notable both for its brevity and for its extraordinary intelligence,"[165] which, as Husserl himself explains in the margins, "goes against every theory of analogization for inter-subjective constitution." The tone here is already, so to speak, Merleau-Pontian: "If I see a foreign hand, I feel my own, if a foreign hand is in movement, this brings me to move my own, etc. But I do not transfer the sensation that I experience to the other living body, neither in the form of the image's production nor in any other form."[166] Confuting the old psychological interpretation, Husserl thus lays the foundation—in a mode that is consistent with the letter from the *Meditations*—for the possibility of the theory of analogy in the original sphere. A resemblance *immediately, originally* ties that body to my own, before any cognition or any analogical reasoning, before any image or any of the games of somatic correspondences or affinities. But what does this "before" mean? The "immediate" or "primordial" resemblance, we could say, which does not follow the body (*Leib*'s) affirmation and does not take it as an object of comparison but is merely the resemblance in which the body discovers itself. My body, in other words, cannot remain indifferent to the mimesis because it appears in it: in the resemblance, beckoning to itself from there, perceiving itself immediately in the body there, it internally perceives itself. Implicated in alterity from the very beginning, I feel or recognize in the livingness of the other body the one that inhabits my own, and in the meantime this sensation extends into a sort of extroversion and doubles itself via analogy. The body does not behold itself but above all lives (is a *Leibkörper*) in another's gaze and gesture; it appears in that gesture and to that gaze, and with that gesture and gaze it consigns itself to itself. Physiognomy would later go on to study this mimicry and recognize the reflection or appearance of an interiority that was already imitative in itself, and it would go on to grasp a series of resemblances specifically in us, who are already similar, that is incarnate in our bodies by a mimesis *we cannot escape.*

21. In one of his annotations to the "Second Cartesian Meditation," Roman Ingarden gave voice to the difficulty raised even by the profoundly discordant voices of Heidegger and Adorno: "How can I be a unique and identical 'I,' constituting, pure, and at the same time constituted, real?"[167]

Jan Patočka later wrote that the problem of constitution is essentially irresolvable and must be acknowledged as such.[168] A different response came from Didier Franck (who, following Merleau-Ponty's example, translates *Leib* as *chair*): "the absolute ego is in one sense identical to and, in another sense, different from the *de facto* ego, . . . due to the double phenomenal status of the flesh [*chair*] . . . because the flesh is always also a body."[169] What is at stake specifically in this double status is the interpersonal and imaginative dimension, which means that this answer contains a list of implicit questions. If it is indeed "absurd to see my *Leib* from without,"[170] this very blind spot is the center of the perspective on the body (*Körper*), and the same immediate, internal resemblance, deprived of the image of the lived body (*Leib*), brings me closer to the other, consigning to me the appearance of the corporeal image. If then the temporal synthesis continually fills in the gap between the actual and the positional, between the pure ego and the factitious one, while this same gap animates it, we can still identify in the incarnation itself the slight but unbridgeable rift: remembrance saturates it and the body (*Leibkörper*) closes it as it reappears in every wrinkle, the at-times minuscule sign of an ever-lost adherence, of the distance that separates the living being from the physical body, that ties it to this body, a deep or barely visible line, an imperceptible fault or naked intimacy of being that separates itself from itself and grows old or dies (or abandons to its own devices that body which had never been alive in itself) both finding and losing itself in memory. Turned toward tomorrow, the ego remains attached to itself, and as a result of the priority of protention,[171] in flowing it "slips" back; it slides into memory, falls back into the past, finding once again the backdrop that guarantees the flux's unity. And this backdrop is the image. And so, immediate perception of the other without images, internal apprehension and memory do not merge.

Or perhaps, according to a hypothesis that at first sight Husserl does not seem to consider, they *should not* merge. If every one of my gestures is in fact immediately similar to the gesture of another, alterity, like an ambiguous filigree, can conceal itself in every appearance of my past. A lack of images can generate any image and, latent or not, my memories can conflate with other images or memories, animated in turn by innumerable acts of mimicry. *Leiblichkeit* is thus the vitality of imitations. And the rationale for this psychic contamination is provided by the immediate presence of what is similar in "my" past: my "first objectification" (memory) is thus an ancient possession, and the imitated alterity contaminates the "flowing-present" itself. There is only the compenetration of fluxes, the mutual contamination of what is extraneous and what is one's own, and every image is the specter of its absence. Turned toward the future, slipping back in time, I thus see myself through a gaze that inhabits my own and captures it via a series of imperceptible imitations. Holding myself back to myself, in retention and in memory, I imitate the strange and remote shadow which calls to me all the more potently from its unreachability. And if the original mimicry becomes confused with the image, even the inanimate *analogon* can be perceived as being immediately similar, and greet me with its wooden or wax hand, leading me to move my own.

Especially in the manuscripts belonging to Group C, in discovering and attempting to grasp the genetic origins of temporality, Husserl conceptualized an irreducible "pre-beginning" ("*Vor*"-*Anfang*), never granted or pre-granted to the ego and therefore constitutively inhabited by the other, which constitutes the basis for the genesis and individuation of the subjective pole and, as its nucleus or "pre-I" (*Vor-Ich*), animates the centrality of the self-conscious ego. But if individuation in memory is itself the imitation of another, it does not remain in an ungraspable past that serves as the present's basis as such: it remains insistent and projects itself onto the present as it is evoked, revived, and rendered manifest in the passing of days.

Alterity does not therefore yield itself only in the "coexistence" (*Koexistenz*) of distinct original spheres and their individuated times, nor is it situated in the common and irreducible origin of the ego and its alter ego, the pre-beginning of temporality and the very source of individuation, but rather it appears in every gesture and expression, it fills every wrinkle, covering the distance that ties the living human being to its body, it is clothed in the intimacy that separates from itself, escapes from its own grasp and "grows old and dies." And as the inexhaustible effort of Husserl's manuscripts seems to attest, the "I" will continue to suffer this unforgiving magnetism when it will split from itself as a "phenomenologizing I" to observe its own mundane life at the last possible level of knowledge. To flow, for the ego, is to tarry, and to tarry among mundane interests is to precipitate. One could also say that the ego is essentially afflicted by vertigo, if the latter consists—according to the classic and ever-enlightening definition—in taking a step that one does not wish to take, in a solecism, in a contradiction or slip of intention (if one could avoid implying with this word the center or identity that vertigo itself perhaps creates). "Enigmas concerning *'innate' character*" are not concealed in the heart of the subject but are displayed in its appearance.[172] And to resolve them, we must once again return to Klein.

22. "The paradox of the non-appropriated 'within' my consciousness necessarily goes back to the paradox of intersubjectivity." This phrase reflects the interpretive bent that Klein manages to impose on Husserl's dictum. One is dealing with what Ricoeur had called the recognition of the paradox as paradox (*la reconnaissance du paradoxe comme paradoxe*):[173] that is, the understanding of that peculiar form of intentionality whereby—as reads another notable passage of the *Cartesian Meditations*—"there becomes constituted for me the new existence-sense that goes beyond [*überschreitet*] my monadic very-ownness [*Selbsteigenheit*]; there becomes constituted an ego, not as 'I myself,' but as mirrored [*spiegelnd*] in my own Ego, in my monad."[174] As we have seen, Husserl arranges the lines of his explication of the alter ego's transcendence in a way that is rigorously coherent with the primacy of ownness (*Eigenheit*), developing it into the theory of appresentation and pairing. The paradox therefore assumes a logically complete form: apperception is, in turn, similar to remembrance, and if the other is analogous to the "I," then the analogy also proceeds from the ego. A single principle is operative in this case, and its variations should confirm it: the experience of the other derives from my experience of what is mine, and I do not need the other to experience my sphere of belonging.

But Klein's reading unsettles this rigid order: indeed, now it is not the thematic of interpersonality that recalls memory as the auto-objectification in ownness. It is instead, as we have seen, the alienating phenomena that ownness cannot reconcile that refer to the intersubjective dimension: remorse, which by opposing itself to memory as an irreconcilable past causes a crisis in the identity of consciousness; and, indeed, vertigo, as a loss of center, an invasion of space itself, as an attraction or nonimaginary fall of my "here." The ego—the center of its own sphere—can think or move itself there, where its alter ego now is, if the latter changes its location. By contrast, the center of an "I" afflicted by vertigo migrates down there, where the other is (in fact or not in fact) located. The "I" that preserves its ownness can—by remaining in its position—imagine itself in the other's place precisely because it could potentially move there, as long as the other moved as well, and consequently by analogy knows that that "there" is a "here," the alter ego's center. A subject prey to vertigo tends, instead, to fall because its "here" is down there and calls to it from down there, transforming its position into a "there." Whereas the "there" of the alter ego reveals itself analogically as a "here," the "here" of my ego vertiginously confuses itself with a "there"—and in the meantime precipitates, because being detached from myself in this exchange of roles, I must fall to continue holding onto myself. This is the paradox of vertigo, which "necessarily refers back to the paradox of intersubjectivity" (or rather, to use Merleau-Ponty's terms, to the exchange of functions between intentionality and its object): on the brink of the precipice, I become another, or better yet, I see myself from a "here" that is by now confused and ungrounded with another's eyes. To not fall, I would have to fall, to truly be "here" (there) and at the same time "down there" (here), I would have to forsake myself and become—since it is only from another's point of view that my "here" is once again such—truly double, both ego *and* alter ego. But by definition the ego holds onto itself and is subject to this vertiginous force. What is it precisely that animates it, that moves it? What is given here is not an internal alterity (there is no schizophrenia) or the pathological presentification of another behind my back or above me (which is the phenomenon studied, in the domain of phenomenological psychopathology, by Karl Jaspers); what is being dealt with instead is a reciprocal slippage and a confusion of the original and the positional, of the living present and of presentified time.

It would therefore seem that vertigo—"which can make us faint and does not let us distinguish anything [*qui peut nous faire évanouir et qui ne nous laisse rien distinguer*]"—produces the exchange that the Husserlian conception of interpersonality categorically rejects. Or perhaps not: just as mediated intentionality, of a higher level, does not erase its immediate counterpart, just as access to the interpersonal sphere goes beyond the primordial stratum without making it disappear, so vertigo would be nothing more than a possibility, albeit an eccentric and pathological one, of the ego's belonging. The real fear and the possible fall (*s'évanouir*) confirm that an ego cannot be in two places (or in two bodies), just as two egos cannot cohabit in a single body. If instead both hypotheses were true, then empathy (*Einfühlung*) and (even before that) ownness (*Eigenheit*) could also be traced back to acrophobia; the very centrality of the ego would therefore prove vertiginous, its every performance (*Leistung*) a slip (*Fehlleistung*).

23. Let us once again read Klein's key passage: "At a level above the sphere of which is my own, consciousness ... is not appropriative; it has the strange faculty of seeing itself no longer simply 'from the outside,' as happens when reflecting upon oneself, but more specifically through the eyes of another, whether that be a specific other or a general, theoretical other. Accessing intersubjectivity decentralizes the world of consciousness; the interlocutor in a dialogue, the former lack of remorse, the void (or any other horrible and unbearable presence) that "draws" into vertigo, are forms of 'here' all while being forms of 'there.'"[175]

What does it mean to see oneself with the eyes of another, to perceive oneself as another perceives me, to understand oneself as another understands me? Once again, Husserl rigorously relates every possible intentional eccentricity to the sphere of what is one's own. And the development of this conception cannot but be coherent, from the lowest level of appresentation to the highest levels of human community, composed—as §56 of the *Cartesian Meditations* explains—of subjects "existing for themselves precisely as I exist for myself, yet existing also in communion, therefore ... in connexion with me *qua* concrete ego, *qua* monad [*in Verbindung mit mir als konkretem Ego, als Monade*]."[176] The other's gaze and my own therefore intersect in a bond that binds us reciprocally and that repeats itself from one monad to the other and extends to animal societies, uniting them in a single community: "If, with my understanding of someone else, I penetrate more deeply into him, into his horizon of ownness [*Eigenheitshorizont*] I shall soon run into the fact that, just as his animate bodily organism lies in my field of perception, so my animate organism lies in his field of perception [*wie sein Körperleib in meinem, so mein Leib sich in seinem Wahrnehmungsfeld befindet*] and that, in general, he experiences me forthwith as an Other for him, just as I experience him as *my* Other."[177] In just the same way, I also realize that the many others are experienced as others by each and every one of them within the horizon of an open, inter-monadic human community, or of a transcendental intersubjectivity.

The interpersonal relation, already based on a close coherence with memory, thus also reveals at this level its reflexive nature: that which I perceive in the eyes of another is, above all, the fact that my gaze is perceiving them, my perceiving being. And thus we could infer that a community is a reciprocal bond among beings, given that the first connection and the matrix for every connection is the return to oneself that further ties the I to itself. In a page dating back to 1930, Husserl recognizes in fact that if the relation to the other via mediated intentionality already implies a relation to that (not only thing but also living being) of which the other is conscious, then I am conscious of this inversion "such that my consciousness, as if in a circle, comes back to itself, passing through the stranger who reveals himself in me."[178] Foreign content that presents itself within the egological sphere thus ends up bringing the "I" back to itself. And a reciprocal inversion of this kind can appear and resolve itself in a reciprocal circularity because it is originally founded on the "coexistence" of my "I" with the other's "I," or "in a common temporal form, wherein every primordial temporality obtains from itself the pure signification of a world that is original and individually-subjective."[179]

It is no coincidence that during his review of the "Fifth Cartesian Meditation," Eugen Fink offers a rigorous development of this significant passage, which not only stretches the Husserlian text all while faithfully respecting its premises—as he is wont to do—but seems to even venture beyond the limits of analogical appresentation, which is to say, of the intentional analysis of alterity. Scheler said: I see not only the eyes of the other but also that the other is looking at me. Not only do I experience their alterity—as §56 of the *Meditations* reads—but I realize that they are experiencing me as other to them, just as I experience them as other to me. Sartre would later go on to say that since the gaze of the other prevails, it places itself before their eyes, hides them, and refers me back to myself. According to Fink, the mode of experiencing empathy possesses, as for Husserl, the "nature of reversibility," or better yet, it creates an "opposing intentional direction" (*hat den inneren Charakter der Reversibilität, des inneren Gegenspiels der intentionalen Richtung*). Indeed, "not only do I experience the other and do they experience me, but I only experience the other if I experience them as someone who experiences (or more specifically, can experience) me."[180] And yet empathy, in the original modal form that Husserl assigns to it, is at heart nothing other than perception ("I see the other, his *Leib* is in my perceptive field, it is a body that shares my primordial nature, despite being such that through its associative resemblance with my *Leib* it appresents a foreign interiority"[181]), and is thus limited—as Fink observes—to a restricted horizon, to a small section of the world. Conversely, empathy should extend to a community located beyond the "periphery" (*Peripherie*) and "border" (*Grenze*) of copresence, that is, it should include the consciousness of the other as absent, disappeared or at any rate situated beyond my perceptive field, in an "inter-subjective zone of absence." Heidegger already resolved the issue of the other's absence (*fehlen*) by considering it a defective modality of being-with.[182] Following a necessarily different strategy, Fink is able to recognize in the total kinesthesia of the body a possibility that Husserl's argumentation singularly overlooks. If it is in fact true that I can move to reach the position in which the other is located, I can also move away till the alter ego disappears, without however ceasing to be conscious of them and therefore constituting them via "a new type of alterity" (*eine neuartige Fremdheit*). Of *what* sort? An alterity that is not perceptibly verifiable will, in its very absence, be a strange presence, stronger than others. But it is equally clear that an absence from the horizon of the perceivable is, in turn, a modality of being that is originally unattainable (the other as such). We could thus suggest, following in the footsteps of Richir, that this absence, which distance renders manifest, *is the absence of the image that offers itself as an immediate mimesis.* The Leibnizian theme of the *Spiegelung*, which Husserl had interpreted as an appresentative mirroring, is thus newly reinterpreted, and acquires a spectral semblance. But this new form of alterity does not, however, cease to be the form of the ego. The primacy of origin is still operative here, as a phantasmic and inexperienceable presence.

24. Let us proceed step by step: according to Fink's hypothesis, this new alterity constitutes the origin of the one within the perceptional horizon already considered by Husserl. And in a scenario where presence is a potential possibility of absence, the latter can never be annulled (that is, reduced to the former). The intersubjective "zone of absence" (*Zone der Abwesenheit*) therefore extends beyond (while including) those whom we see, who surround us and at the same time belong to the great community of the absent: "present inter-subjectivity" (*anwesende Intersubjektivität*) is nothing but a reductive modality of "inter-subjectivity in general" (*Intersubjektivität überhaupt*).[183]

The step taken by Fink, who in overcoming, so to speak, a spatial boundary, frees interpersonality from the limits of analogical apperception, could render the singular faculty of seeing oneself through another's eyes in a rigorous sense thinkable and coherent with the Kleinian notion of the decentralization of consciousness. We have seen that this faculty cannot be reduced to mere reflection, to the distance that separates the positional from the nonpositional, to which appresentation, by contrast, remains tied. But then how should we conceive of presence and copresence on the basis of absence, on what variations or modalities of the latter? To think of absence without mistaking it for a temporary lack, not yet filled, without reducing it in other words to a potential presence, means to conceive of it in copresence itself and to conceive of the latter in a way that is altogether novel: to truly understand presence as a modification or possibility of absence, that is, without losing or erasing the latter, means to think of it as both a strange and familiar apparition, here, now, of that which never ceases to be lacking. The Sartrean view whereby absence is a structure of being-there (*l'absence est une structure de l'être-là*) and to be absent means to be already given for myself (*déjà donné pour moi*), just as the sender of a letter is already called back within my horizon by the address,[184] is thus literally overturned. It is in the very proximity of the perceived that an uncrossable distance persists, one that cannot be erased by the movement of my body (*Leib*). And I can do my best, arrive exhausted down there, at that point on the horizon, reach the place in which the other clearly stood; but first I must know that every presence, whether distant or near, always harbors and at the same time derives from an absence that I will not reach even by the efforts of my imagination.

It stands to reason, then, that the nature of reversibility or of intentional counterplay (*Gegenspiel*) must also change. How? Consider Husserl's view: I analogically recognize in another's body (*Körper*) a lived body (*Leib*), and therefore I can infer that the other also analogically perceives my body as *Leib*. And if *my consciousness, as if in a circle, returns to itself by passing through the foreign figure that discloses itself within me*, it is by virtue of the *Körperleib*, or in other words, of the exclusive bond that, by tying together the physical body and the living being, becomes the linchpin and matrix of the concrete ego's individuality, and therefore of every interpersonal connection and, in an ever-broader context, of community as a whole. Here, where copresence is the principle of interpersonality, "the unicity of this 'I' that reigns in the living body, is a fact in the living body (the only one) that does not leave any other possibility." Wherever absence reigns and copresence constitutes a particular modality thereof, the union of the *Leib* and the *Körper* and the dominion of the ego can also lose their stability and privilege: the power of the "I" that reigns alone over its living body yields to another *strange faculty*. In that case, "to see oneself . . . through the eyes of another" does not imply "passing through the foreigner in me," but more specifically—and precisely because I do not see myself in the act of looking, because my gaze, in turn, is not part of its own perceptive horizon, because the impossible vision of the *Leib* is turned into evidence of the *Körper*—through the eyes of someone who, for me, is currently *absent*, that is, by a foreignness irreducible to any analogy.

Access to this absent intersubjectivity—or the appearance of alterity as such—decentralizes consciousness, throwing its world into disarray. In this case, my body both is and isn't mine, it occupies the space of another, it reveals itself as the locus of an exceedingly strange coexistence and of an absolute doubleness. And the copresence of the other who in this very moment turns toward me is also summoned up and included in the primary relation to absence. The stranger's eyes behold me and, appearances notwithstanding, they grope about in the dark since I am not where, in fact, I see them. The unbridgeable distance between us separates me from myself.

25. What are we to make, then, of the constitutive centrality of the ego, if its horizon is inhabited from the very beginning by absent figures and every presence is in the grasp of the inappropriable? It is by distorting them in the direction of vertigo, of decentralization, of possession that one could recall Husserl's words: transcendental subjectivity is intersubjectivity; the possibility that there may be another resides within me and with it the possibility of duality. The very formulation of the "Fifth Cartesian Mediation," §44, according to which the second ego "is constituted as 'alter ego'—the ego indicated as one moment by this expression being I myself in my ownness [Ich-selbst in meiner Eigenheit],"[185] defines the structure of a subject who looks at himself with the eyes of an absent other. This means, however, that the synthesis of identification is produced in relation to *absence* and that the scission of the "I" and the nonactuality in which I recognize myself owe their origin to it.

Reflecting on "the immense problem of phenomenological intersubjectivity," the most distant and authoritative voices have sustained that "my" "I" is altogether different from the primitive experience described by Husserl, and perhaps it is not even the necessary, constant "I" that is numerically identical to itself. Instead, as Adorno has written, it is mediated to the highest degree and intersubjectivity is "the real condition for being I, without which the limitation to 'my' ego cannot be understood."[186] As Derrida explained even in one of his last works (*On Touching*), in order for the experience of one's own body that allows one to say "this is I," "this is my body" to take place, a certain introspective entropathy, a certain intersubjectivity must have already introduced the other as well as analogic appresentation. Every form of auto-affection must pass through something that is foreign, and so it is for the experience of the touching-touched body.[187]

For my part, I will hazard the following: the condition for appropriation is the absence of the other, from whom the very possibility of analogical representation derives, and with it the appearance of the "I"'s identity. And we can read Merleau-Ponty's famous argument, altering and integrating it into our own: if the sentient and the sensible are always "slightly decentered,"[188] if I will never be both touching and touched, if in trying to touch myself being touched "the hinge between them ... remained irremediably hidden from me," and if this gap is in reality "spanned [*enjambé*] by the total being of my body, and by that of the world," it is however precisely the lack or absence of the other at the origin of this tension vis-à-vis oneself, it is the void between "the two *almost* concentric circles" that is then found in the disjunction that leads me to find myself tactilely, and it is only from the perspective of the absentee that "I am always on the same side of my body."[189]

The domain discovered by Fink is therefore not situated beyond copresence, but on the contrary includes the latter, superimposing itself on it perfectly. And thus, to think absence does not mean losing sight of presence but discovering instead the absent alterity in the copresent one. What remains to be defined, however, is this not-being-there; it remains to be understood how absence can reside in that "common temporal form" in which, according to Husserl, "every primordial temporality" is "an original and subjective-individual world." Fink intuited that what was at stake here was the problem of transcendental intersubjectivity's temporal structure. Not only that, but he also brought intersubjectivity's "historical character" (*historischer Charakter*) to the fore, noting that the contemporaneity of egological poles (which in Husserl is a precondition for their copresence) cannot but be relative, in other words, that "the other does not merely live in my own time, he is not just my contemporary, but is also my equal in age, or older or younger than I am."[190] A new type of "intentional modification" (*intentionale Abwandlung*) thus serves, via a play of analogies or a partial sharing of lifespans (since the remote past of the other, which exceeds my own, is only comprehensible via an analogy with a more proximate past that, by contrast, is identifiable with my own), as a basis for an understanding of intersubjectivity as "intersubjectivity through history" (*Intersubjektivität durch die Geschichte*).[191]

It is precisely spatial distance that naturally implies temporal difference: someone has left my perceptive field well before I first opened my eyes, while someone else will be born when I will already be too far from their gaze. We can therefore say that intersubjectivity has its origins in the story of a disappearance, and the intentionality that it demands is paradoxically subject to the vortex of absence: it is fundamentally eccentric and vertiginous. And if the zone of absence (*Zone der Abwesenheit*) does not merely extend beyond that which is currently perceptible, but insists on presence itself, if every presence, however proximate, always harbors and originates from an absence, if the distance of the absentee animates the vicinity of the perceptible, it is—to use Benjamin's famous formula—by virtue of an authentic "spatio-temporal intertwining" (*Gespinst aus Raum und Zeit*).

One can therefore speak of a temporal structure of intersubjectivity or even of coexistence, by which one may mean the warp of absence, inseparable from the weft of visible presence. And one must add that presence—mine and another's—is an "auratic effect," a *Nimbuseffekt* in the sense given to the term by Helmut Plessner: it is the existence of "something that must be and act here without, however, being 'here'" (*etwas . . . das da sein und wirken soll, ohne "da" zu sein*).[192]

3
Habit, Mask

26. The scene is, once again, familiar: Scottie has followed Madeleine into the museum and discovers her absorbed in contemplation, in her crepuscular state, before the large portrait of Carlotta Valdés. We see the painted image in front of Madeleine, seated, and then Scottie, who appears behind her and does not seem to notice it. Hitchcock was the master of subjective, or at least apparently subjective, points of view: the stylistic signature of *The Wrong Man* (1956), as Rohmer and Chabrol have observed, is a false subjectivity that is at the same time a fake exteriority; it is a point of view—that of the protagonist Balestrero (Henry Fonda)—which corresponds to our own because it is external to itself.[1] Here, we are not behind Scottie, but our gaze is immediately drawn, like the detective's, to the details arranged before us: Carlotta's bouquet of flowers and hairstyle, which are identical to Madeleine's. Because, by now, she is Carlotta: she is not simply admiring her but, far more than that, she *sees herself through the eyes of the dead woman*. Scottie is there, a spectator summoned by Carlotta's absence, before one and behind the other, and so both seen and unseen by the dreaming and ungraspable young woman. From that old painting, Madeleine scrutinizes her prey.

Now, of course, she is not at all Carlotta Valdés, and she is not Madeleine, either: instead, she is Judy, the actress of the hoax orchestrated at the ignorant detective's expense. But in any case, whether she be Judy or Madeleine, she is the one who sees herself through the eyes of an absent other (Madeleine or Carlotta). Now, of course, *D'entre les morts* is nothing but the twentieth-century metamorphosis of Rodenbach's *Bruges-la-morte*. There, Hugues Viane, "lonely and idle,"[2] the initiate and priest of a cult dedicated to a deceased woman (the stylized Ophelia of Fernand Khnopff's frontispiece), could encounter his beloved via a series of relic images (a youthful photo, a more recent one, a painting "whose shining glass alternated between concealing and revealing her, like an intermittent silhouette") and therefore find her once again in a living figure, the actress Jane Scott, to live out with her his impossible dream and finally recognize—in a moment of "solemn" lucidity—the deception of the mask and the falsity of the (necrophilic) sentiment: "She was no longer the figure of the dead woman." As is well known, the symbolist writer had built his story around the quiet, watery city of Bruges, which determines and orients the actions of the protagonist ("Bruges was his dead woman. And his dead woman was Bruges").[3] He combined the images of the city, the sights and glimpses that illustrate the novel, into a single dream "whose phases are nothing more than nostalgic reflections of souls and forms long departed."[4] Bachelard has thus rightly spoken of an "'Ophelisation' of the city as a whole" since the canals' melancholizing water surrounds and binds together the houses and the streets and, quiet or nimbus-like, dictates and dominates the entire story.[5] By contrast, Boileau and Narcejac's raw material is deceit: and using it, by amalgamating what Rodenbach had kept separate—that is the cult and the spectacle, the examination of truthfulness and the production of its object—they obtain Flavières's dream, or that catacomb-like Paris capable of being resurrected in a fluctuating, cocoon-like San Francisco, in the specter conjured up from beyond the Ocean thanks to the artifice of a student of Murnau's. A trick was needed, and in fact many tricks were needed to be able to say a second time: "Ah! Always that greyness of the streets of Bruges!"[6]

Judy thus manages to pass as Madeleine, to replace her, and she succeeds thanks to this painting, to the puppet-figure of Carlotta and to the story of Madeleine's fascination with her (if Madeleine identifies with Carlotta, then Judy can simply dress like Carlotta to become the former). It is a double and somewhat intricate hoax, a redundant farce that perhaps accidentally escaped parsimony's law, but that reveals itself as an effective trap since it is based on the formula, or better yet is made of the authentic "tissue" (*Gespinst*) of interpersonality.

Scottie has followed Madeleine all the way into the museum and now he stands there behind her, observing her while remaining unseen. Judy's situation with respect to Madeleine/Carlotta is decisive, however. If in the scenario concocted by the murderer, Madeleine is in fact possessed by Carlotta, and lives and sees herself as Carlotta or through the latter's eyes, then for Judy, Madeleine is not merely Elster's wife, just as Judy herself is not merely a role for the actress who plays her ("Judy . . . was, in a sense, me, trying to become the Hollywood person, trying to be Madeleine, needing to be loved, and willing to be made over" as Kim Novak would go on to reveal). Judy incarnates the

Madeleine/Carlotta dyad, that is her (Madeleine) who is impersonating the same person (Carlotta) that she (Judy) is also impersonating, and her living present is a copresence in which mask and identity merge, both animated by Madeleine's absence. Putting on that costume, delving with Madeleine into the story of Carlotta Valdés, Judy *truly puts herself in the shoes of those who put themselves in other's shoes*, an actress disguised as an actress who, while playing a role, does not play it and sees herself as she is, with her hair tied back like Carlotta's, just as one who is absent sees herself (Madeleine, perhaps a highly contrived Madeleine, but in any case—just like her gaze—a *truly absent one*). And therefore, Judy (alias Kim Novak) enters, so to speak, into herself; she becomes herself because she does not limit herself to playing Madeleine's part (Scottie would easily find her out), but sees herself with Carlotta's eyes, which are now Madeleine's, and which "grope around" and do not pretend. And so the entire lie is, for her, the truth, the imposture is the authentic love (precisely the opposite of what we find in Rodenbach). Her affliction is simultaneously false and true: a trick staged for him, certainly, but it is much more than a trick in her eyes, which see his and return to her from that enchanted gaze, the gaze of one who, already the victim of a game, encloses her in that game, staring at her from an anticipated tomorrow turned into destiny. One who sees oneself through the eyes of another and tricks them is not immune from being tricked. For this reason, looking at Ferguson, she—Robert L. Stevenson's words are particularly apt for Judy—"she hung over the future and grew dizzy; the image of this young man, slim, graceful, dark, with the inscrutable half-smile, attracted and repelled her like a chasm."[7] The powerful atmosphere of the film arises from this inextricable knot.

Two egos will perhaps never end up in the same body or a single soul in two bodies, but an actress can impersonate an actress and herself, and a soul can *become* itself ("Judy . . . was, in a sense, me") in a body that is a pure mask. Who is Madeleine, who seems like Carlotta? Actually, it is Judy. And Judy? She is the one who keeps herself in a difficult equilibrium *entre les mortes*, between Carlotta and Elster's wife. She is the one who lives under the gaze of one and the other, and in that greenish atmosphere she welcomes and attracts Scottie into the cemetery to then surrender to him, in that same light, in a hotel room that will turn out to be her grave.

So long as Elster's wife is alive, Judy can play a role (imitating the woman in the painting in order to be Madeleine); once she is dead, Judy can no longer imitate Carlotta or Madeleine but must leave the stage ("It is too late"). But could a being of absence ever disappear? Thus, Scottie continues to pursue Madeleine, wandering in his vertiginous state. And since he cannot but meet her again (seeing as an absentee cannot be missing, someone who has disappeared cannot disappear), he meets Judy (without recognizing her) and dresses and transforms her once again. And Judy could live on, if only she could merely be a mask; he could love her, if only the mask could live. But by now (the crime has been committed), the absence has been reduced to a lack of life: Judy cannot dress up as Carlotta, she cannot play Carlotta through Madeleine, she can only make herself up as Madeleine, a Madeleine who can no longer imitate anyone. By now, the mask only conceals an identity, or indeed death: Judy/Madeleine's final glance, with the necklace, in that room, is a desperate plea: it is now merely the glance of Elster's accomplice—and her tragedy is an impossible comedy.

And so Scottie Ferguson, who can neither love Judy nor let her go, demands a confession of her, "[He has] to go back into the past. Once more, one last time." He must go through the scene with the culprit, to replace his own bewitched "I" with a self-conscious one: he must retrace his steps without being able to erase them in order to finally be free and himself. He makes Judy/Madeleine climb the tower once again, and follows her, defying his own vertigo: this time, he succeeds, because the sight deception (Judy/Madeleine) is evidently not a deception, and so he can and must look down the staircase once—"Did you notice the distortion?"—and then again. Vertigo cures vertigo, or else does not tolerate repetition. And so both reach the top of the bell tower. We know who she is, but what about him? Of course, he does not spare her anything, not even an interrogation that is as cruel as it is superfluous. Perhaps in the hope of a final denial, and out of love for Madeleine, he forces Judy to admit everything, leading her to make a useless attempt ("when I saw you again I couldn't run away, I loved you so! I walked into danger and let you change me again because I loved you and wanted you!") only to finally answer: "Too late, there's no bringing her back." Who is he, we may ask, who responds the way she had responded? And who nevertheless embraces and kisses the culprit, the woman who could only throw herself, trembling, into his arms? The identificatory function suddenly changes: the old characters once again reappear, as well as seduction and, once more, the necrophilic passion. What had happened at the foot of the tower happens once again at its summit. And just as Madeleine had cast her gaze toward the tower's top while in Scottie's arms, so Judy must now look down the stairwell. She can hear steps growing nearer, and indeed in the darkness a nun appears, but in the meantime she flees out of fright, and falls. "Nothing excites vertigo . . . This was not foreseen," Madeleine had told Scottie, before climbing up there, and it was Judy speaking. What was unexpected was love, and when the two embrace at the top of the tower, Judy is now definitively Judy and, precisely with that kiss, she once again merges with Madeleine. Then someone appears on the staircase:

it is not the ghost of Madeleine, and it is not her that Judy fears. It is Madeleine who hears Judy climbing up, or rather it is Judy who, falling prey to her own deceit, sees herself, sees her own "here" "down there," and truly, or once again, precipitates.

In an alternative ending, never actually used but shot for the purpose of averting censorship, Elster is arrested. But the original screenplay does not foresee any other scenes and remains silent regarding the fate of this, not exactly secondary, character. But it is a conspicuous silence. It is precisely by his absence that the murderer dominates the entire narrative, as if he had foreseen and orchestrated even the finale, as if it was once again him pulling the strings here, at the top of the tower, even without being there.

So who is Scottie? In the last images of the barely illumined darkness, from up there, standing on the cornice, he looks down, and does not close his eyes.

In Boileau and Narcejac's detective novel, Gévigne has already been dead for a while by the time Flavières discovers and at the same time rejects the truth: "So this woman who shared his room was Renée . . . [. . .] No . . . No . . . [. . .] She had merely trumped up this story to get rid of him, because she didn't love him . . . [. . .] 'Madeleine,' he murmured beseechingly. She dried her eyes [. . .] 'I'm not Madeleine.'"[8] The roles are inverted, or rather they respect their *fin de siècle* model: in *Bruges-la-morte*, Hugues, taken by a sudden frenzy or fulfilling his city's imperious mandate ("a dizziness swept through his head"[9]) strangles Jane, who had made herself guilty of touching and desecrating a sacred relic, a braid of hair belonging to the deceased—the unattainable origin of every mimesis, which in the instant of the desecration opportunely transforms itself into vindictive locks (evoking Maupassant) and an instrument of death.[10] It is therefore not Renée who throws herself (like Judy) into the arms of the necrophile but Flavières who, unable to bear the conflict ("'You're lying . . .' he groaned"[11]), grabs Renée by the neck and kills her to grasp the object of his desire: he loves Madeleine ("Because of Pauline, because of the cemetery, because of your dreamy airs"[12]), and now he can finally kiss her, in that lifeless body. But to do so, he must ask permission of the policeman who is already alongside him and has already had him handcuffed. If for Hugues, alone in his room, the two dead women had become "identified in a single one," while around him the sounds of the city streets died down and Bruges "was beginning to once again be alone," Flavières's room is now packed with the sorts of people that gather at the scene of a crime. Nobody makes a sound. The people present are joined by the silent absentees: Renée, of course, but also Madeleine, Pauline, Gévigne, and alongside them Hugues and Jane. And Flavières? Who is he, or through whose eyes does he see himself, if for him the dead Madeleine is Renée and the dead Renée is once again Madeleine or perhaps, finally, Pauline? The object of love and the object of the investigation coincide, like the idol and the actress that plays her, when identification itself is a form of vertigo, and the community of monads is a conflation of life and its absence.

27. Scission animates the identification of the transcendental ego. And the most authoritative and distant voices have highlighted its difficulty. Refuting it, the young Sartre conceived the notion of a pure consciousness, one that is neither substantial nor positional, one that is transparent to itself, defined exclusively by intentionality and not weighed down by the ego. "Superfluous and detrimental," the "I" is in fact not only the object but also the product of reflection and therefore a passive figure, capable of only illusory activity. The ego "is the death of consciousness," or rather the enemy who "must fall before the stroke of the phenomenological reduction."[13]

Before Sartre, Adorno demonstrated the paradoxical status of the phenomenological ego, which is both pure and concrete, the subject and object of reflection which, according to Husserl, *can and must* recognize that it remains one and the same over the course of its scissions. Adorno observes that if the transcendental ego were the simple form of the multiplicity of empirical experiences, it could not auto-objectify itself; if instead it were truly "my" ego in a sense that was not merely formal, then it *should* not auto-objectify itself.

After having stigmatized, during the course of the summer semester of 1925, the "unphenomenological" tendency that—going against the motto of "returning to the things themselves"—would have induced phenomenology to overlook the question of consciousness's being, Heidegger directly asked Husserl a question concerning the absolute ego's mode of being in a famous letter from October 22, 1927: "In what sense is it the *same* as that of the factical ego; and in what sense is it *not* the same?"[14]

We are already familiar with Ingarden's observation: "How can I be a unique and selfsame 'I' that is constitutive and pure, and at the same time constituted and real, if the properties attributed to the two are mutually exclusive and therefore cannot coexist within the unity of an object?"[15] And even if this "great difficulty" were hypothetically surmountable (in spite of the principle of non-contradiction), "how would one understand the unity of an objectuality, whose elements (constitutive consciousness—constituted objectivity) are unified into a single and identical object by the intentionality of one of them?"[16] To this matter, Ingarden concludes, "nobody, as far as I am given to understand, has drawn attention."[17] With the exception, we might remark, of the very same Husserl. He demonstrated that he was not at all unaware of it when he defined the scission of the self-observing phenomenologist and tried to unite the two intentionalities—the one of the ego always interested in its own goals, and the phenomenoligizing or impartial one—by affirming that in reality the latter is also interested, even if only "to see and to describe adequately" (*zu sehen und adäquat zu beschreiben*),[18] that is, uniquely in its own disinterest (with regards to itself). It is a curious attempt, one might observe, to salvage the unity of a subject that is its own object of intention (both constitutive and constituted), placing alongside the pure ego a "pure" (or "purely phenomenological") "interest" that is still possible where any involvement is excluded.[19] An attempt that (much like the well-known figure by Giotto presenting the very triptych that depicts it) reproposes the scission within the framework of transcendental living and, by revealing that disinterest is an interest in (dis)interest, finally confesses and performs its own *mise en abîme*. The phenomenologist's impartial *habitus must* chase after itself *ad infinitum*.

28. In reality, and in accordance with an illuminating paradox, the figure of an authentic, pure disinterestedness had occurred to philosophers at the beginning of the twentieth century via psychological studies of the supreme instant (*instant suprême*), which recognized in the epileptic fit's intellectual aura or in the emotions of the dying an exaltation of memory capable of reconstituting in a single panoramic representation the events of an entire existence.[20] Referring back as well to the testimonials of alpinists who had survived life-threatening falls, first Victor Egger and later Bergson chose as a privileged theme the mnemic shortcut, whether in the prodigious forms of the panorama (Bergson) or of the rapid succession of images. As Georges Poulet observed, "this Leibnizian affirmation of total recollection and of the identification of the latter with consciousness" could not help but intrigue Bergson, and the same applied to its correlate: the sensation of beatitude experienced by the dying in relation to their own existence.[21]

One might say that, in falling, that man has lost his footing and forsaken vertigo to acquire an until-then unknown serenity, a for the first time true and absolute disinterest, experiencing no longer fear but a sort of "metaphysical curiosity" (*metaphisische Neugier*).[22] In more Bergsonian terms: his detached gaze reconnects with the past, which the force of habit (that is, of attention and action) made him overlook. "Placed before the vision of *mobilité universelle*," Bergson explained to his audience at Oxford in 1911, "some of us will suffer from vertigo . . . they are used to *terra firma*. . . . They need 'fixed' reference-points in which to ground their thought and existence."[23] The visions of the dying shine light instead on the idea of a conversion of attention directed toward life, freed of practical concerns, that "will thus embrace in an undivided present the entire past history of the conscious person."[24] One must, however, go beyond Poulet and add that the idea of an enduring present (*présent qui dure*) has its paradigm in the history of precinema, more specifically in that of the moving panorama (*mouvant panorama*). One may also recall the critique of the cinematographic mechanism of thought, which was developed between 1900 and 1904 before finally being set forth in a famous chapter of *L'évolution créatrice* (1907). By combining the generic movement of a machine with the immobile and personal attitudes captured by photography, cinema realizes and illustrates the ordinary procedure or the fundamental illusion of consciousness,[25] which associates immobile snapshots of reality with an abstract and uniform becoming. Four years after *Creative Evolution*, the nineteenth-century rotating disc is therefore Bergson's chosen model for a vital conversion, from which cinema however remains precluded because "the mechanism of our ordinary consciousness is cinematographic in nature."[26]

It is Gilles Deleuze's famous thesis that would go on to unsettle this framework: with its decisive technical evolution, with its editing and mobile camera, emancipating itself from uniform and abstract time, cinema becomes genuinely Bergsonian. Its images are no longer snapshots in a series, animated by abstract movement, but mobile sections of *durée*, like the movement-image in the first chapter of *Matter and Memory*. Nor is that all. According to Deleuze, it is precisely Hitchcock who (with his "mental images") pushes "the movement-image to its limit," and in the case of *Vertigo*, even beyond movement itself into the domain of the time-image. By revealing that which is vertiginous "in the heroine's heart" and transforming the eminently common pathology of the protagonist into that strange contemplative state that dominates the entire narrative,[27] *Vertigo* bears witness to a duration that is neither subjective nor tied to internal life; it demonstrates that "time is not within us," that it is we, rather, who "inhabit time" and that "subjectivity is never *ours*."[28]

It would seem possible at this point to recognize the formula of a purer disinterestedness by underscoring in the cinematographic effect the separation between vertigo and the identity of the subject, recognizing in the "moment" (*Weile*) of the counter-zoom a dreamy and impersonal *durée*. If the free fall caused by vertigo lends a paradoxical serenity, the interaction of the dolly with the lens releases both from individuality and death; it does not enact a "conversion of attention," which would orient it once again toward a person's undivided past, but a metamorphosis of the phobic engram into a spectacle that is enjoyable beyond empathic participation, or in the most complete of detachment. The vertigo effect thus replaces the vertiginous attraction and the solitary contemplation of the dying with—as Benjamin taught—a truly distracted reception (*Rezeption in der Zerstreuung*) for which there is no supreme moment.

29. This "interest in disinterest" is however once again vertiginous, and it defines the "I" that, all while separating itself from itself, keeps itself to itself. "Actuality and egoity," as Enzo Melandri has explained, "converge but do not perfectly coincide," and in any case "an imperceptible but essential fracture persists between the *ego* and the *cogito*."[29] If, as Husserl asserts, through a reflection of a higher order or an identifying synthesis, "I can and must" recognize that a selfsame "I" is involved in every reflexive action, that egological life itself is nothing other than this division of a single "I," precisely that unique ego of which I am conscious—one must add—is both mine and already no longer mine, it is "numerically one and unique with respect to 'its' stream of consciousness" and is now also divided from the act that is observing it and that perceives itself unreflectively.[30] It is precisely the unique and the selfsame that appear in a scission and from a perspective that, while illuminating them, evades and grasps them.

In *The Transcendence of the Ego*, Sartre showed the magical nature of the "I" and explained why man "is always a sorcerer for man," and "we are sorcerers for ourselves, every time we consider our I."[31] He furthermore separated Husserl from Husserl to save the immediate, transcendental, and impersonal consciousness of the self, by freeing it from the reflexive and transcendent figure of the ego. The ego makes its appearance only "on the occasion of a reflective act," but no earlier.[32]

Nevertheless, one must insist, the ego appears and manifests its power. And unreflective self-consciousness cannot be autonomous—as Sartre admits, following Husserl, it could not exist without its reflexive counterpart[33]—because it is betrayed precisely by its immediate self-evidence, because it is *precisely as self-consciousness* that it contains the formula of reflexive identification, which consigns it to the hands of its product, and by virtue of which it necessarily "from its first arising, . . . makes itself *personal*."[34] If the ego is "the death of consciousness," and if, to cite the almost unchanged formula found in *Being and Nothingness*, "it is consciousness in its fundamental selfness which under certain conditions allows the appearance of the Ego,"[35] then it is death itself that rises before consciousness, as a *"power independent* of the one who produces it" (Marx), to capture and dominate it. The ego is merely a product; its power—one may admit, following Sartre—is magical and impure, because it is the spontaneity of consciousness that is productive. But, originally tied to itself, the latter forces itself into a relation with its product, "by a sort of vertigo, by a spasm of spontaneity."[36]

30. For this reason, identification constitutes an irresistible attraction. And the ego itself, numerically one and corresponding to a person, only offers

itself to itself from a point of view that is already foreign and eccentric, via a living, current gaze that by holding itself to itself slides toward the positional, the past, the nonliving. The very unity and ownness of the ego is intersubjective (*intersubjektive Eigenheitssphäre*) and its vertigo extends (immediately, without the intervention of an image) to interpersonality in the proper sense.

Identical to itself, the ego is now once again attracted by something outside itself, by the stranger who presents himself in the identifying vision as another I-myself (*Ich-selbst in meiner Eigenheit*). It is precisely the development of this magic that cannot but be coherent, from the first level of appresentation to the higher levels of human community, composed of individual and concrete subjects (monads), "existing for themselves precisely as I exist for myself," and are therefore bound to me and among themselves by an essentially fascinative "connexion" (*Verbindung*).[37] The Leibnizian principle of the absolute singularity of every monad, which in its hypothetical guise informed the theory of analogical apperception, undergoes a hallucinatory metamorphosis here.

If Husserl accuses Descartes of having missed the transcendental turn, Heidegger accuses Leibniz (and therefore also Husserl) of having based the monad on a Cartesian model, understanding it as a substance enclosed in a sphere that includes the entire world. One would have to write a history of the theodicies of consciousness and of the monadologies abandoned by their first creator, who by his departure allowed for a conspicuous or apodeictic affirmation of the ego, whether still substantial or pure, or of a neither internal nor external *Dasein*, imposing modern projections of harmony or community. §60 of the *Cartesian Meditations* and those of Husserl's manuscripts which were precociously inspired by Leibniz would thus be united in a constellation that would at first sight seem bizarre when compared with the distant and diversely brilliant attempts of Renouvier and Tarde. In its various semblances, identification (or universal imitation, contagion, Renouvier's solidarity) would reveal itself as a specific correlate of the personal subject's centrality, "a member of a community of monads,"[38] which renews the old metaphysical setting of the single common world. What would appear all of a sudden, alongside the words *community* and *society*, is the recent, more or less recognized or respected paternity of nineteenth-century psychology and of the theories of hypnosis and suggestion. Not even Heidegger's "being-with" (*Mitsein*) could perhaps escape this vertiginous fascination.

At least from "What is a society?" (1884) till *Monadology and Sociology* (1893), for Gabriel Tarde, the theological becomes social, but society in the meantime becomes patently more magical. A suggestive, harmonious relation mutually binds the monads who imitate each other and distinguish themselves by imitating each other, dazed, somnambular, drawn by the opposing magnetic forces of belief and desire. Everything is social and society is imitation: imitation is a relation of repetition and difference (that is, invention) and identity is made up of a minimal quantity of the former and a maximal quantity of the latter. But a dream that does not explain itself can easily take a turn and lose itself in a nightmare, and what all of a sudden emerges out of Tarde's universal sociomorphism is a foolish and dangerous "crowd" of minions lacking inventiveness (or identity), a true social pathology that undoes the felicitous economy of imitation.

To fill in Cartesianism's lacunae and solve the difficulties of psycho-physical parallelism in a preestablished harmony, Renouvier had recognized (in *Nouvelle monadologie*, 1899) that the external relations between monads presupposed consciousness as an internal relation of representation, that is, as a relation "of the subject to the object, within the subject," which is "a distinction and at the same time, an identification."[39] Hence his perspicacious theory of vertigo: a scission of temptation and will, the latter renders the subject "pour lui autre que lui, l'homo duplex'" and makes him fatally take the step that he dreads (as Renouvier writes in the above-cited passage in the *Traité de psychologie rationelle*, "the central question is that the dreaded movement is precisely the one that is most likely to occur").[40] But since consciousness is itself an internal division, the pathological crisis can only be seen as an aberrant form of the more general phenomenon, that is of "normal vertigo, in which a modification of the organs is provoked by the imagination of a certain movement." Will and action—as Renouvier would go on to add—are not one, as Maine de Biran's substantialism claimed: rather, there exists between them a "small, but inevitable"—or, perhaps one could say, magnetic—interspace of imaginative passion.[41]

What is essential is not a difference intrinsic to the object or relative to its condition, which would expose it to the sights of desire or to more or less well-founded repulsion. The peril does not lie in this or that entity that I have good reason to fear and that, nevertheless, or rather for that very reason, attracts me. Even before that, it is the attraction itself that inspires fear, it is the identifying attitude or passion of consciousness that confers on its object a potentially mortal allure. Even in distant times and contexts, there was a medical distinction, proposed by Erasmus Darwin and later taken up by Purkinje, between physiological and pathological vertigo, which however remained excluded from the tests conducted by the scientist on himself.[42] But now it is identification itself, the primary structure of the "I," that reveals itself to be attractive or magnetic, which means that regarding "abnormal" vertigo one could say, using Georges Canguilhem's formula, that despite denying and logically coming after the normal form, it actually precedes it and constitutes its existential basis. For this reason, Lasègue, even without citing Renouvier, was able to use the term *mental vertigo* (*vertige mental*) for a specific type of alienation. While similarly concealing the source of his inspiration, Alain—as we have seen—thought to normalize vertigo by relating it to the habitual. And yet the very subject of every habit and mastery is still, existentially, in peril: excessive, incongruous, and fumbling, it ventures beyond its bounds and remains perpetually, whether in a way that is conscious or not, authentic or not, exposed to the abyss.

The tendency to find the primary fact of consciousness, its scission, in suggestive mimesis is something Tarde and Renouvier have in common and which dominates their work. The tendency to combine interpersonality and personal consciousness in the name of imitation or scission unites the distant stars of Tarde and Husserl. The idea of reintegrating instead the scission within the norm of self-consciousness, thus distinguishing it from alterity and pathology, is something that Husserl and Renouvier unexpectedly share: the psychological interspace of the imagination, brief, but inevitable, corresponds to that of the analogy or of the "as if," which in the *Cartesian Meditations* separates the ego from the alter ego. And it is in such an interval that attraction can exert its force and that the cogito ambiguously holds onto itself, identifying itself with the mask of its own past.

What remains to be understood, in this peculiar sketch we have put together, is the role of *Dasein*, which is originally both *se ipse* (*Selbstheit*) and "being-with" (*Mitsein*). We have already evoked Klein's phrase concerning acrophobia and thrownness (*Geworfenheit*). A decade or so before him, Jean Wahl had in passing compared Renouvier's vertigo with existential anguish.[43]

31. The past of the "I" does not exist as if the "I" were already there to assume it. The past is instead the nonliving, the lack of actuality or presence in relation to which the ego is formed and lives. This is the origin that Husserl attempts to capture with his "surrealistic delirium of . . . *Ur-*" and which goes back to the "enigma of that which is innate."[44] What is at stake is the archi-past, which doubles and precedes the temporality of the ego or of the trace that Derrida placed in plain sight, taking phenomenology to the extreme, and which produces the same "as the self-relation in the difference with itself, the same as the non-identical."[45]

Post-Heideggerian interpretations of Husserl recognized that the truth or perfect individualization of the ego is its death and they retrospectively discovered the possibility of all possibilities at the very heart of the individualizing consciousness. As Derrida has written, "the appearing of the *I* to itself in the *I am* is therefore originally in relation to its own possible disappearance.

I am means therefore originarily *I am mortal*."⁴⁶ Melandri had by then already expressed himself using similar, perhaps less sophisticated, but all the more clear terms: "The fact that the ego implicitly contains its own death within itself, and this not as an accident, but as the fulfillment and perfection of its own immanent motivation, means that saying "I" can sometimes have a convincing accent of truth."⁴⁷ And yet, by means of a brilliant reversal, Derrida added the decisive annotation: from the perspective of the living ego, death is not a point of flight or a fulfillment, it is not merely an accident because it is not just a possibility, but (the possibility of) an accomplished fact. "The statement 'I am living' is accompanied by me being-dead and the statement's possibility requires the possibility that I be dead—and the reverse."⁴⁸

The perspective of the ego as a living being or *Leibkörper* is in fact that of someone who is looking at himself through the eyes of another who is currently absent, who belongs to the past and is not living. Derrida cites Edgar Allan Poe's Valdemar. We can say that the words uttered by the famous living corpse ("I am dead") reveal that the proposition "I am alive," more specifically "I," is precisely a slip of the tongue: I said "alive" because I meant "dead" and meant to say "dead" because by saying "I," I meant "another." But that is not all: I said "alive" and meant "dead" because subjectivity is constitutionally afflicted, to cite another page of Poe's, by the "demon of perversity," so irresistibly attracted by death as to confuse it with life.

32. The structure of the transcendental ego, or of a society of subjects identical to each other, is attractive or magnetic. As an example of the "crisis of presence" (or of personal identity), Ernesto de Martino borrowed from Georges Dumas the peculiar example of Captain Victor, who would suddenly throw himself on the floor crying out "To me, granite!" only to then slowly rise, looking around at everyone defiantly. As he would later go on to explain, he thus intended to demonstrate his attachment to French soil: "I was overflowing with patriotic love and wished to show it."⁴⁹ And it was indeed a notable exhibition of such sentiments, given that "the soldier's proper position is cataleptic rigidity, auto-hypnosis via the black line of the rifle against the wall to which he presents arms";⁵⁰ and one could also define it as a crisis that arises out of an excess of military conditioning, or a loss of one's senses caused by inflation. A perfect monad, this man had to impersonate the hallucination of the identical so decisively as to exhibit it on the stage of presence itself: surrendering to the fascination of the "fatherland" (the tomb of one's fathers or a granitic affirmation of origin), that is, to the past as such or to the "first determination," he transformed his drama into a psychological comedy.

Indeed, within the domain of intersubjectivity or of monadic society, the zero point or orientational center of the singular ego is the Earth, to which Husserl dedicated the pages of the famous manuscript D17 at the end of May 1934. The Earth, it reads, is not a body among others and cannot lose its sense of *Ur-*, of archi-plane, of "experiential ground" (*Erfahrungsboden*) and of "the original immobile arch" (*die Ur-Arche Erde bewegt sich nicht*) of the common world (*Mitmenschheit*), much as my lived body (*Leib*) cannot surrender its originality. Just as a single soul cannot inhabit two bodies, just as there cannot be two "I"s in a living body or two living bodies in a single body (*Körper*) or in the same place, so there could not be two Earths. And even if I were to reach the Moon or Venus, I could not have another Earth, nor could the now distant Earth simply be an ordinary body. Two Earths could only be two fragments of the same Earth, inhabited by mankind.

But if it is precisely the center of the transcendental ego that is afflicted by vertigo, one can understand how the Earth too may move, or rather, as simple earth, may split to attract me to it. Dizziness—which some may sense before an earthquake—is both the sign and the symptom of a momentary separation, capable of reducing the center of the common world to a simple vibrating body with respect to which I perilously oscillate. But it also simultaneously testifies to a constant and otherwise concealed attraction: my very own "here" attracts me from "there," from the viscera of the planet, from the nucleus towards which ideally I plummet, falling to the ground, for the reason that the Earth as archi-plane, as the transcendental origin of *kínesis* and the foundation of community, exerts its imperious magnetism, thus demonstrating its perfect integrity. The empirical proof of vertigo discloses an original tension, and since an evident force is also in a certain sense unmasked and precarious, this very appearance can in turn result in a characteristic malaise: "Then I, always, I extend my hands, one and the other,/towards a cliff, a tree, a stem! . . . to a trifle, here, to not fall into the sky!"[51] If dizziness therefore occurs in the community of monads, if the Earth is one and there is no need to get to the moon to experience vertigo, it is because the grounding itself is hallucinatory and uncertain. Although Henri Wallon studied the loss of equilibrium in the horizontality of large open spaces, already before him, Charles Féré, Charcot's student, had diagnosed the most pedestrian of acrophobias in a subject who, despite avoiding climbs and cliffs, regularly suffered dizziness spells when he did not sense anything above him.[52]

Suspended between climbing and falling, fear is not an imaginary distortion in this case; rather, it corresponds to the real eventuality that identification may also find itself faced with itself, unable to escape. Only an ulterior reflection would perhaps be capable of concealing this semblance and, overturning the original spell, opening a way out. Taking up de Martino's earlier research, Elvio Fachinelli explained the vertigo suffered by a patient of his over the course of two days as an ("aborted, incomplete, unrecognized") attempt at an almost magical cure for an earlier psychic breakdown (the fact that in this case the sensation of dizziness increased "in an analytic position" does not contradict Ferenczi's theory[53]). For its part, the commonplace evoked by Renouvier, according to which vertigo cures vertigo (Cox believed that provoking a dizziness spell and bringing the patient to full circulatory collapse was the best way "to correct erroneous ideas," while Frank, among others, recommended the rotating machine as an antidote to epilepsy) finds confirmation in the specific case of acrophobia, and suggests that the first memory engrained in the victim's memory (Bachelard's engram) is in fact only the second, which intervened to placate the first, and that the perilous moment has been erased by an identical one to then resurface in a new instance of vertigo. Perhaps only a subsequent reflection could dissimulate this appearance, or hold back the second spell to keep the first from happening. It is by following in Gilbert Cohen-Séat's footsteps, and through him in Renouvier's, that Siegfried Kracauer has recognized in vertiginous suggestion the specific effect of cinema, which is "denied to other media."[54]

33. As Sartre rightly affirmed, "it is exclusively in magical terms that we should speak of the relations of the I to consciousness."[55] But we must add that this does not mean that "unreflected consciousness must be considered autonomous."[56] At least against the pretense of saving an anonymous, transparent consciousness from the spell of the "I," Derrida's consideration regarding Husserl's original genesis is valid: "This pure spontaneity is an impression. It creates nothing."[57] It is precisely its being "*consciousness* in each of its phases"—precisely the fact that the retentional phase is conscious of the preceding one without objectifying it and that the original is already self-consciousness "in the original form of the 'now'"[58]—this nonpositional transparency bewitches consciousness, tying it immediately and irremediably to its derivative.

Recognizing the magical nature of this structure means studying the exercise that isolates activity from passivity to tie them together in a circular enchantment, and distancing oneself from Derrida's perspective, which sheds light on living presence through its relation with absence, which discovers the play of difference by keeping it within the fascinating field of the *arché*. It is precisely the obsession with origins that demanded the truly surrealistic discovery of an irreducible trace on the basis of which originality could be conceived. There can be no *Ur-stiftung* if not on the basis of its residue, and there is no pure constitutive subjectivity: "the constituted constitutes the constituting and inversely; the absolute monad originarily welcomes 'the other.'"[59] Granting alterity a transcendental status, the philosophy of *différance* thus distinguishes itself from phenomenology as a fulfilled version of its promise: passing "à travers le texte de Husserl" it attains, radicalizes, but also stabilizes the position that the latter had reached in the Group C manuscripts, recognizing the original as a "pre-beginning" (*'Vor'-Anfang*) and a primordial extraneity.

The critique of presence and spontaneity, that is the critique of the consciential paradigm, is thus unable to efficiently move toward this *Vor-* or toward the supplement on whose basis the origin itself becomes conceivable. Observing that the very mythology of the *arché* is nourished and supported by its own presupposition, it aims instead at disclosing the relation to death (*rapport à la mort*) hidden beneath a thick metaphysical covering to bring it to light and exhibit it as such. It does not see in death the *télos* or perfection of the ego, or something that is "originally" in relation to it; it does not conform to the "rules of transcendental genesis," but interrogates them by asking which habituality refers to a subjective pole and how a *héxis* can be limited to egological centrality. From its point of view, both one and the other, both ego and death, reveal themselves as the specific products of a vertiginous relation.

A reading that confronts Husserl's texts not as mere objects of reflection but as "'that through which' . . . to think the very things to which Husserl referred while writing,"[60] must "explain the constitution of the 'I'" on the stage of its history to conclude that "complete individuation," "the *télos* of personal life is death" and its foundation "is on the contrary the seed of the *Ur-ich*" or the "substrate of habitualities."[61] Instead, we observe, reading Klein, that this very "consciousness of the signification of the perfect individuation" is produced through the eyes of another, and that therefore every "'biography' understood transcendentally" is nothing other than "a spectacle for a consciousness."[62]

34. It is on the basis of the definition of the temporal structure of consciousness as a consciousness of identity that, in the *Studies in the Phenomenology of Constitution* and in the "Fourth Cartesian Meditation," Husserl develops his theory of *habitus*.

This transition from the self-transparency of consciousness, from retention and therefore from memory to possession has seemed fascinating and problematic in equal measure to his students and scholars, and to Ingarden in particular. Finding numerous affinities (*persönlich sehr sympathisch*) between the passages on habituality in §32, he reformulated in his *Kritische Bemerkungen* to the *Cartesian Meditations*, in new and fitting terms, Aristotle's old objection:[63] if every act of (constitutive) consciousness is coherent with its (constituted) object, to "have a habit" would generate an infinite regression (*Führt dies nicht auf einen "regressus"?*[64]). Clearly adopting Husserl's lesson and the term *Durchleben* (living through)—*Als Ich, der ich dies und jenes erlebe, dies und jenes cogito als derselbe durchlebe*[65]—in light of his notion of "non-difference" between the process and the object of consciousness,[66] he thus proposed as a viable solution in the form of a reinterpretation of the theory of habitualities. Not unlike the act that captures them, according to Ingarden, habitualities are characterized by a peculiar "living through" in themselves, that is, they yield themselves by going through and prolonging themselves in self-knowledge, in that which we are "experiencing." Understood as a constant reference to oneself, as the experience which we live, possession should not have recourse to a different possession. If the peril of a *regressio* is thus averted (just as Husserl avoided it at the level of the stream of consciousness, denying it an intentionality vis-à-vis itself), it nevertheless seems clear that by virtue of the same principle of "non-difference," every *cogito* that the "I" lives would thus immediately acquire the status of *habitus*. This is indeed what Ingarden hypothesized, intending to proceed along this path, indicated at the end of §33 of the *Meditations*, which fully identified the phenomenology of self-constitution with phenomenology in general, while at the same time conceding that Husserl himself would have rejected the hypothesis of the existence of *Durchleben*'s acts (*Indessen weist, so viel ich weiß, Husserl die Existenz des "Durchlebens" zurück*[67]).

Indeed, the assertion of §31 ("the ego grasps himself . . . as *I*, who live [*erlebe*] this and that subjective process, who live [*durchlebe*] through this and that cogito, *as the same I*"[68]) referred exclusively to the pure "I," originally self-evident in every act of consciousness. Ingarden, by contrast, transposes and pushes *Durchleben* into the domain of possession and thus of the concrete ego. This gesture is replete with consequences. The very theme of reflection (or of memory) as a "first objectification" is thus dethroned from the primary role that Husserl had assigned it and tacitly replaced by that of the habituality of all conscious actions. This wholesale placement of cogitation within the domain of *héxeis* has implications for the very process of identification: the ego, both "pole" and "substrate," is now disseminated in a variety of *habitus*, which are themselves subject to an implicit and decisive metamorphosis.

35. One might be led to believe that in his attempt to rewrite the "Fourth Meditation," Eugen Fink considered Ingarden's objections so intently as to make them his own and enlist them, so to speak, to defend Husserl's position. Indeed, he keeps the ego's fundamental role as substrate intact, conceiving its identity, however, as habit, or as a primary *héxis* in which various *habitus* have

their origin: categorizable in "three fundamental forms" (stances, convictions and volitive actions; involuntary dispositions, which determine the ego's tendencies; passive but voluntary dispositions, attributable to the kinesthetic organization and mobility of the *Leib*); these are all "supported and made possible by the main, fundamental habituality of the 'I,' that is the habituality of the identical being-I."[69]

All while respecting Husserl's pronouncement that "the enduring Ego himself . . . is not an experience [*Erlebnis*] or a continuity of experiences,"[70] Fink nevertheless points out that the identity of the ego cannot, in turn, be made up of habitualities. Some random *habitus* does not live itself, it does not freely self-constitute itself as both a process and an object of consciousness, but rather takes its origin from the cardinal *héxis* or the identity of the pure ego. "The persisting, the temporal self-perseverance [*Sich-Durchhalten*], of such determining properties of the ego" does not derive from every one of its actions a stable property,[71] but is already habitual, in its very own being identical: particular habitualities do not form it, "they merely concretize it."[72] A fundamental *habitus*, neither objective nor concrete, thus strengthens the domain of the cogito by imparting to it a primary stability, whereas the phenomenology of self-constitution seems to superimpose itself directly—and not as a subsequent consequence, as Husserl writes at the end of §33—upon phenomenology in general.

Now, if this fundamental "habituality of the selfsame being I" allows the ego to "find itself"—without running the risk of a *regressio*—"identical throughout its passing," and along with the past to seem stable and unitary, what truly distinguishes its "self-perseverance" (*Sich-Durchhalten*) from Ingarden's *Durchleben*? Why should this first *habitus* not be, in other words, *one* of many, simply "a habit . . . the habit of saying 'I'"?[73] One could also conceive of the ego as a primary *habitus* and even overturn the "inflection of being into having, of 'I' into mine" into that of having into being,[74] of mine into "I": the relation between *héxis* and the properties of the subject will remain inviolate, and will lose none of its ambiguity.

36. In 1957, Gerhard Funke, previously a specialist of Maine de Biran, dedicated chapter 1 of his *Zur transzendentalen Phänomenologie* and most importantly the essay (based in part on Brand's work) "Transzendentalphänomenologische Untersuchung über 'universalen Idealismus,' 'Intentionalanalyse' und 'Habitusgenese'" to the phenomenological problem of *habitus*. A year later, he published his great study on the notion of "habit" (*Gewohnheit*) as a monograph in Erich Rothacker's *Archiv für Begriffsgeschichte*, ending the main part of his study with a chapter on "Das Ich als Substrat von Habitualitäten

(Husserl)." He did not cite Fink's (still unpublished) revision, but attentively read Ingarden's *Bemerkungen* and proposed an original solution: he forcefully reiterated *habitus*'s noncorrespondence with absolute subjectivity (which placed him at odds with Fink's hypothesis of the subject's self-identification) and responded to Ingarden by recognizing that habitualities could not be true transcendences. "In the self-genesis of the ego with its *habitus*, the self-apparition does not depend on the 'matter' or the 'quality' of the relative constitutive intentional lived events (Ingarden) but is 'the simple fulfillment of the act that can lead to the constitution of an objectivity.'"[75] The latter is precisely the hypothesis that Ingarden rejected, since it would introduce a second reality that all while arising with the act would transcend it. But Funke manages to avoid the formation of another transcendence (and, therefore, once again, of an infinite regression) by making a further distinction: "If the acts of objective intentionality need to be connected to a transcendence in immanence, the genesis of *habitus* does not have this nature in this form."[76] *Héxeis* are therefore not "transcendent noemata," and yet they do not flow by without leaving a trace: they are "remainders" (*Sedimente*: the Husserlian term also dear to Merleau-Ponty) of lived experiences that form a "second transcendence" (*zweite Traszendenz*) "alongside" (*neben*) the first one and which therefore have the particular characteristic of being experienced in an immediate manner.[77] To circumscribe their domain, Funke develops the concept of "paratranscendence" (*Paratrascendenz*), coined by Oskar Becker in an openly pro-Nazi context derived from Heidegger,[78] in order to define, under the natural sign of birth ("literally: 'nature' means birth [*Geburt*]"), the (paraontological) equality of "essence" (*Wesen*) and sameness of "character" (*Wesen*), that is, the belonging to a people, to a race, to a certain landscape. "Blood or race," Becker writes, "is, in Aristotle's words, 'nature in the sense of appearance,' the very same *eídos* realized in organic procreation, since *génos*, origin, determines *eídos*, appearance."[79] Funke ties this terminology back and adapts it to Husserl's theme, clearly making *Wesen* (essence or character, behavior) morph and resolve itself into *habitus*. The "I" as the substrate of habits therefore manifests itself in the stream of consciousness, but does not entirely coincide with this stream (it is not its self-evidence or its original self-experience): rather, it is equal to the precipitate of its transformations. The latter are not transcendent, but almost: they resist, unmovable (or irrevocable), they form that which remains positively untranscendible (an *Unentstiegenheit*, as Funke writes, once again borrowing Becker's term), that is, the precipitate of "paratranscendence";[80] and if their persistence does not derive, as it does in Ingarden, from a special action, it is because it originates in retention. For Funke, that which is preserved by retention without being objectified is in fact neither perfectly immanent nor transcendent but precisely paratranscendent. *Habitus*, therefore, does not coincide with the immediate self-evidence of consciousness but rather derives from it: "Egological habits constitute themselves only because consciousness remains consciousness in all of its phases."[81] Because consciousness of something is always also, originally, self-consciousness, and because as a result it holds itself back and moves forward retentionally, *héxeis* form and manifest themselves in a very particular way, which differs from that of external objectivity and is proper to *Durchleben*. It is therefore only because consciousness is retentional that a *habitus* is formed, the continuity of the ego can manifest itself, and a subject can display "an abiding style with a unity of identity" and be endowed with a "personal character."[82]

Funke's interpretation seems to thus rigorously adhere to Husserl's view. All while reaffirming that *habitus* does not coincide with absolute subjectivity, it nevertheless ties the phenomenology of self-constitution back to phenomenology in general, thus dissolving the problems of the former (the formation of habitualities, the potential infinite regression) in the domain of the latter. By keeping them distinct, he resolves the thematic of *habitus* by integrating it into that of the stream of consciousness, thus reducing habitual perseverance to the identity of the "I" understood as an identity of being and appearing. For this reason, Funke is able to correct Ingarden's perspective by appropriating Merleau-Ponty's words, shedding light on the problem of *héxis* in the sense of the "absolute contact of me with myself," as indicated in the *Phenomenology of Perception*:

> Alongside all experiences and reflections, one thus also finds an "I" which originally knows itself, which is nothing other than self-consciousness and which is conscious not through observation or objectifying deduction but through direct living [*unmittelbar Durchleben*]. One can thus say that "self-consciousness is the very being of the mind in practice." And, indeed, such a genesis is *causa sui*. . . .
> The *habitus* is not constituted as a sense but is formed genetically, "the absolute contact between me and myself, the identity of being and appearance cannot be posited, but only lived, prior to any affirmations."[83]

The driver behind this definition of pure "living" as an adoption of *héxeis*, which recalls and translates Becker's language (the essential "equality," *Gleichung*, of *génos* and *eídos*) into Merleau-Ponty's terms (the identity of being and appearance), is nevertheless the concept of "paratranscendence," which is untranslatable precisely because of its functional role, which is efficient—in that it allows one to isolate habitualities from "noematic *intenta* which are correlatives of actions"[84]—by virtue of its peculiar amphibology: for indeed, it transforms the retentional (both in view and nonobjective) into that which, all while remaining "alongside" and insuperable in every act of transcending, must be lived. "Everything here," Funke reiterates, "concerns 'interiority' and 'living' [*Alles kommt hier auf das 'Innesein' und das 'Durchleben' an*]."[85] But one could wonder whether *habitus* (habit or second nature) may truly be a "second transcendence," if it can legitimately subsist in a genuinely Husserlian context, which cannot be that of *Dasein*'s ecstatic constitution, if, that is, a legitimate transposition of Becker's terminology can be applied here given that immanence and transcendence already nearly merge in the "original vicinity" by definition. One could also wonder whether with such an *Innesein* (in which one recognizes Scheler's voice) one is not reintroducing a surrogate or parody of an outside where a "pure contact" (*contact absolu*) should realize itself. Brand soon responded to Adorno's criticism, which was directed at the immediate nature of self-comprehension, arguing that "for Husserl, immanence . . . is neither interiority [*Innerlichkeit*] nor an 'inside' [*Drinnen*] but an original closeness [*Urnähe*] or—as one reads in *First Philosophy*—the proximate figure of pure life, the self-clarification of self-estrangement in and through reflection."[86] Funke—who read Brand's book on the Group C manuscripts—conceived instead the para-transcendent constitution of *habitus* all while maintaining at the same time the claim to an immediate experience.

Beyond the domain of reflection, Ingarden shed light on the field of living through (*Durchleben*), which transforms every action into habituality. Fink tried instead to salvage the role of the ego's identity by transforming into a fundamental *habitus*. For his part, by confining retention to the domain of *héxeis*, Funke defined *habitus* as an insurmountable residue of the flow of consciousness, and assimilated the ego as a substrate of habitualities (the theme of §32 of the *Meditationen*) to the identical pole of lived experiences (that is, in §31)—shifting thus the problem of interiority and associating the latter with *Durchleben*.

Thus, through a series of subtle and at times Byzantine distinctions, the *habitus* of the pure "I" has been interpreted either in the sense of consciousness's identity or of single dispositions. It is as if it were impossible to follow the articulations of Husserl's text, that is, to conceive together and at the same time distinguish concrete habituality and the identity of the pure ego.

37. Klein reads "Ingarden's critique and Funke's extraordinary construction," which have "assumed a different position" faced with the impossibility

of reducing *habitus* to a mere content of consciousness.[87] He does not take up the stratagem of paratranscendence, however, believing it to be impossible to establish a conformity between the subject and unthematized retentional residue, nor does he hypothesize, as Ingarden does, that habitualities constitute themselves via peculiar acts of consciousness. He advances instead a radical hypothesis: if the actual and direct experience of *habitus* implies "a having of my own having," it consequently demands a transposition to the intersubjective dimension. If the ego "obtains for every act that emanates from it a new stable property (*bleibende Eigenheit*)," these properties constitute the appreciable characteristics of the "I-for-others," that is, "from an initially external perspective that is only possible after a shift to an intersubjective point of view."[88] The intentionalities required by *héxeis* are therefore not special: rather, they come from another ego. And it is not transcendence that introduces itself into *Durchleben*, but habituality that implies a leaving of the self and a diversion toward alterity: "On both levels, it is clearly necessary to deviate via an objectification since, when placed before myself, I come to realise my own having."[89] Since *habitus* is an emanation of self-consciousness, it "has no 'actuality'"[90]: it is not in any way its own object, it is not a noematic content, but it is not self-evident (like consciousness) either, and hence it does not cease to be objective. It implies an eccentric point of view, and appears before a gaze that turns to itself from another's point of view. It is only thus, after all, that one can explain the transition from the habituality of the pure, nonobjectual "I" to the empirically perceivable dispositions of a personality.

It seems that Klein is pushing to its extreme a position that Husserl had arrived at when he noted, in *Studies in the Phenomenology of Constitution* (§58), "in reflecting I always find myself as a personal I," nevertheless at the beginning of this experience of oneself, which later "continually grows," "there is no constituted, given 'self' that would be available as an object, and of this self which is still completely hidden to itself, only others can have a certain understanding through *Einfühlung*."[91] *Habitus*, we could say, remains hidden (or untimely) and unappropriable, since it is unable to evolve—precisely because of its continuous growth—from a situation that is perpetually initial. But at the same time, and for the same reason, it demands a transition to another's gaze. The originality and astuteness of Klein's interpretation reside in the fact that it does not attempt to avoid or exclude the *regressio*, but instead accepts the problematic and paradoxical status of habitualities and resolves it by tying it to the Husserlian theory of *Einfühlung*, in a way that is coherent with the passage in the *Studies in the Phenomenology of Constitution* cited above.

To follow and develop this characteristic logic: I see myself, "as a 'fixed and abiding' *personal Ego*,"[92] through the gaze of another. As an identical being, I can only then see myself as a *persona*. If consciousness is consciousness of identity and if identity implies stability of possession, there is not a single ego that does not possess this diversion or eccentricity, and it is precisely "the absolute contact of me with myself," which remains inseparable from *héxis*, that requires this nonactual vision, which is deviated through alterity. If *habitus* defines the permanent style and character of the pure "I," there can be no centrality of the subject without a fundamental eccentricity and the passage through alterity must be a correlate of identity. In every case, I, as an identical being, see not only that the other sees me but "see myself through the eyes of another." And what is more, this does not mean that I identify with the other, as if the latter were endowed with a simple centrality; rather, if to be oneself, to be "centered in oneself," implies already from the beginning a deviation and alterity, it is because the alter ego—that is, "I myself in my ownness" (*Ichselbst in meiner Eigenheit*[93])—cannot appear if not via this turn or deviation. There is no identity without another's gaze, just as there can be no other's gaze without identity (coherently, the Husserlian theme of analogy *must*, *pace* Lipps, hold together alterity and identity, originality and nonoriginality).

Self-consciousness inflects itself in a *habitus* that is externally perceptible and, as we have seen, internally opaque. Once again: I must see myself through eyes that are not my own in order to reach myself. Thanks to this detour through exteriority, my "here," in this case, flees downward and attracts me from down there. Identity reveals itself to be kinetic and this dynamism is the key to every habituality. In other words, identity itself, which is inseparable from *habitus*, is vertiginous. For this reason, a latent vertigo precedes the objective one—the dizziness is already within me, even if I do not suffer from it and remain calmly grounded, that is, surrounded by objects and points of support above (Féré) and around me (Wallon). For this reason, vertigo is always secondary and, emerging and concealing its latency, always already first: it is both exposure and defense, peril and cure. Holding oneself back means letting oneself go, passivity and activity, voluntary action and pathological attraction become one under a common denominator, as Renouvier had rightly recognized. And in order for there to be a pole of attraction there must be not only another pole but an entire community of monads attracted to each other or subject to a mutual enchantment (hence the imitative magic that animates that which is social and therefore that same social machine "for manufacturing . . . , above all, vertigo [*machine sociale . . . à fabriquer . . . du vertige*]").[94]

But that is not all: if *habitus* does not become synonymous with retention, it is nevertheless a coherent and necessary development thereof; and every point of view that remains caught in itself, even without objectifying itself, regularly precipitates toward itself. Sartre's fascinating hypothesis notwithstanding, we must reiterate that a transparent and impersonal consciousness lacking an "I" could not therefore isolate itself: it is precisely immediate self-consciousness that prolongs itself into personal unity (just as the solution to the infinite regression at the level of consciousness is inextricably tied to the solution at the level of *habitus*). It is specifically consciousness, "which makes possible the unity and the personality of my I,"[95] that remains in any case tied to its product. To attain pure impersonality, perhaps we should forgo, as Deleuze suggested, the very term *consciousness*. Undoubtedly, we should free ourselves from the old cage, the mechanism that continues to inevitably be set off when *héxis* is reduced to possession and isolates the terrified figure of the self, the subject *qua* selfness, making it revolve around itself.

38. To break the primacy of the primordial ego one would have to destroy the *Vor-* of alterity, to cancel the preliminary game of the other, that despotic and spectral figure which from its absence makes me say "I am I," "this is my body," that is, to affirm identity "as the self-relation in the difference with itself, the same as the non-identical."[96] One would have to do away with this relation between alterity and origin to attain a difference without origin or identity.

We know that Foucault took up and radically transformed the concept of *historical a priori* which Husserl used to define the transcendental condition of that which has a history, and of history itself, keeping instead to that which in turn "does not escape historicity" (that is to say, the transformable totality of conditions which, in the *Archeology of Knowledge*, define the "enunciative function": "anonymous, historical rules, always determined in . . . time and space").[97] For Foucault, the work of the scholar, or rather of the archivist, does not revolve around the apodeictic affirmation of the self; it neither restores like *habitus* nor follows the continuity of the pure ego on an empirical level, it is not our own "becoming conscious" (*prise de conscience, Besinnung*) of ourselves, "philosophers of the present." Marked by the impossibility of describing the rules of its own discourse ("it is not possible for us to describe our own archive, since it is from within these rules that we speak"), it comports instead "a privileged region: at once close to us, and different from our present existence, it is the border of time that surrounds our presence, which overhangs it, and which indicates it in its otherness; it is that which, outside ourselves, delimits us."[98] According to this theory, we live within a system of rules that remain ungraspable to us in their current state but that are nevertheless circumscribed and indirectly illuminated by a describable and analyzable alterity.

What is clearly at stake here is the model of knowledge and subjectivity that marks the distance separating Foucault from the phenomenological undertaking, and which hence seems applicable, via a potentially permissible simplification, to our problematic context. We cannot have our own *habitus*, certainly, but the latter—we might hazard in an as-of-yet imprecise and provisional manner—is defined by an exteriority or by a limit zone which, in its alterity, belies the canon of consciousness, the unity of its flow and of history or of the continuity ordained for the *télos* of death, based on the *Ur-Ich*, and which in forming a historically defined field of inquiry could not have the characteristics of the original experience of a nonoriginal.

One understands how Klein, who had made his attempt by pressing against the perspective of transcendental idealism from within, could both admire and decisively refute Foucault's very different strategy. "Sartre is still a man of the 19th century," as the author of *The Order of Things* once said, distancing himself from phenomenological humanism. Having read the aforementioned work, Klein wrote to André Chastel on August 31, 1966: "I admire ever more the blindness of intelligent people, and in his case it seems proportional to his intelligence, which is no small thing."[99] And a few days later he protested once again, somewhat in jest: "Read Foucault, at first with admiration, then with indignation, and finally scandalized. If the philosophical world does not react, I declare this country to be in a state of decadence. You see, my temperament isn't particularly Ricoeur-like, having rather a tendency towards intolerance, at times."[100]

Indeed, here, where no indirect intentionality is possible, the very framework of intersubjectivity irreparably collapses. "Alterity," as such, is describable: it is not "irreducible to *my* ego," nor does it have "the form of the ego." And that which it indicates is not coherently an ego or a *habitus* but merely its limit, its discontinuity and difference. To cite the famous phrase, "The description of the archive . . . deprives us of our continuities; it dissipates that temporal identity . . . it breaks the thread of transcendental teleologies. . . . It establishes that we are difference, that our reason is the difference of discourses, our history the difference of times, our selves the difference of masks. That difference, far from being the forgotten and covered over [*recouverte*] origin, is this dispersion that we are and make."[101] The polemical aim of this passage is well known and perfectly clear: "All the concepts of metaphysics . . . *cover over [recouvrent] and coincide* with the strange 'movement' of this difference," Derrida had written two years earlier in *La voix et le phénomène*.[102] From Foucault's point of view, this formulation fully corresponds to the foundational function of the subject, or in other words to the self-conscious awareness (the *prise de conscience*) of which we are capable only thanks to a tiring *dressage*, having for a long time been habituated to "seeking origins ... to projecting teleologies."[103]

An old custom has formed the figure of phenomenological consciousness: *habitus* as the property of the pure ego, we might say, is nothing but its imprint or its transcendental residue. And we stick to this convention, Foucault suggests, "as if we were afraid to conceive of the Other in the time of our own thought."[104] To therefore free ourselves of ourselves, we should no longer seek the "relation to oneself in the difference from oneself," conceiving "the same as the non-identical," or seeing in the other the irreducible figure upon whom our presence is founded or the excluded figure who forms and arms our identity. It is not, in fact, the absolute monad that constitutively admits an unattainable alterity, but the other who resides in our very own temporality. And the problem of the constituent's constitution with respect to the act that constitutes him turns out to be a false problem, if the *historical a priori* is no longer (as in Husserl) the universal unconditional, if alterity and origin are no longer synonyms, if we are not the actuality of consciousness or the reflected magic of the "I" but merely the pure difference between the actual and the describable.

"Nothing excites vertigo more than fear," but nothing, neither fear nor the vertiginous grip of death, is actual for us, since everything that is knowable points at us from its alterity. Now, if we cannot describe our archive, if we cannot free ourselves of the rules that delimit us, that which we describe is instead proximate to us: it is precisely that which we possess, or rather the whole of that which continuous *exercise* has conflated with our possessions. Since we have surrendered to the habit of having a story by mistaking it for our own story, dissembling it with lineages and evolutionary curves, within the confines of the tradition that it itself has projected, and finally insisting, facts notwithstanding, on the "truly apodeictic" evidence of the horizon of all facts. The brilliant transformation of this tradition into an archive (that is, of the ego into an archivist, of *habitus* into a difference of masks) is Foucault's discovery or lesson.

Neither Judy nor Carlotta, nor Renée, nor Pauline: "No, it was Madeleine who was different from other women: she belonged to a different species. And just as she had seemed somewhat lost in the role of Pauline, so now she seemed lost in that of Renée,"[105] as if she were not in the end the forgotten, hidden, or disguised origin, but the dispersion that we ourselves are, the difference wherein the community of monads loses and dissolves itself.

Boris Sidis once wrote that "the cultivation of the power of habit-disintegration is what constitutes the proper education of man's genius."[106] There is a habit that projects teleologies, reconstructing derivations and traditions by separating life from death, but there is also a technique capable of overcoming the usual terror and of thinking alterity within our thought. It is the technique, the fiction or attitude capable of making us enter into the cemetery of Passy, in that "strange land, at the edges of life," which now, precisely while we follow the alleys and distractedly gaze at the flowerbeds, at the inscriptions, or fix our gaze on a bouquet of flowers, becomes "the border of time which surrounds our present." Gazing through the shot's subjective point of view, we are no longer ourselves. We are close and yet far and different, as we observe from a different region our sunny necropolis.

4
A Singular Rapture

39. Radicalizing Renouvier's ideas (and thus subtracting them from the influence of the old psychological ideodynamism), Jankélévitch recognized vertigo's place at the heart of action, freedom, and *habitus*, and explained that it transports us beyond all indecisions, beyond "our internal Rubicons," toward the shores of the *fiat*: "the act will not come about through speaking but through acting, and therefore, *daring.*" What indeed does the verb "to dare" express if not "the supplement of energy which is always necessary to break a habitual adaptation and confront the vertigo of initiative?"[1] Capable of not hesitating, of acting, resolute or free to subject himself to the attraction of action, man, Jankélévitch explains, is an apprentice sorcerer: a sorcerer, because he is the master of his own decisions, subject to a freedom with incalculable consequences and that is therefore vertiginous; an apprentice, because "consciousness proper would not suffer from vertigo . . . if it were free to not have willed what it willed, if it could not only destroy the willed thing but annihilate [*nihiliser*] the fact of having willed [*voluisse*]."[2] This would be impossible, "by virtue of the indestructibility and eternal identification with oneself of that which was [*fuisse*]."[3] Of course, the register is quite different, and Husserl's name does not even appear in these pages; it seems at times, however, that the rigor of the phenomenologist shines through the inspired French prose (which can happen to a *demi-sorcier*), revealing a dramatic nature, as if the *ductus* of the *Cartesian Meditations* (of §32) and the disinterested observer all of a sudden lost their sovereign detachment to confess that their performance is based on itself. To the Husserlian dictum made famous by Merleau-Ponty, "the reference of phenomenology back to its own self [*Rückbeziehung der Phänomenologie auf sich selbst*]," Jankélévitch responds: "There is indeed good rea-

son to suffer from vertigo! [*Il y a en effet de quoi avoir le vertige!*]" The adjectives "enduring" (*stehend*) and "permanent" (*bleibend*) hint at the less composed tone and inflection of "fatality, irreversibility, indestructibility," or the "eternal identity to itself of the having-been," while the "permanent style" (*bleibender Stil*) and "personal character" must confront the impossible ordeal of *regret*, with its host of commonplaces: "A second to say yes, and a lifetime to regret it. . . . Isn't the meta-empirical fatality of regret contained . . . in this impotence of our omnipotence? But let us clarify: it is the impotence itself that creates the omnipotence; our current strength is procured at the price of our future weakness."[4] It is the impossibility of being canceled that constitutes the act as such.

It is precisely irreversibility that is the salient feature of remorse in the "excellent description" (Klein) that Jankélévitch gives of it: "Remorse despairs . . . to annul, and the torture of irreversibility here consists, not in forgetting, but in the impotence of repairing."[5] If repentance is an attitude with respect to a now distant past and is therefore already a solution, remorse is instead "the fault itself, the fault that is unresolved" (*la faute elle-même, la faute non résolue*):[6] "remorse is thus much more than recollection; it is the complete, literal, and 'textual' past; it is the real presence, total survival."[7] Nevertheless, this undeniable reality does not overcome but favors dreams: the irrevocability, the uniqueness of the flow or the impossibility of swimming against one's own current, of passing through the same stages to confirm to oneself the clarity of the trajectory and, even before that, to objectify it as a trajectory (once again: the impossibility of having a *habitus*), "gives to our lived time an I-know-not-what of the unfinished, of the oneiric, and the unreal . . . Did I really live it?"[8]

We are familiar with this atmosphere, which pervades the entire film: and one could define it (the hypothesis would not be unjustified) as a climate of remorse, caused by the presence, in Madeleine, of an unassumable and insurmountable *habitus* (Judy, Elster's mistress and accomplice), which, intact, resists her role play. Madeleine's dream would not then be Carlotta's but rather the more prosaic truth of Judy or of a literal past (the pact with Elster) which underlies her every phrase and gesture and continuously remains "before her eyes." And the mask would be the expression of this strange detachment from oneself, of the difference between living actuality and the past, of the "imperceptible but essential rift" from which the dense oneiric climate emerges and spreads, for everyone. The deceit or *Schwindel* orchestrated by Elster would in other words be safe from Judy's repentance, coinciding with the dream and the demand for remorse. Did I truly live it? Doubt dictates the words of Judy/Madeleine, the accomplice in the (already decided, perhaps already executed) crime, who impersonates (or sees herself through the eyes of) the victim. "Am

I also a murderer?" is the imperceptible but pressing question that underlies every phrase and gesture, which translates perfectly (without second thoughts) into "am I still alive?" "'You're not dead' . . . Her eyes turned towards him. Their gaze came from afar. 'I don't know,' she said softly."[9]

It is a doubt that is very similar to the dismay that for Sartre arises from the hybrid nature of the ego, that of a passive creator ever outdone by its product, all while being this product ("Hence the classic surprises: 'I, I could do that?'"[10]), and yet also being quite different: in a coherent and only apparently odd way, Klein understands it as an "awakening" or an "unexpectedly becoming conscious [a *prise de conscience*]."[11] In fact, it is doubt that awakens me from the dream of identity, throwing me into the eccentric dimension of intersubjectivity and revealing to me, from that alienated point of view, that my very own "I" is merely one among many: "the partner in the dialogue" (as in Merleau-Ponty, or like Kant for Herz), "the error that becomes remorse" (as in Jankélévitch), and "the void . . . which 'attracts' in vertigo" (as in Hitchcock) are (as in Husserl) "forms of 'here' all while being forms of 'there.'"[12] But they demonstrate, in all of its dramatic exasperation, the irreparable and unappropriable that animate the very constitution of the subject. Now, for the first time, I look at myself, I see myself through another's eyes, and I see my own possessions, that which I cannot appropriate and which possesses me, that which holds me in its power, being irrevocably mine. That is, for once I cannot appeal to my own disinterest, I cannot exercise *epoché* because everything is already suspended; I must suffer instead the vertiginous constitution of my own identity and see myself as a looming presence, both past and strange, or in other words see myself through the eyes of one who is absent. "For you . . . death is the opposite of life . . . but for me . . ." If Judy cannot repent, if her impossible dream envelops Scottie and spreads throughout the city, unable to ever fully engulf it, it is because the *Schwindel* masterminded by Elster coincides with the very awakening of the subject.

40. In the theater scene in *Torn Curtain* (1966), Hitchcock reproduced a conspicuously vertical vertigo effect, without recourse to rails or dollies. Paul Newman and Julie Andrews are separated by a crowd that (just as in *The 39 Steps*, 1935) flees, panicked, toward the exit: turned toward her beloved, she desperately tries to resist the clamorous wave of people overwhelming her. The camera frames her face and the outstretched hand of the actress (another of Hitchcock's engrams) which for a moment draws nearer while growing more distant, before being carried away.

What is vertiginous is intersubjectivity and the very identity of the ego, and what is equally vertiginous is the community of monads. These are *realiter* separated from mine,[13] and they all coexist with mine inside a common worldly time (and in that of an "intersubjectivity throughout history," to use Fink's expression) by virtue of the bond that mutually holds them together. And if *Einfühlung* is not reduced to the horizon of perception, then presence is a form of absence. And absence is the unappropriable irreversibility of presence, the netherworld of presence itself which contains it as such; and therefore everyone is and is not, and the auratic essence of subjectivity, which Madeleine displays and dramatizes, is the organizing principle of the society of monads. She does not attract the already compresent gaze of the other but convokes it as such, casting a preliminary spell: the coexistence of the community, the time of interpersonal relations, that which Husserl (in the *Pariser Vorträge*) calls "an intersubjective transcendental community . . . the transcendental ground [*Boden*] for the intersubjectivity of nature and of the world" is nothing other than this inescapable call.[14] Every presence gives itself in absence, and possession is always an impure magic. If Madeleine is not entirely within herself, if she has lost her *compos sui*, it is because she takes a step into the distance of dreams and from that distance calls the other to her, to her own presence. But she who establishes and seemingly controls the relation also passively suffers it. She cannot live as a pure mask: when the very structure of subjectivity appears, whether as deceit or as a scenario to play out, the absence that animates her must necessarily be filled in. Judy (inevitably) ends up falling into this trap. And Scottie's dreamlike state—that risky disequilibrium that Elster was able to fix and extend into a lengthy, guided suspension of disbelief—even that cannot endure.

41. When Madeleine offers herself as a pure mask, when Judy, by putting on the necklace, reveals that "we are difference . . . our selves the difference of masks,"[15] Scottie Ferguson realizes instead that behind Carlotta's legendary death another death was hiding and being planned, that the suicide concealed a homicide and the marriage concealed the lovers' complicity. We know that by putting on the necklace, Judy silently begs him to revoke the principle of identity. And it would seem that she is making a desperate gesture; or, as Scottie believes, hers is merely a *lapsus*. In any case, he is the necrophile, and she requites his love.

"It seemed as though there wasn't a truly enamored woman who did not wish to be killed by her lover at the climax of pleasure. What a singular rapture!" wrote Rachilde about the novel of Edmond Cazal (Adolphe d'Espie), *Le vertige de la volupté et de la mort*.[16] Going back to a note by Jankélévitch, we can say that the *lapsus* is not a blow dealt by the unconscious to the subject master of itself, but one of those acts that Aristotle—in a passage that would end up being so important for Thomas Hobbes[17]—defines as "mixed":[18] it is an action carried out in a state of waking, but which in itself no one would choose; it is voluntary despite being absolutely involuntary (it would thus be the *lapsus* that explains its refusal and the unconscious, not the other way around). It is in fact the will itself that now finds itself constrained, the freedom that it finds bound to it and cannot restrain itself when it should. And that which now constrains or vertiginously pushes it into death's arms is death itself, as an irrevocable signature of the self or a stigma of subjective identity.

In that room, with that pendant around her neck, Judy is thus truly Madeleine: "The statement 'I am living' is accompanied by me being-dead and the statement's possibility requires the possibility that I be dead—and the reverse."[19] But for Scottie it is clearly "too late": she who in the neon green light says, "I am alive—I am dead" is no longer Madeleine. If only he could accept her offer, the proposition "I am alive" would pair itself with the other in the desired sense, and to be dead would mean living as a pure mask. But he refuses and pronounces the condemnation that alone can fill in the vital void of the *je*. He refuses, because only in death will the living (*Leib*) that the mask conceals be identified with a *Körper* (not living, dead), and the *persona*'s absence will transform itself into substance (Boileau and Narcejac's logic is the complementary inverse: he says "you are Madeleine," she denies it and thus—this is Renée's *lapsus*—offers herself to him and dies). Now, if "it is too late," it is because Madeleine's mask demands to constitute itself, in turn, as a substantial subject, because Judy (the homicide has occurred, after all) wants to be *that* mask (once again a person) and not another; disguised as Madeleine, she proposes to conceal herself, or rather, for the same reason and irremediably, to once again be herself (precisely as Renée). Even when she believes that she is hiding, whether dressed as Madeleine, or even earlier in her shabby clothes, in a different neighborhood, in a small hotel room, she is already undressing and offering herself to the gaze of (or better yet, sees herself through the eyes of) the detective who will recognize her sooner or later. The *lapsus* is the ambiguous, decidedly contradictory action, because it is an action caught up in and late with respect to itself. A pure mask would be pure difference. But the impersonal *se ipse* is not granted any possibilities; its every instant is already lost or out of joint: and thus it produces its own void, reacts vertiginously and coincides with the fall. For one and for the other, it is always too late, death has already occurred.

42. In an essay written in 1943, undoubtedly influenced by Heidegger, François Cuzin laid out his radical thesis: it is "to my experience of myself that the death of the other refers back, as to the only thing which can clarify

it."[20] This definition of *Einfühlung* is both rigorous and estranged, capable of explaining in what sense the ego "indicated as one moment by this expression [alter ego] being I myself in my own ownness,"[21] and, at the same time, in what way I can constitute "him [another person as another myself] as constituting, and as constituting in respect to the very act through which I constitute him."[22]

Cuzin does not avoid the Husserlian limit of originality, but explores it by both maintaining and stretching its limits. For him, the ego is exclusively and totally itself and is, in its identity or totality, "constituted in and on the basis of death." This means, however, that the end of the other discloses "the need for a point of view . . . which cannot be other than a subjective point of view." Death is "the absolute condition of subjective existence," and reveals that transcendental consciousness itself has "an empirical sense and destiny."[23] In other words, it coincides with the appearance of subjectivity, of selfness, of egoity in alterity, that is, of the other as the ego that I am. In this sense, then, the other's death, which is radically foreign to my experience, refers to my self-experience. The other dies, demonstrating his own subjectness, and "I recognize myself as a subject." It is thus precisely when a subject "is never given to another subject" that a common sphere of belonging is given and intersubjectivity becomes possible: "The only way for a subject to be accessible to another subject is to inherently be part of the constitutive act of the subject proper. And this is precisely what happens at the death of the other."[24] Irreducible to just any phenomenon, inexperienceable in itself, it therefore constitutes the condition for my presence to myself: "To affirm the death of the other, but to not affirm it as a phenomenon . . . means to affirm that I am not myself, this I which I know myself to be, if not because the other dies."[25]

If I see myself through the eyes of another, whether that be a specific other or a generic one, he will always be the one who ceases to be. And what comes first is not the individual point of view, but the intersubjectivity that constitutes the subject as a personal subject identical to itself, it is the death of the other that presents the "I" to itself, and it is only in death that the other presents himself to the "I" and participates in its constitution: that which Fink calls the "habituality of the identical being I" is granted precisely via the other's death. This death is, finally, the true disappearance from the horizon of perception, the absence of the other that persists in its own conspicuousness.

Recognizing in cinema "a non-Cartesian operator or, better yet, a trans-Cartesian one," Jean Epstein recalled the famous reaction of a diva to her moving image thus: "Incredulous, disappointed, scandalized, Mary Pickford cried seeing herself for the first time on screen. This means nothing other than the fact that Mary Pickford did not know that she was Mary Pickford, she did not realize that she was the person whose identity millions of eye-witnesses could still testify to today."[26] The actor's weeping is one of disorientation, of protest, and of liberation. It is a lament against the image that (beyond any doubt or feeling of unreality) has substituted itself for the living body, one that expresses a desperate refusal of its new authority. But it is also, for the same reason, a lament against all identification on the part of one who, with her surprise, reveals the masquerade that is identity, breaking away at least for a moment from the ties of the inter-monadic community. And she thus testifies to the (real though denied) possibility of a gaze that would finally be free of interest, no longer empathic, devoid of participation. In cinematographic vertigo, the vertigo of identity is canceled, and the actor could finally look at herself through the eyes of another without having to be herself, without having to cling to her own mask in filling it with life. Mistaking a mannequin for an alter ego at the Panorama on Friedrichstrasse, Husserl had experienced the fright of resemblance or mirroring, of the inanimate semblance and therefore of himself. He had been frightened because he had recognized himself in the lifeless counterpart. Then, celluloid replaced wax, and the Mary Pickford who moved on screen would go on to acquire a completely novel autonomy and life, to which the actor too would have to adapt. Those who witness the life of images, who recognize in the diva her very own image and their own lives in the moving images, who confuse their own crepuscular state with the slowness of the film and the dreamy atmosphere of San Francisco, are not confusing that which is mortal with its semblance but with another being, which does not die even in dying and whom they no longer fear.

5
Chasm

43. "It is as though thought becomes dizzy pouring over the emptiness of the verb to exist." In the very moment when he breaks away from ontology, Levinas actually quotes a prominent passage from Heidegger's *Kant and the Problem of Metaphysics*: "The being is known to us—but Being? Are we not seized with vertigo [*Schwindel*] when we [try to] determine such a thing, even if we should comprehend [*eigen fassen*] it properly?"[1]

For Heidegger, to ask this question about the meaning of being means, as is well known, to go where Husserlian phenomenology (despite the principle "to the things themselves!") had failed to reach. According to Heidegger, the latter had conquered its territory by sidelining or better yet by warding off as a contradiction the ontological problem of intentional content,[2] thus leaving unprobed the very *residuum* of the *reductio* or of the "annihilation of the world" (*Weltvernichtung*), pure consciousness,[3] and consequently its concrete aspect, the personal subject as a permanent substrate of "stable properties" (*bleibende Eigenheiten*). To take phenomenology beyond this limit, to ask the question overlooked by Husserl, meant looking down—and experiencing the vertigo that Kant experienced before unconditional necessity[4]—into the ontological abyss (*Kluft*) that separates the "sameness [*Selbstheit*] of the authentically existing self . . . from the identity of the I maintaining [*durchhaltend*] itself in the multiplicity of its 'experiences.'"[5] For this reason, in *Sein und Zeit* the critique of the Husserlian ego (which in §10 is combined with that of Dilthey and Scheler's personalisms and would later go on to trace its roots back, as in the summer course of 1927, to the transcendental, psychological, and moral personality in Kant), follows the positive solution of the problem of *Selbst*—that is, of the "scission" (*Spaltung*) of the reflecting subject, of his identity or difference vis-à-vis himself—formulated in terms of (authentic or inauthentic) modes of being: *Dasein* will thus always be the same, since it will always have to be its modes of being. And these modalities, which inherently all go back to the authentic or inauthentic one, are distinguished in the most radical of ways from the "'properties' present-at-hand" (*vorhandene "Eigenschaften"*[6]) which are highly reminiscent of Husserl's *bleibende Eigenheiten*.

The *Kluft* was therefore supposed to be an irremediable fracture and mark an equally profound incomprehension. Reading *Being and Time* with a sense of regret and astonishment, Husserl recognized in the structure of "care" (*Sorge*) or of being-in-the-world only a superficial and unfounded reworking of the theory of intentionality and recognized in the general design of the book an obscure and at the same time overly simplified anthropological transposition of phenomenologico-constitutive analysis, which ended up depriving it of "philosophical value."[7] Already in 1936, Edith Stein attributed to Heidegger a pretentious refusal of the terms *I* and *person*, convinced as she was that by the word *Selbst* he actually meant to convey precisely "man's being a person [*Personsein*]."[8]

Naturally, from Heidegger's point of view, it is only via a forsaking of intentionality for the sake of *Sorge*, that is to say of the ontologico-existential *a priori* of being-in-the-world (*In-der-Welt-Sein*), that *Selbstheit* or property could be conceived as an authentic "always-being-mine" (*Jemeinigkeit*) of *Dasein*. Refuting the notions of intentionality and consciousness, he therefore also had to reject the notion of *héxis*; he had to clarify, as we have seen, that the authentic "decision" (*Entschlossenheit*), which is the care of care, is "not an empty *habitus*." Certainly, §29 of the *Studies in the Phenomenology of Constitution* constitutes a perfect response to §60 of *Being and Time*: the "absolute stream of consciousness" (*absolute Selbstheit*) of the pure I does not form "a *habitus* as what had become customary."[9] But an ontological chasm nevertheless separates the two explanations.

44. A series of question marks drawn by Husserl on his copy of *Sein und Zeit* punctuates, in the margins of §64, the radical redefinition of the concept of selfness which subtracts it from the classical principles of the "subject" and the "ego-substance" (*Ichsubstanz*). With one of his characteristic quips in the domain of philosophical terminology, Heidegger substitutes in these pages the original notion of "the self's stability" (*Ständigkeit des Selbst*) for the "presumed permanence of the subject," that is, the canonical *Beharrlichkeit*. The latter—after Wolff's modern version: "an enduring and modifiable subject is called a 'substance' [*Subjectum perdurabile et modificabile dicitur 'Substantia'*]"[10]—designated in the "Transcendental analytics" the ("persistent and permanent"

[*bleibend und beharrlich*]) substance or substrate of time in general, and Edith Stein, for example, turns to it in her faithfully Husserlian definition of the psychophysical individual—that is, of the soul as the "bearer" (*Träger*) of "permanent properties" (*beharrliche Eigenschaften*).[11] This "stability of the self" or "self-stability" (*Selbstständigkeit*) is distinct from the continuity of the subject of experiences because it goes back to the existential that is *Sorge*, to the structure of care and to the authenticity of *Dasein*'s being as care.

Heidegger's recognition of an "original stability and totality of self" (*ursprüngliche Selbstständigkeit und Ganzheit*) in "maintenance" (*Standgewonnenhaben*) or in "persistence of a state" (*beständige Standfestigkeit*) has therefore dethroned the permanence of the ego or of *habitus*, that is, the "solidarity with . . . the past" of a subject still definable in genuinely Kantian terms (*stehend und bleibend*).[12] The having-been—one reads in a passage that sounds like a parodic critique of retention of the permanent "I" (*bleibendes Ich*) or of pure consciousness as a "residue of reductions"—"is not a remnant of myself that has stayed behind [*ein zurückgebliebender und liegengebliebender Rest meiner selbst*],"[13] just as my future is not exclusively before me. Faithfulness to the past can therefore be rethought or better yet grounded in a sense of "anticipatory decision": in *Being and Time*, to happen means to assume the having been, whereas the past arises from the future.[14] "'Backward-forwards!', Günther Anders observed, could be Heidegger's motto" (*"Vorwärts-zurück!" könnte Heideggers Devise sein*).[15]

45. The first thing that Heidegger's critique takes aim at is the definition, given at the end of §49 of the *General Introduction to a Pure Phenomenology*, "of the whole *spatiotemporal world*" (*die ganze räumlich-zeitliche Welt*) as "*a merely intentional being*" (*blosses intentionales Sein*).[16] Contrasting this "inadequate and external" characterization with the discovery of *Dasein* as being-in-the-world,[17] he carries out a radical (or merely nominal and unjustified, from Husserl's point of view) transformation of intentionality in the sense of specific transcendence or of being for-the-sake-of-itself, and ties the relation to the entity back to the "*transcendence*" as "*a fundamental determination of the ontological structure of the Dasein.*"[18] Consciousness, for Heidegger, includes the object in its halo (*Bewusstseinshof*), and can therefore take aim at it, make it the object of its intention; subsequently, the same spiritual gaze will potentially be able to direct itself toward *cogitatio* to grasp it reflexively in a new *cogitatio*.[19] *Dasein*, by contrast, does not exist initially to then occasionally turn itself toward external entities. The entities with which it deals are instead intraworldly, that is ever already exceeded by *Dasein* which, in encountering them, moves toward the world or, in other words, always once again toward

itself. And if such a phenomenon does not correspond to a form of behavior or to "an isolated tendency in a world-less subject,"[20] but to a fundamental constitution of *Dasein* as *In-der-Welt-Sein*, it is as care or transcendence, precisely in its being the transcendent itself, that *Dasein* must always be *"its own, it has itself"* (*es sich "zu eigen" ist, es "hat sich selbst"*).[21] Now, insofar as it is this "having itself" (*sich "zu eigen"*), *Dasein* can also lose itself: if in general it has lost or not yet conquered itself, it is only because its essence comports the possibility of authenticity or of the appropriation of self.[22] As a "counter-possibility" (*Gegenmöglichkeit*) of "non-Self-constancy" (*Unselbst-ständigkeit*) or of abasing indecision, "the *constancy of the Self*" (*Selbst-ständigkeit*) thus existentially means "anticipatory resoluteness."[23] The problem of *regressio* is thus resolved *a priori* (possession does not follow possession but precedes and originates from itself): precisely according to the scheme of anticipation, as one reads in *Vom Wesen des Grundes*, freedom is the *"reason for reasons,"* but "not . . . in the sense of a formal, endless 'iteration.'"[24]

46. The *Seinsart*—*Dasein*'s *"kind* of being"—"*requires*" (*fordert*) an ontological interpretation capable of conquering the being of this entity despite its own *"tendency to cover things over"* (*Verdeckungstendenz*).[25] Now, what is it that lies at the basis of this need, what makes or stabilizes stability itself? If inauthenticity entails appropriation, it is precisely anticipation, one could gloss, that imposes in turn the "fall" (*Verfallen*) and slips beyond itself. Every possible arbitrariness must therefore be removed: necessity must coincide with the "highest instance" (*höhere Instanz*) of possibility, to which the projected structure of comprehension will also correspond. If the *original totality* can be grasped, its stability, which is not a property that is simply "available" (*vorhanden*), must be related back—as a having and possession of self—to the thematic of finitude (of being-toward-the-end). Hence the role that Heidegger gives (already especially clearly in the summer course of 1925[26]) to the end as the removal or impossibility of the incomplete. In more exact terms, "the coming-to-its-end of what is not-yet-at-an-end (the extinction of its absence) has the character of no-longer-being-there [*Nichtmehrdasein*]."[27] Now, if this conclusion "is defined as death," that which renders death the "extreme" and definitive possibility is precisely the fact that it fractures the being-ever-before-oneself or the incompletion of *Dasein* as care. In the 1925 lectures, like later at the beginning of §47 of *Being and Time*, this theme leads to a not-so-subtle and completely altered reinterpretation of the famous maxim of the *Letter to Menoeceus*. *Dasein* has ended, but when it reaches its totality it is no longer a *Dasein*: "Death marks the loss of the being of the there. The transition to no-longer-being-there lifts Da-sein out of the possibility of experiencing this tran-

sition and of understanding it as something experienced. This kind of thing is denied to actual Da-sein in relation to itself."[28] Now, it is precisely this impossibility—the impossibility of experience, which for Epicurus casts death and dying (as a passage between life and death) into nonbeing—that coincides here with the anticipatory structure of care: precisely as the possibility of no-longer-being-there, *Dasein* is in fact always before itself. "Care as being-ahead-of-itself is as such and at the same time a being-possible. 'I can,' or more accurately, I am this . . . 'I can die at any moment.'"[29] The possibility of not being there is therefore constant and indeterminate, and *Dasein*, which cannot experience its own death, is already always moribund: "*sum moribundus*. . . . The *moribundus* first gives the *sum* its sense."[30] According to the modality of anticipation, death—or "dying" (*Sterben*) as a "mode of being" (*Seinweise*) of *Dasein*—can now be assumed phenomenologically as a constant possibility (of impossibility), one that is both indeterminate and certain and in which *Dasein* looms over itself. Thus, care (*Sorge*) or the specific transcendence of *Dasein* is nothing other than being-toward-death. And since what is at play here is the existential concept of the future, since in attaining itself being is futural (*zukünftig*) in the original sense, the ecstatic nature of temporality will be fatally dominated by death. In other words, the *Dasein* outlined in the second part of *Being and Time* (§§61–66 and §§78–83) is moribund as a being which in its original *Selbstheit* is temporality itself. And—we must admit—that what is also logically inseparable from the theme of being-toward-death (as a logical development of it) is the interpretation of the *Critique of Pure Reason* developed beginning in 1927, both in university courses and in *Kant and the Problem of Metaphysics*. As is well known, it culminates in the clarification of the nexus between transcendental apperception and time as pure intuition, between receptivity and spontaneity, or in other words in the theory of temporality as "the primal structure of the finite self as such" or "pure self-affection."[31] It is here, finally, where time is the form of *Dasein* as transcendental, and in forming the original "moving from oneself directing oneself to . . . to return to oneself," it also "preforms" or temporalizes worldly succession, that the technical phrase of the *First Critique* can finally be recovered and salvaged—as happens with *héxis* in *The Essence of Reasons*[32]—on the other side of the ontological *Kluft*: "The 'fixed and perduring' I goes so far as to mean: the I, in the original forming of time, i.e., as original time, forms the letting-stand-against of . . . and its horizon."[33] Since time is "*a priori* having-to-do-with the self and simultaneously self-standing . . . pure original receptivity and original spontaneity" (*aprioriorischer Selbstangang und zugleich Selbständigkeit, reine ursprüngliche Rezeptivität und ursprüngliche Spontaneität*), the self "must," in realizing itself, "*be able to understand itself in each concrete moment as the same futural self which has already been [zukünftig-gewesen].*"[34] *Vorwärts-zurück!* is the moribund's motto.

47. *Dasein* is a moribund and mineness (*Jemeinigkeit*) identifies with dying (*Sterben*) not as an anonymous *exitus* but as a mode of being, that is "with death, which at its time is only *my* dying."[35] It would seem as though anti-hedonism were reaching its culmination here. If "Epicurus does not say that the death of others must not afflict us, but only that we should not fear our own,"[36] because in dying we no longer sense, or rather we are no longer ourselves, Heidegger writes instead that in dying "I will be my ownmost I. I myself am this possibility, where death is my death. There is no such thing as death in general."[37] With the phrase that everyone remembers: "Death is the possibility of the absolute impossibility of Dasein . . . the *ownmost nonrelational possibility not to be bypassed.*"[38] What is less well-known is Husserl's gloss on the passage, which is once again characterized by a question mark and whose tone is particularly drastic: "The possibility of death is [in such a way] ever presupposed and never clarified."[39]

One must now understand the reach and validity of such an objection by carefully examining Heidegger's argument. It is initially tied to the theme of *Mitdasein*, which in turn appears in §26, from a critique of *Einfühlung* as a "bridge from one's own subject, initially given by itself, to the other subject, which is initially quite inaccessible."[40] Indeed, faced with the unexperience-able nature of death, where the totality and disappearance of *Dasein* coincide, one must, according to Heidegger, consider the death of the other, whereby "an end of Dasein becomes 'objectively' accessible." "Dasein can gain an experience of death, all the more because it is essentially being-with [*Mitsein*] with others. This 'objective' givenness of death must then make possible an ontological analysis of the totality of Dasein."[41] But this "must" depends on a rhetorical hypothesis, which Heidegger immediately rejects, and in an enlightening manner: *Dasein*'s coming to an end refutes, in fact, a constitutive possibility of quotidian being-with, that is, its "representability" (*Vertretbarkeit*).[42] If in its "with-world" (*Mitwelt*), *Dasein* always encounters (whether directly or through the mediation of the entities at its disposal) the being-with of others, and "one Dasein can and must, within certain limits '*be*' another Dasein," by contrast, "*No one can take the other's dying away from him*" (*Keiner kann der anderen sein Sterben abnehmen*).[43] Death cannot be substituted for or reduced to "in-being" (*In-Sein*) as "being-with" (*Mitsein*): it is not an inner-worldly phenomenon, for what is at stake in it is the very being of *Dasein*.

"In dying"—one reads again in §47—"it becomes evident that death is ontologically constituted by mineness [*Jemeinigkeit*] and existence."[44] From this, in fact, proceeds the argument of §50: "Death is a possibility of being that Dasein always has to take upon itself [*sich übernehmen*]"; and hence, once again, we have the development of well-known formulations: "In this possibility, Dasein is concerned about its being-in-the-world absolutely. Its death is the possibility of no-longer-being-able-to-be-there. . . . Death is the possibility of the absolute impossibility of Dasein [*Tod ist die Möglichkeit der schlechtinnigen Daseinsunmöglichkeit*]."[45]

Emmanuel Levinas had to insist on this point, correcting Jean Wahl: death is not "the impossibility of possibility" but rather, in Heidegger, "'the possibility of impossibility.' This apparently Byzantine distinction has a fundamental importance."[46] The distinction, we might say, is nevertheless a relation, and in Heidegger the possibility of impossibility of *Dasein* remains in fact tied to or superimposed on the impossibility of the "potentiality of substitution" (*Vertretungsmöglichkeit*). Death is the possibility of impossibility, but as such it is nothing but the obverse of the impossibility of possibility (of being substituted). This impossibility of substitution is characterized by reciprocity: it defines for everyone the difference (or rather, the analogy) between the experienceability of another's death and the inexperienceability (or the possibility of impossibility) of one's own (or of the other's death as one's own), between the ontic level and the ontological level, the death of the other and "dying" as a "potentiality-of-being of *his being*" (*Seinsmöglichkeit "seines" Seins*).[47] It therefore keeps the possible and the impossible in a relation according to which the experience of the *exitus* must be conceived, in terms that are still Husserlian (or analogical) as the original experience of a nonoriginal inexperienceability. No one could replace the other, that is, no one could separate themselves from themselves to experience objectively their own death. But at the same time, everyone can (objectively) experience the death of the other, that is, everyone can (authentically) assume their own death. Only the ("ever presupposed and never clarified") relation between the ontic evidence of the other's *exitus* and its own-most possibility of being, only this implicit and negative reference of the "objective" experience of another's death to the totality or, better yet, only the preliminary, double projection of totality on the *exitus* of another, of the authentic end of *Dasein* on the end of being-with (and vice versa), recovers death as the property and totality of being. Anders's irony concerning this death of mine (or at least mine more than anything else) is therefore not unjustified: "Heidegger transforms the grammatical possessive pronoun into a true property deed, which is supposed to console him in the same way in which the victim in the *Thousand and One Nights*, by crying out "my murderer!," was supposed to become the master of death as he was of his own slave, thanks to the peculiar power of the possessive pronoun just uttered."[48]

Strictly speaking, in fact, nothing—if not a presupposed coincidence between the extinction of absence, that is totality, and the extinction of life—guarantees that the "objective" experience of another's death is in relation to *his* mode of being or to *his* being at the end, that is, to a *Jemeinigkeit* which for its part depends instead on death (and on its transformation into *Sein-zum-Tode*). In fact, precisely here a *Kluft* opens up, which Levinas's words shed light on: "In death, there is indeed an abyss between the event and the subject to whom it will happen."[49] Nevertheless, in Heidegger, there is one last, strange analogy that seems to persist and which is based on the impossibility of substituting not experience, but the original inexperienceability, not on perception or the immediate mimesis of the living but on the impossibility of the latter as well as of every *Gegenspiel*, or rather on the paradoxical transformation of mirroring, now born of a vitreous opacity: he who dies is he who does not return the gaze, thus demonstrating to me, who sees myself in him, that death is only and always mine. And so, precisely here—in this difference between another's death and one's own, between death as a fact and being-toward-death, here, where the problem of the soul's relation to the body is overcome at an existential level—a bond is formed on the basis or by virtue of the common denominator of "no-longer-being-there" (*Nichtmehrdasein*). The pronouncement of §48 of *Being and Time*, according to which "the coming-to-its-end of what-is-not-yet-at-an-end (the extinction of its absence) has the character of no-longer-being-there,"[50] owes its appearance to the so-called objectivity of experience and finds the condition for its possibility in the formulation of §47: "In the dying of others that remarkable phenomenon of being can be experienced that can be defined as the transition of a being from the kind of being of Dasein (or of life [*Leben*]) to no-longer-being-there."[51] The very completeness of *Dasein* is thus situated on the threshold of the experienceable/inexperienceable. It keeps itself on the worldly horizon of quotidian *Mitsein* as a negative virtuality thereof (hence the need for a rhetorical hypothesis): the medium of no-longer-being-there (*Nichtmehrdasein*) renders the ontically experienceable ontologically unassumable and transforms the impossibility of assuming that which remains merely objective (the other's death) into the duty to assume the inexperienceable (one's own death), thus transforming the unassumable into that which is most properly and authentically assumable. But, above all, pure dying (*Sterben*) is at the end related to the so-called objective evidence of nonbeing, that is to the *exitus* (*Ableben*), which dictates the domain of the possible and anticipation as such. The latter, we could say, is nothing but the anticipation of the experienceable, in other words, it is "objectively" the observability of another's death, the evidence of death, *Ableben*, which precedes *Sterben*. Thus, pairing (*Paarung*)—which, as Merleau-Ponty said, is "hardly a metaphor"[52]—seems to make a distorted reappearance here, as the numinous relation of the living person with the dead one who makes a moribund of the former. We could conclude from this that precisely this bond ties together the articulation of *Dasein*'s modes of being, solving the problem of Husserl's "splitting" (*Spaltung*)—of the tension between the factitious and the pure ego or, adopting Fink's terminology, among the three egos (the worldly one, the transcendental one, and the theoretical one, which deals with reductions) that form a single unity—in the stability of the *Selbst* (or in the triple preeminence of *Dasein*, as Reiner Schürmann would have said: the ontic, the ontological, and the ontico-ontological), and lastly submitting it to the same demand of ontological interpretation.[53] On the other hand, Heidegger himself concedes dying's dependence on death (*exitus*) at the very moment in which he differentiates them and specifies that *Dasein* "is always already delivered over to its death ... it dies [*stirb*] factically [*faktisch*] and constantly as long as [*solange*] it has not reached its demise [*Ableben*]."[54] The anticipation of one's own death therefore also has an end; the possibility of impossibility shows itself (confirming Wahl's interpretation) to, in turn, be possible; and dying (*Sterben*) also ends and is distinct from *exitus* just as the mode of being called life (*Leben*) remains circumscribed by the "so long as" (*solange*) and by the "no longer" (*Nichtmehrdasein*).

It is then as if the thanato-maniacal formulas cited by Marcel Mauss in his study on "suggested death" or owing to "pure imaginative power"[55]—in which (from a point of view internal to being-with) "the social nature of man very directly intersects with his biological nature"[56]—acquired in this case an ontologico-existential tenor, that is, a universal and definitive one: "That Dasein dies factically means at the same time that it has always already decided in this or that way in its being-toward-death."[57] Just as the native truly dies for fear of the end, Heidegger's *Dasein* constitutes itself preliminarily as the subject of an actual death (*Ableben*), but only on the basis of an anticipation of death that is once again a magically efficient projection of the demise itself.

In Anders's words: "Heidegger's *Selbst* does precisely this: it represents life itself as a manner of suicide."[58] "Forward-backward!" is the formula of such vertigo. Heidegger managed to suffer it ("When we try ... to grasp such a notion") or to endure it, so that it might coincide, as it had to, with the subject's totality or *Jemeinigkeit*; and in suffering it—that is, by entering into its "circle" (*Kreis*) and fixating his gaze on the "circular being of Dasein" (*zirkelhaftes Sein des Dasein*)[59]—he could not but think: "I am this ... 'I can die at any instant.'"

48. It was Hannah Arendt who recognized in the fear of a "violent death" the "objective limit" of the experience that characterizes the generation of World War I, and therefore of German philosophy of the 1920s and its double tendency, on the one hand to "interpret in an extensive sense this fear, transforming it into anguish on account of death, and on the other to consider this fear as fact that reveals the much more universal and central phenomenon of anguish."[60] The reference to Heidegger is clear (and precise: "the fateful destiny of Dasein in and with its 'generation'"),[61] and what is equally clear is that the adjective "moribund" (*moribundus*) can aptly define the being of *Dasein* mobilized or better yet "thrown" out onto the battlefield, amid a with-world (*Mitwelt*) of corpses. Now, this "violent death," anonymous and decided by others, is also in effect a form of dying in another's stead: its fear is dictated by the resolution of war, its anticipation resides in the relation of sovereignty, and substitutability is thus its most essential trait. This substitution does not, of course, pretend to relieve another of their dying,[62] but rather to restore it to them in return for an anonymous and undecided end, precisely as *his*. Indeed, one dies by another's hand and therefore in another's stead, since one is already exposed to death instead of someone else to live in their place: it is this relation of power (of sovereignty or subjection) which, when referred to the repulsive foreignness of the corpse, constitutes or produces, in the return to the self, the subject as its own (as the subject of this relation, who is restricted to it). The principle of "your death, my life [*mors tua, vita mea*]" applies here to those who have died in place of the sovereign, that is, to the potential losses from within a supply of substitutes (each of another and, at the extreme, of a single other), whose existence is nothing but a lack with respect to no longer being there. But one must add: the true decision of this power (physical death) is always already made and therefore in the air, latent, and therefore its actor—as Benjamin argued—is, yes, sovereignly undecided. Sovereignty and indecision coincide, because the force of the former is mythical and consists in superimposing one's own apparatus on the ancient dominion of nature, of god, or of universal chance, in demanding precisely that which these have always disposed (the simple eventuality that death should remove a sovereign from his indecision or the victim from his power reveals the truth about this demand). What is incumbent is not in fact death itself, which "is not there" and in its absence is not fearsome, but sovereign indecision, that is, the power that constitutes itself by covering over absence, dissimulating it, and transforming it into a lack.

In the "anticipatory resoluteness," which seeks to grasp precisely this latent and spectral presence (the philosopher, as we know, always arrives *post festum*), *Dasein* is situated and remains on the level of unsubstitutability, in the sense that the latter ends up being shifted, or anticipated, from death to the decision itself. This decision can indeed be anticipatory only because in death it grasps itself, or better yet, it agrees with itself; it can be anticipatory precisely *après coup* (abusing Kimura Bin's terminology, it is *ante festum* only because it is *post festum*): that is to say, under death's spell, undergoing the insuperable experience of others' deaths, approving it (unable to do anything but approve it) and at the same time surrendering to its dominion. In Heidegger's words, precisely "when fear has subsided, Dasein has to first find its way about again";[63] thus, "when Dasein, anticipating, lets death become powerful in itself, as free *for* death it understands itself in its own *higher power* . . . which always only *is* in having chosen the choice" and therefore becomes free to die.[64] In other words, it is only by giving its own assent, by choosing that which is (or will be) chosen, by taking the (latent, sovereign) decision that concerns it, that *Dasein* can decide and thus become the subject of an anticipatory decision. Therefore, if death is now mine it is only because I have made the decision mine, because the subject (as the center or substrate of habitualities) has become the one who chooses (the choice already made), since—and *après coup*—the decision and being of *Dasein* coincide completely. It is only by virtue of this unsubstitutability, that he who is indeed wounded by a bayonet or poisoned by gas dies (as does the one who sees him), and the same person dies because "he has already decided . . . concerning his being-toward-death." And only now does fear (both physical dread and pure trembling) reveal existential anguish as its form of compensation; the inauthentic emotional situation recalls the authentic one, and the incompleteness of the "not yet" (*Noch-nicht*) or of the "before oneself" (*Sich-vorweg*) can be transformed into a totality. Only now does a liberty without conditions emerge precisely from the sovereign bond, just as a boundless possibility emerges from *Dasein*'s "*higher instance of its potentiality-of-being.*"[65] Forming a subject worthy of its historical destiny (Wahl's observation concerning the ambiguous simultaneous presence of realism and idealism is fitting here: "Heidegger wishes to deny subjectivism, but the problem of death is posed exclusively in its relation to the subject"[66]), modeling it after the mold of the power of death that subjugates it, Heidegger reaches the final ridge. He delivers his simultaneously vertiginous and apologetic version of phenomenology, disclosing an anarchic perspective (Schürmann's brilliant interpretation) and a diametrically opposed one—thus lending himself to a caricatural interpretation like ours, but even before that to the "bestial seriousness of fascism" (Benjamin), that is, to an attempt to eliminate every ambiguity, which replaces the potentiality of the transcendent with the para-transcendence of *Dawesen* (Becker).

For this reason, the ontology of *Dasein* would go on to be defined in 1933 and knowledge in general would go on to be defined as a "service" (*Wissendienst*) on equal footing in terms of "necessity and rank" with work (*Arbeitdienst*) and the military (*Wehrdienst*).[67] Certainly, as Husserl observed while reading *Being and Time*, not only death but universal chance is also insuperable. But it is precisely the most violent exposure to chance that is *not* casual. And for this reason the *Dasein* that takes it on as its obligation will speak in the first person, identifying with the people and the state, and—burdening itself with the decision, fully making itself a substitute, that is, "in the basis of its being ... fate"[68]—will finally be able to say "ego." Now, truly, "*in saying I, Dasein expresses itself as being-in-the-world*" (*im Ich sagen spricht das Dasein als In-der-Welt-Sein*);[69] "Siding with Carl von Clausewitz, we affirm, 'I declare myself to be free of the thoughtless hope of salvation by the hand of chance.'"[70] And now, finally, he will be able to return whence he came, that is, to the battlefield, to reconquer, as an "unsubstitutable" totality, as a *völkischstaatliches Dasein*, the authentic dimension of *Mitsein*, that is, a world that he had not lost "by epoché, in order to regain it by a universal self-examination,"[71] but to which only death consigns him and from which only death removes him. "Every individual, even and all the more so when he avoids it, shares this decision [*entscheidet darüber "mit"*]";[72] and in this sense, "its historicizing is a co-historicizing and is determined as *destiny* [*Geschick*]. With this term, we designate the historicizing of the community, of a people."[73] In this case, the experienceable and the inexperienceable (presence and absence) will coincide: every person will be able to "die" (*Sterben* and *Ableben*) authentically and in another's stead. Forward is backward. From the "Self-Assertion of the German University" of 1933 (or from certain notes belonging to the same period as the *Black Notebooks*) one gets a barely hidden sense of *Being and Time*: the freedom to die both originates from the death of the other and anticipates it. This anticipation is nothing other than a killing, and the destiny of the community easily manifests itself in a gathering of murderers. But that is not all: if the sovereign power of war constitutes itself by masking itself and imitating a power or assuming a role that does not belong to it (the anonymous one of chance, or the transcendent one of a god), this mask (the whole of historic destiny or of the mythical god) must fall, while violence reveals itself in its most expansive and terrifying truth, and death becomes a lack of the sense of defeat or removal. "For the generation that has gone through, the central experience of the forms of totalitarian dictatorship, even more clearly than that of war ... murder is not at all the worst that a man can do to another man and ... death is not what man fears most ... on the contrary, the assertion according to which 'if there were no death there would be no fear on this earth' should not only be amended in the sense that alongside fear there is also intolerable suffering, but even turned upside-down in the sense that if death did not exist man would be unable to endure this intolerable suffering."[74] Perhaps one could then recognize in this phase the true situation of *Dasein* "whose being is concerned with being itself" and, interpreting the "possibility of impossibility" in the subjective sense of the genitive, to finally affirm that it is in the domain of the intolerable, and every one of its possibilities, that death affirms itself as the only, ultimate, authentic possibility.

49. Wherever dying is unsubstitutable and irreducible to "being-in" (*In-Sein*), temporality affirms its supremacy: it coincides with the fundamental stability of *Dasein*, it is the "original structure of the finite self."

As is well known, in 1962 Heidegger pronounced a lapidary statement concerning this primacy: "The attempt in *Being and Time*, section 70, to derive human spatiality from temporality is untenable."[75] Now one could add that this attempt also dictates the ingeniously forced interpretation of the Kantian notion of affection in a prominent section of *Kant and the Problem of Metaphysics*, which completely overlooks space precisely in the thesis according to which "space and time 'must always affect' [*affizieren*] the concept of representations of objects."[76] And most crucially we must observe that this unsustainable attempt actually goes back to the first chapters of *Being and Time*, and therefore pervades the book's entire structure (and therefore the very notion of clearing [*Lichtung*], which makes its first appearance in §28). Indeed, it is based not only on the results obtained in §23, and is coherent with the definition of the notion of in-being, but is already irrevocably sketched out in §24: "*Space is neither in the subject nor is the world in space*. Rather, space is 'in' the world since the being-in-the-world which is constitutive for Dasein has disclosed space."[77] "Has disclosed" is here a synonym (or synecdoche) for both thrownness (*Geworfenheit*) and the temporality of *Dasein*, and therefore contains *in nuce* the famous formulation of §70: "*Only on the basis of ecstatic and horizontal temporality is it possible for Dasein to break into space*. The world is not present-at-hand [*vorhanden*] in space; however, only within a world does space let itself be discovered."[78] It is specifically the subordination of space to temporality which later explains the primacy of spatial representations in the quotidian existence of *Dasein*. The "dependence" of *Dasein* on space "in the Articulation of concepts and significations has its basis not in some specific power that space possesses, but in Dasein's kind of Being," Heidegger writes, only to then correct himself in the margins of the so-called *Hüttenexemplar* (in a note that announces the idea of time and space's co-originality, that is of the "time-space" (*Zeit-Raum*) later developed in *Being and Time*): "No opposition; both belong together."[79] In other words: *Dasein* loses itself in space, and spatiality, whose origins go back to temporality, is one of its abasing modalities.

Insofar as it "possesses itself" or "has itself," *Dasein* can lose itself and be dependent on space.

The theme of *Mitsein* is also coherent with this subordination and this dependence. If it is true that the mode of the other's *Dasein* is not encountered in the "simple care" (*Besorgen*) driven by "circumspection" (*Umsicht*), but rather precisely in "caring for" (*Fürsorge*), which is guided by "consideration" (*Rüchsicht*) and "indulgence" (*Nachsicht*), it is also true that others manifest themselves in their own peculiar ways on the basis of the same usable elements, and that *Dasein*'s "understanding of others already lies in the understanding of being."[80] The being-in of *Dasein* is already a being-with: the other is encountered "in the surrounding world" (*umweltich*), in its being-with in the world,[81] and substitutability belongs to the *Umwelt*.[82] The encounter with the other therefore remains internal to the constitution or opening of *Dasein* just as, in the latter, spatiality remains subordinate to temporality. It is therefore precisely the existential primacy of temporality (that is, the concatenation: mineness [*Jemeinigkeit*], authenticity, totality, anticipation, being-toward-death) that also dictates the authenticity of concern (*Fürsorge*): "When they devote themselves to the same thing in common, their doing so is determined by their Dasein, which has grasped itself. This *authentic* alliance first makes possible the right kind of objectivity [*die rechte Sachlichkeit*] which frees the other for himself in his freedom."[83] This bond (the decision shared by everyone, to use the terms of 1933) is the self-grasping of *Dasein* which—according to the order of its existential constitution—depends on spatiality. Once again, the two go together: dependence on space and freedom as a bond to oneself and a possession of self, the subordination of spatiality and anticipation or authenticity. *Dasein* grasps itself because it depends on space and vice versa. The impossibility of grasping oneself spatially corresponds to the possibility of anticipation.

Thrownness (*Geworfenheit*), which as Klein wrote is revealing of being just as vertigo is revealing of space, also in turn possesses a spatial nature. The "existential determination" (*existentiale Bestimmtheit*) of *Dasein* includes its "situation" (*Situation*) and "in the term '*situation*' (position—'to be in the position of'), there is an overtone of a spatial significance [*schwingt eine räumliche Bedeutung mit*] [which] is also implied in the 'there' of Dasein."[84] To comprehend is to "embrace" (*umfassen*), and that which transpires vibrates or "oscillates together" (*mitschwingt*). If in its abasing modality *Dasein* depends on space, it is because this modality is essentially spatial, because *Dasein* is thrown before all else into spatiality.

50. It is well-known that Heidegger defines the spatiality of *Dasein* as a "de-distancing" (*Ent-fernung*). *Ent-fernung* characterizes *Umsicht* because it

discovers and brings closer not one entity or the other but the distance as such or as a relation—later ascertainable and measurable—between worldly presences. "Dasein is essentially de-distancing . . . it lets beings be encountered in nearness." In other words: *"an essential tendency toward nearness lies in Dasein"* (*Im Dasein liegt eine wesenhafte Tendenz auf Nähe*).[85]

Dasein can therefore cover and discover any distance (whether brought nearer as such or de-distanced), but "this de-distancing . . . is something that Dasein can *never cross over*" (*diese Ent-fernung kann das Dasein nie kreuzen*), nor can it place itself within it, precisely because *"it is essentially de-distancing, that is, it is spatial"* (*weil es wesenhaft Ent-fernung, das heisst räumlich ist*).[86]

If *Dasein* crossed its own horizon, it would already be beyond itself: and it could, by moving within its own de-distancing, that is, by crossing its borders, experience its own death in another's, reducing it to an ordinary fact. Expressed more simply and precisely, *Dasein* would not be spatial (*räumlich*) and its being would not be ordered according to the principle of *Jemeinigkeit* and of death. But spatiality remains subordinate to temporality, and the *Dasein* that cannot cross its own de-distancing (*Ent-fernung*) can—for the very same reason—anticipate its own end as the possibility of impossibility, it can decide, repeat itself and, at the same time, historicize itself within a common destiny.[87]

Dasein therefore essentially tends toward proximity because it is always "futural," transcendent, reaching toward or rapt in the distance, always beyond itself and therefore tied to itself, "free for its own death." As one reads in *The Essence of Reasons* (and in "Distance and Nearness," the contemporaneous supplement to the *Metaphysical Foundations of Logic* course), man is "a creature of distance" (*Wesen der Ferne*): "It is only through the original distance [*durch ursprüngliche Ferne*], which he forms for himself in his transcendence with respect to every other being, does a true nearness [*wahre Nähe*] to things grow in him. And only knowing how to listen in the distance makes one mature [*zeitigt*] in Dasein as oneself [*als Selbst*], the awakening of the response of being-there-with [*Mitdasein*] in being-with [*Mitsein*] with which it can renounce egoity, to conquer itself as an authentic self [*eigentliches Selbst*]."[88] And as a bond that ties *Dasein* to itself or to space, this "freedom" finally reveals itself to itself as "that which renders the bond and obligation in general possible."[89]

The dependence of proximity (that is, of *Ent-fernung*) on original distance reflects the dependance of spatiality on temporality, or in other words, the relation that Heidegger must institute between the modes of being of falling and of authenticity in order to affirm the *Selbstheit* of *Dasein*. The authentic modality is coherent with the original distance or temporality of *Dasein*, whereas the inauthentic one adheres to spatiality. Now if *Dasein*, as an indivisible self, is not reducible to a "self-point from which it moves away" in falling,[90] it is precisely because the latter coincides with the unapproachable de-distancing (*Ent-fernung*). And if authenticity is a "modified grasping" of falling (of spatiality, of *Mitsein*), this is temporally possible as an anticipatory decision since *Dasein* has, so to speak, already always fallen into its spatiality. Spatiality creates the abyss, it is the "vortex" (*Wirbel*) of thrownness (*Geworfenheit*).[91] But that is not all: the relation between spatiality or *Mit-sein* and temporality or anticipation—and therefore the very possibility of the anticipatory decision and of destiny—corresponds to the relation between *Sterben* and the mere *exitus* which is "'objectively' accessible." Spatiality (or the manner of in-being) is the domain of death as an "'objective' givenness," it is the *Ent-fernung* of death (*Sterben* brought nearer as *Ableben*). Therefore the appropriation of the self—*Selbstheit* or *Jemeinigkeit*—is the anticipation or vertigo of *Sterben* projected by another's demise, spatially incorporated into the horizon of the experienceable.

If, as we have seen, *Dasein*'s existential *situation* (its "situation," its "being in a certain situation" or "in position") reveals the spatial meaning implicit in *Da*,[92] if the dependence of the *moribundus* on space exists, it is because of the suggestion of death (*exitus*), and the original distance itself comes in turn from the dead person's proximity: via a modified grasping this proximity is constituted as an authentic possibility, and therefore experienced (within the domain of spatial determinations) as a merely objective appearance of the latter. A truly characteristic or vertiginous circle encloses *Dasein*.

51. One thus reaches the "objective limit" that Hannah Arendt recognized in the fear of a "violent death." We can hence call the temporality of *Dasein* temporal vertigo (*Zeitschwindel*), and say that unsubstitutability (the exclusively objective, spatially determined experienceability of another's death) is the disjunction (both a fracture and a first apparition of the *Weile*) that produces vertigo, that is, individual subjectivity and intersubjectivity itself, and which finally demands to be interpreted ontologically, returning on stage disguised as a being who is originally *se ipse* and being-with. We can call violence or the power of war the production of death as a limit of being, or of fear (including in its authentic modality of existential anguish) as its vertiginous attraction which posits and preserves *Selbstheit* and the totality of *Dasein*, notwithstanding any scission. Whether it be actual or latent, war is indeed nothing other than an enormous factory of (corpses, and therefore of) the moribund. It is capable of mobilizing and inscribing in a temporary manner ("can put animals into this state for a time")—it is a manipulated "suspension of life,"

as Furio Jesi put it[93]—that is, in an exemplary way, all of the forms and possibilities of being under the liminal sign of death. Rethinking in his own way the widespread subject of popular literature during or right after World War I (Edmond Cazal, for example, wrote in *Voluptés de guerre* [1918] that the voluptuousness of sacrifice and death, the inebriation of killing, is more obscure and passionate than any other), Roger Caillois identified in the vertigo of war the same "essential phenomenon" that Heidegger had expressed most clearly in "The Self-Assertion of the German University" in 1933: if this frenzy takes hold of and irremediably carries subjects, it is not in fact because of an imitative magic, of a nature that is in turn social, but because the subjective identities and the community that the war itself produces and brings together are magical and vertiginous. And if there is no second vertigo capable of stopping it, it is because (or so that) it presents itself precisely thus, as the vertigo of war, that is, as the *first* vertigo, whereas it is merely derivative. This is, in fact, its lie: it is neither the first nor the second (which, as Renouvier taught, could cure it) but both the "demand" (*Forderung*), the production and the concealment of the first. One must therefore discover this first vertigo so that a new, therapeutic, or finally weakened one may be produced. But in actuality this simply means the following: it is necessary for vertigo to stop presenting itself as *first*, and for it to immediately appear as second, that is, as an overt trick or spectacle.

"Vertigo is an inversion or a contamination of proximity and distance," wrote Henri Maldiney.[94] One must add that if it later turns out to be unbearable for the subject, it is because it coincides (*pace* Kant and Heidegger, but not Herz) with the irruption of spatiality itself, with its drawing closer as such. Consequently, it is tension and falling, that is, the end or the impossibility of anticipation: an effectively possible transformation of dying (*Sterben*) into death (*exitus*), of the moribund into a corpse; it is a contamination of the original *Ferne* or a (de-)severing of the very *Ent-fernung*, a spatial proximity of temporal distance; it is a distancing of all proximities or the suspension of all presences in an outdated time, it is Madeleine and, bound in the same embrace, the absent Carlotta, it is the halo-like atmosphere of Bruges or the auratic and powerful one of the film, which develops "with the vagueness of the circle and the peremptoriness of the line."[95] One falls, then, because every proximity comes from afar just as every distance comes from up close, because the death of the other is the point of inversion, the cornerstone of de-distancing, because it is *Dasein* itself in its *Selbstheit* that is tacitly (or, thinking back again to Renouvier, normally) vertiginous. It is not the height that is unbearable, but the subordination of spatiality, the ontological "chasm" (*Kluft*) that separates it from temporality.

6
Surface

52. "The alpinist holding onto a rock-face," Klein observed, "is no longer able to refer space to his *here* as its center. The entirety of space, space itself, irrupts into the subject's consciousness."[1] Maldiney echoes his comments, arguing that "vertigo is a limit-situation, a pre-cosmic situation in which we are in the grip of space,"[2] or, according to a better-known formulation, "of the entirety of space, which has collapsed into itself, in a universal retreat around and within us. . . . Man is not the center, nor space a place. There is no longer any *here*."[3] In ordinary life, "we experience the space of our presence in a tension of 'proximity-distance' that is outlined on the basis of a determined region of our body in action."[4] But if a man stands on a mountaintop or on the peak of a cliff, then he is endangered, "he exists in the peril of space; and if he does not maintain a precise limit between proximity and distance, this danger takes the form and substance of Vertigo."[5] For Maldiney, the overcoming of this state consists in the affirmation of rhythm, which happens all of a sudden, without mediation, right when "everything spins in a universal flight that does not open onto anything or onto oneself, as Fozio evokes it in his description of Santa Sofia."[6] "After vertigo, the rhythm [*Après le vertige, le rhythme*]." Or, notwithstanding, after vertigo, the fall. "It is significant that Vertigo ceases after the fall and that it always presupposes a foothold. Just as the fear of darkness strikes those who do not trust it, Vertigo does not afflict those who abandon themselves to space. It occurs when the body lifts itself and feels its hold, just as oneiric death corresponds to the start of awakening."[7] But perhaps it is possible that the fall does not come as a result of vertigo, that it is instead the latter, which precedes the rhythm, that comes after the "free abandonment to space [*le libre abandon à l'espace*]" as a loss or limitation thereof—it is proba-

ble, in other words, that the man who tottered up there, leaning out from the tower in *Il Grido*, could not, by throwing himself down, escape his own situation and put at an end to his anguish, since this serenity was already with him, although too close to be within his grasp. The end of vertigo would thus precede its beginning, like the immortal opening of a space without limits or footholds; it would thus paradoxically make an appearance precisely when Aldo "totters, leans out, as if trying to resist," like the mystery of a cure enclosed in the harbinger of the illness, in the "typical absence" that announces a fit. But this means that the spreading of the halo-like domain (the atmosphere in Passy) is the appearance of a purified aura, one that is without death, and still unknown.

53. We know that Alois Riegl distinguished the principle of "near vision" (*Nahsicht*) from that of "distant vision" (*Fernsicht*), thus illuminating the entire history of art as a continuum existing between the polarities of tactile and optical vision, between Egypt and Byzantium. Under Riegl's gaze, the haptic gaze of Ancient Egypt settled on the surface, almost touching it, closely following the contour of figures and appreciating their light bas-relief. By contrast, the man of late antiquity admired or conceived his works from further away, and he announced the purely optical solution of the mosaic by transforming that tactile, solid, impenetrable background into a refined fretwork, or else sculpting figures in greater, seemingly more rudimentary relief, with their play of light and shadow (or color-rhythm, "*Farbenrhythmus*"), which was more legible from the distance of vast urban spaces. Under Riegl's gaze, over the course of millennia, the beings once pressed down upon by the dark stone of the crypts and temples of the Valley of the Nile, forced every time into impossible contortions to show their less fleeting profile (the head from the side, the bust straight on, the legs from the side), would thus have emerged with great effort, at first only partially—conquering on the decorated tympanums of Greece the intermediate distance of normal sight (*normale Sicht*)—to then separate themselves entirely in the great sculptural works of imperial Rome, where "a niche of free space" now separates them from the white of the marble and their distant forms throw sharp shadows on the background; they become visible and clear, like stably determined units, almost ready to roam the golden Byzantine skies. Conquering for themselves or bringing closer (or de-distancing) all distances, sweeping through the entire spectrum of visibility, humanity would have thus never ceased to know beings and entities in their distinct individual definition.

54. Following Riegl, Wilhelm Worringer compared an Ancient Greek funerary frieze with a fifth-century one from Ravenna: "Almost equal in the

austerity of the surface [*Flachestrenge*], the two are in fact at the opposite ends of an evolution . . . the plane of the Ancient Greek relief has a tactile meaning [*Tastebene*], whereas that of the later one from Ravenna is visual [*Sehebene*]. The figuration of the Greek relief emerges from an absolute surface [*absolute Fläche*], the other from an absolute space. . . . If we wish to grasp its essence, the naked surface of the Ravenna frieze's background must be observed as if it were a uniform shadow . . . or a golden background, like a mosaic's."[8]

Inspired by Riegl's teachings, but equally so by Husserl and Heidegger, Sergio Bettini took a further step forward, lending a new and radical meaning to the expression "absolute surface." He brilliantly recognized in Rome and discovered in Venice a chromaticism that goes beyond the oppositional relation with the surface, one that is deprived "of the relation knowable via the *tactum intrinsecum*," that ties the spectator to the artwork at a distance that is in turn objective although infinitely extendable: "Venice is born between air and water . . . it concretizes itself between these two limitless dimensions. . . . The entirety of Venice's form is color, which is to say surface. . . . No unifying number, no restful equilibrium . . . only effects of light . . . the light . . . the *locus* of moving splashes of color . . . where volume becomes lost, and the very scale of weights and substances, now unanchored, oscillates infinitely."[9] According to Bettini, in Venice as in Ravenna, the true heir of late Roman antiquity, the desubstantialization of the figure first attained during the epoch of Hadrian finally established itself. It is, in fact, in imperial frescoes that the "surface of the work dissolves into splashes of color that match and combine with each other," yielding novel combinations: "Architectural works, whose depth was originally a *trompe-l'oeil*, come to the surface, place themselves on the same level as the sculpted figures, which once stood out, artistically emerging in the foreground, and now take their place as part of the background, inserting and dissolving themselves in it."[10] Thus, the sculptures of the Arch of Constantine are indeed also "delineated by very deeply sculpted outlines, which go so far as to create areas of emptiness—of very strong shadows—between one and the other, separating them conspicuously from the background." And although their "character had been noted by Riegl, who however had interpreted it as a sign of an increased spatiality. . . . We know . . . that the signification of these deepening grooves is not spatial, but markedly chromatic . . . and that the basis of the image is no longer the sculptural background, but this optic, chiaroscuro-like surface, which thus came into being."[11] This surface, which now harbors forms "unrelated to the 'environment,'"[12] while the background emerges and the foreground meets it in its depth, is for Bettini the "absolute surface." The new usage of Worringer's term (*absolute Fläche*) thus bears witness to an essential theoretical change, which removes the keystone from Riegl's evolutionary arch.

The absolute surface revokes every relation between proximity and distance; it implies the disappearance of spatial meanings and concepts. Neither far nor close, lacking any support, it is the impossible *Ent-fernung*, the insubordination of spatiality to temporality; and if perchance it were down there, it would never end up "at the bottom," it would never induce vertigo: it could never be the "there" based on which *Dasein* understands its "here."[13]

For us, it is on the absolute surface, not in the background, or by covering it, that the pure mask frees itself and oscillates infinitely, the mask both clothed and stripped by Ferguson, obtained via the countermovement of a *maquillage* that is only a *démaquillage* (Rohmer).

55. She barely emerges from the greenish light as he turns and looks at her. We are both him and her and neither him nor her, we are the encounter, on the stretched, invisible white canvas, of the luminous silhouettes. Thus, we both are and are not the figures absorbed into the background of the ancient fresco. It is not, in fact, from temporal distance that spatial closeness comes; it is space that temporizes, time that gets muddled in things. And no one lives and no one dies, we are without destiny, without bonds, we are not the masters of ourselves or even the same, we are nothing but the faint appearance of that silhouette, of that almost inebriated face, of that small, changeable vibration, we are their only and unrepeatable occasions.

The film seems to capture us with the slow movement of its entanglements, with Scottie's hypnotic roaming, "part-robot, part-zombie,"[14] and the shot from the point of view of his car guides us, slow and undulating (or dancing: "Melancholy waltz and languid vertigo!") through a San Francisco that is in its own way old, luminescent, and crepuscular ("Your memory in me glitters like a monstrance! [*Ton souvenir en moi luit comme un ostensoir!*]": Baudelaire, once again), just like the readers of *Bruges-la-morte*, who follow Hugues's uncertain gait and "feel the presence and influence of the city, will experience more vividly the contagiousness of the waters, will themselves become more aware of the tall towers, their shadows lengthening over the text."[15] The director's dynamic imagination, as Bachelard might have put it, skillfully attracts ours, while the all-too-calm flow of the Flemish canals passes by the Quai de Courbevoie and mixes on the shores near the Golden Gate Bridge with the waters of the Pacific and the San Francisco Bay. But the pure effect, which gathers and frees every enchantment, is not itself vertiginous, and by showing itself finally lets us go. The background, over there, between the walls of the buildings, rises to the surface, while the support slowly disappears into the distance, and the stairs flee all while getting nearer. And nothing offers a foothold anymore and everything—whether person or thing—will henceforth be merely light that wanders in light, just as images once reached the screen carried on a cloud of dense vapor and uncertain reflections. Everything finally appears as artifice, and cinema is truly nothing other than cinema, everything is pure technique, which—as Klein would have wanted—finally takes the floor: "Did you notice the distortion?" And so, we are no longer "here" and will not be "there"; space is not our cage, there is no center or rotation, no chasm. And we are neither together nor separate. We have neither past nor future, we cannot say "forward!," "backward!," or "forward-backward!" because everything slips on itself and everyone becomes muddled: Judy, Madeleine, Carlotta, Pauline, Renée, Kim, Jane, Hugues, and anyone else with or within them.

But the eyes do not fumble and they realize, just now, that ontology is a form of politics, and that politics and ontology are nothing but technique. The latter cannot, in fact, be reduced to one or the other, and proclaims with its display: don't hold back, let yourself fall, scatter the violent fiction of the self in this new, true fiction. Know that if he, the lover relegated to the reign of identity and death, will not be able to accept her entreaty, and she, who would like to abnegate herself, will be implacably stripped bare by her mask, you, however, have managed, since the very beginning, to receive both within yourself. Death marks your ungraspable actuality, but the subjective image flows in itself, beyond itself, it is already beyond that borderline. Therefore, only be the untimely vertigo that follows, precedes, and cancels itself out. Live nudity alone, be the life of small sensations, lose yourself in an aura without the dead or in the difference of masks. "Lose the prey by grasping at the shadow." Such is indeed the dream of indeterminacy dreamed by the attentive eyes, extending it into the deadly dream of determination.

56. "Lose the prey by grasping at the shadow . . ." Or better yet: let go of both one and the other "in favor of that which is no longer the shadow and not yet the prey: the shadow and the prey coalesce in a single flash."[16] It will not be easy to accept the surrealist invitation, so similar to Jean Epstein's non-Cartesian spirit—and capable of defying Henri Bergson's recommendation to the members of the *Society for Psychical Research*: "One does not let go of one's prey for what is perhaps nothing but a shadow."[17] Under the dominion of death, temporal vertigo binds the subject to its corporeal "here" on the basis of an (ungraspable, unassumable, distant in its very proximity) "non-here," it shuts the being in space at the very moment when this space emerges as such, or as insuperable, in the perilous attraction. Renouvier's intuition, according to which our actions are normally vertiginous, is thus worth returning to.

Every action of the subject identical to himself derives from the fear of death; it proceeds from the conclusion that he fears and chases, it is the action suggested by and exposed to death. The dominion of *exitus* produces both the action and the subject and identifies property (possession) with quality to transform it into "the distinctive quality"—to once again cite Klein's 1953 *thèse*—or the "visible marker of singularity itself."[18] This relation is indeed the relation with the other. It makes the moribund appear in the "here" that is a "there" and, even before that, from the "not-here" that mythically inhabits the dead man's "there," tying the death (of now) to the life (of before) as the absence of life, and thus making a "here" of the "there." It corresponds to the violent technique that lays hold of beings, that produces and dominates every single thing and the very "worldliness" of the world.

But precisely in conspicuous naturalness or in pervasive force, a weak point nevertheless hides. The relation does not in fact escape—it could not escape—the very appropriation it produces. This means that it can, in turn, be grasped, shown, exhibited in a fiction. We can consequently define as *pure technique* the modality of grasping that displays life as a relation to the dead individual and that keeps to vertigo itself, fixating on it, keeping itself in a strange, precarious, and unrepeatable equilibrium. The cinematographic effect thus reproduces in a tranquility without footholds the same vertiginous mirroring and shows to one who looks at himself through the eyes of an animate figure the suggestive *rapport* that constitutes and determines him as an individual subject. Only here does the bond loosen, and indeed "the self with which one has the relationship [*rapport*] is nothing other than the relationship itself ... it is in short the immanence, or better, the ontological adequacy of the self to the relationship."[19]

We therefore recognize amid the tricks, scenes, lights, and machines, among the dollies and lenses, the thin pole of the tightrope walker. Its consistency is of the most labile nature, that is, genuinely speculative. Before the exhibition becomes lost in the canon, before the solution is reduced to a trick and the technique to a cliché, thought must intervene to obtain, with all of its ability, a new vertigo effect, to assemble in a novel manner, as has been said, the very same tools of the Husserlian laboratory. One may thus recognize Heidegger's own effort and, in *Being and Time*, the radical self-exhibition of the vertiginous *Dasein*. One can thus grasp, seemingly against the author's will, a hint of fiction in the profound transformation of intentionality into care or into *Dasein*'s transcendence, and appreciate the mutation of the most concrete of fears into existential anguish or into an overcoming via excess that, by grasping the anticipation itself, will demand the abandonment of its theme, so that even the name of death, that menacing presence which has now been dissolved into a modality of being, may disappear (as indeed happens in his later writings). We can therefore recognize in the motto "forward-backward" the principle of an optic distortion and read it as if the two terms had to be pronounced in unison, in a decidedly Hitchcockian way. If then, Heidegger notwithstanding, authenticity reveals itself to be a masquerade, it is because pure technique never becomes confused with the semblance that it projects (whether that be a wax mannequin, a figure on a screen, or the horizon of being). The vertigo effect is not empathic; it only coincides with the attention that discloses it ("a track-out combined with a forward zoom"), it is a countermovement, a challenge to the *Weile*, the translation of vertigo into appearance or the transformation of fear into thought.

57. Now, fear is not anxiety, and it is not vertigo either. Instead, fear stokes vertigo and transforms into anxiety. In the famous chapter of *Being and Nothingness* on the origin of nothingness, Sartre returns to Heidegger's distinction and situates the vertiginous moment in the transition from the mere fear of falling—which concerns external circumstances, which touch me as objects of the world—to anxiety, understood in the Kierkegaardian sense and, via the secularization and generalization carried out precisely by Heidegger,[20] as an anxiety before oneself. If I can be afraid of a precipice, which appears to me as something "to avoid," my reaction to this sentiment is of a reflexive nature and prefigures a series of subsequent actions ("I will pay attention . . . I will keep myself as far as possible from the edge of the path") determined by external conditions, but which are also indeterminate, which are possibilities that are entirely mine.[21] Nothing could in this case force me to do or not do something, nothing could stop me from jumping a moment later into the chasm. Thus, Sartre continues, if to avoid fear I have sought refuge in reflection, the latter places me before the possibility that "will emanate from a self which I am not yet." And what is vertiginous is precisely this perception of this dependence of the subject that I am on the I that is not yet me and that does not depend on the one that I am: "I approach the precipice, and my scrutiny is searching for myself in my very depths."[22] The fact that the possibility of suicide may later render one's motives apparent (to put an end to anguish) and that these may seem insufficient, undetermined, that anguish may therefore transform itself into indecision and subsequently into the decision to draw away from the precipice, does not do away with the disjunction that separates the actuality of my being from my future being, or which divides the present from the past. Some ten years after *Being and Nothingness* (and almost twenty years after *The Transcendence of the Ego*), Sartre would go on to write the splendid

chapter of the book on Jean Genet, "A Dizzying Word." Genet, it reads, is not born "an actor and a martyr" but becomes one the day he, an adopted child, is caught reaching into one of the kitchen cupboards. From the moment when "a voice declares publicly: 'You're a thief,'"[23] the poet's life is marked, defined by a paradoxical situation with no way out. From the moment in which "the dazzlingly evident present confers its meaning on the past,"[24] Genet is "read, deciphered, designated": "He has *vertigo*, in the strict sense of the word. When we stand on a precipice and suddenly feel dizzy, we feel that we are slipping away from ourself, that we are flowing, falling. Something is calling us from the bottom of the gulf. That something is ourself, that is, our being which is escaping from us and which we shall join in death. The word is vertiginous because it opens out on an impossible and fascinating task."[25] Everything here, we can further add, as in the case of "bad faith," goes back to the "intrastructure of the pre-reflective cogito [*intrastructure du 'cogito' préréflexif*],"[26] that is, to the pages in which *Being and Nothingness* takes up the central idea of *The Transcendence of the Ego* and the coherent distinction between consciousness and the "psychical": because consciousness, ever being an immediate consciousness of the self, is tied to its reflection, precisely this link is an impossible and irrefutable task; vertiginous fascination is still always the magic of immediate, nonpositional self-consciousness, of the "fundamental selfness" which in turn produces the magic mask of the "I." It is indeed at the level of this product or "of our person as a transcendent psychic unity" that *Being and Nothingness* must illustrate the notion of *héxis*, shifting it, in Husserlian terms, from the domain of absolute selfness to that of *habitus* in the sense of habit. The forcing is obvious and perhaps not all that justifiable. But here, compared with the 1936 article, vertigo is already the protagonist, the magic of the ego finally has a definite name. The transparency of the *cogito* contained, in fact, a latent and inevitable question, which has now been asked openly: the essence is known to us, but what about being? When consciousness tries to grasp such a notion (the support of being) it is seized by *Schwindel*. When Sartre quotes *Being and Time* ("the 'how' (*essentia*) of this being . . . must be conceived in terms of its existence (*existentia*)"), when with the same anti-Cartesian gesture with which he defines a prereflexive *cogito* he takes up the ecstatic, nonconsciential definition of *Dasein* to find a consciousness of ecstasy and, imitating Heidegger, writes that "consciousness is a being such that in its being, its being is in question,"[27] he suspends consciousness up there, between the towers of Notre Dame. One could perhaps define the existentialist as a troubled and shocked phenomenologist, subjected to the trial of the chasm.

58. But precisely phenomenology can easily become the art of roofing. The attempt to grasp being can be supplanted by the technique that allows one to grasp vertigo.

Let us recall and briefly go back to Klein's thesis: the history of art and of artistic theory has also been a lengthy interpretation of the passage in the *Nicomachean Ethics* which defines *téchne* as *héxis*, as an ability and capacity that historically exists between the extremes of the rule or *routine* and genius, which is irreducible to any rule (between the lower limit of necessity and the upper limit of freedom, as Ravaisson once put it). As an explicit return to Aristotle and therefore a vindication of medieval commentators with respect to humanism, which was then in decline, as an affirmation of art as a "factive habit" (Benedetto Varchi, who borrows Aristotle's terminology verbatim), mannerism marks a paradigmatic moment in this development and one of utmost tension. It is the moment in which the theory of the *artes* is transformed into an aesthetics of artifice, that is, of the work which, in provoking wonder, draws attention to the act—or better yet to the manner, the how, the *maniera*—of its coming into being, to the mastery or grasp of a technique. The latter must therefore affirm and discover itself every time as the *recta ratio*, all while exhibiting itself in ever more singular and stunning virtuosities, paradoxically soaring beyond every norm, that is, above the emptiness of contingency. The artist, Klein explains, must therefore defy and overcome the vertigo of chance with ever more ingenious and dissimulated (*sprezzatura*) artifices and adaptations, only to once again reveal the arbitrariness of his own gesture: "If it is true that art is the 'power of opposites' and that 'its principle lies in the person who produces it, not in that which he produces,' the artificial style must *render palpable* that the artist *could have done it otherwise* every time he creates something."[28] One can hear the barely veiled Sartrean echo of the possible, indeterminable *mine* here, and when Klein affirms that "mannerism illustrates Aristotle," the assertion brings to mind the canonical formula of *Being and Nothingness*: it may seem licit to believe that the vertigo of the artist occurs on the border that separates *habitus* as norm from the being "for itself" of invention, and that the "for itself" is opened up, torn apart by irreducible genius; and that every artifice owes its origin to the dependence of what the artist is on what he is not, thus revealing in that very *sprezzatura* the anguish of freedom. With its typical "little perceptions" (*petites perceptions*), reanimated by the pages of treatises or flickering in the awe-inducing style of Michelangelo and reflected in the caprices of Arcimboldo, the style of the sixteenth century seems to concern us closely. For Klein, it prefigures in fact the attempts to integrate the aleatory into the necessary (Mallarmé, Valéry), or to the reach the nucleus of necessity starting from the arbitrary (Juan Gris's cubism); it announces the more forceful irruption of chance, whether baroque or modern: "*Art brut*, children's art, the art of alienated figures and 'surrealism' . . . this is what mannerist Aristotelianism set the stage for in the moment of its complete self-consciousness [*prise de conscience*], which was also a complete self-questioning."[29]

Art is a *habitus*, and vertigo, I reiterate, is a sudden "becoming conscious" (*prise de conscience, Besinnung*) which breaks *héxis*'s continuity and the integrity of the sphere of what is my own (*Eigensphäre*). As Klein wrote in a different essay, art is akin to laughter because it produces, with the complicity of the other, an unrealizing effect. But art is technique, and when technique becomes the "production of effects," when it is "oriented towards and defined by the effect," then, Klein remarks, it has interiorized the other's point of view (or complicity)—it is already in itself "inter-subjectivization."[30]

Up until now, I have described the vertigo effect as a moment during which technique exhibits itself and the director declares his own mastery or, one could also say, his own style; and I have also hinted at the notion of cinema as the transformation of vertiginous movement into spectacle (or also into an "ideated sensation"). In reality, the two are but one: here one is not merely dealing with art as a joyous transfiguration, with art that, like laughter, turns the austerity of reality into a joke by taking a step toward intersubjectivity, that is, by engaging the other's complicity and consent; nor is one dealing merely with cinema as an effect that provokes and guides others' reactions. Now, in fact, it is precisely the effect, cinema as a technique of intersubjectification, that operates by "mannering," by drawing attention to its mode or style, that hovers over contingency and grazes the *regressio* or stylistic void of the "how" of a "how." "Mannering what? Clearly something that has already existed, and something of great value, at that," Roberto Longhi would have said; and even if it isn't necessarily "Leonardo da Vinci's and Michelangelo's two cartoons in the Palazzo Vecchio,"[31] then it can at least be the zoom in *Rebecca* and Murnau's *unchained camera technique*. If the doorman, the drunk and dreamy hero of *Der Letzte Mann* (1924), "can no longer tell whether the chair he is sitting on has suddenly whirled into space or whether it is space that has started turning around him," and the camera sucks us into a vertiginous sinkhole with its visual whirl,[32] Hitchcock, by contrast, uses a counter-zoom to capture that raving apparatus: by freezing and thus showing the first effect as such, he keeps himself in suspense, resisting vertigo, avoiding exponential mannerism while he searches for and obtains, beyond the interiorization of the other's gaze, via a new step, a question that is almost rhetorical but anything but gratuitous (and which also defies the rules of the interview), a novel complicity and a confirmation of his feat: "Did you notice . . . ? Do you know how we did that?" "Wasn't that . . . ?"

It should be noted, however, that the question addressed to the director-accomplice tends to confirm a deeper and more general agreement concerning cinema itself. One could say that for both the vertigo effect, which grasps and puts cinema as such on display, is nothing other than cinema itself, in its elementary simplicity. "Effect" means "cinema," because cinema continues to exist if it produces its effect. And the technique that, while producing the effect is at the same time turned toward its "how" by the interiorized gaze, is not—we might add—a reflection on the technique but an immanence of the effect: it is *a technique that grasps itself while producing its effect and in producing it exposes itself, its own self-grasping, as an effect*. Since the effect is that of self-exposure and the exposure nothing other than an effect, the technique itself cannot be unrealized and transformed into something that can only trigger laughter: in the very moment in which vertigo becomes a spectacle, artifice appears in all of its seriousness. And this is no pose, given that it can be traced precisely to the structural homology of the subjective self and of artifice, which is also the origin of the specific possibility which psychologists, along with critics and phenomenologists, have called "identification": "If cinema produces its effect, this occurs because I identify with its images."[33] When the structure of *habitus* and, even before that, of the *se ipse*, of consciousness as self-consciousness, of being (or of consciousness's being), whose being is concerned with this very being, is vertiginous, the pure effect, the vertigo effect or the transformation of vertigo into an effect is precisely this: a self, the being of a consciousness or a grasping of the self, a passing through oneself which shows, by breaking the unity of that which is one's own, by tearing apart habit, appearing both to itself and to others and no longer to a self or to its alter ego. It is having itself that is disclosed as an artifice, it is the vertigo of selfness, immobilized by a counter-oscillation which (by calling attention to itself) makes it ready for analysis. This pure technique is in fact balanced between the unrealizing procedure and the seriousness "of that which is," between comic revocation and the irrevocability of destiny, between the ecstasy of the indeterminate and the dream of death; and by keeping itself at this intersection, it shines light on the opposites of painful factuality and laughter, of liberty and norm, on the correlation between the empathic and the irreplaceable. Klein once called this particular intelligence humor. He, the philosopher of vertigo, as well as of laughter and of art as effect, and even before that, the philosopher of the destruction of the starry sky as a transcendental reduction, made recourse, debating also with Paul Ricoeur and Adolphe de Waelhens, to the complicity of the other with a very serious witty quip: "I almost wish to call phenomenology a philosophy of humor."[34]

59. "There, on that sunny boulevard, Flavières once again experienced the attraction of darkness and realized why Madeleine had struck him right away."[35] The introduction to and the interpretation of Boileau and Narcejac's passage was written by Rodenbach: "in this study of passion, I have striven to evoke the spirit of a particular city as main character, a city associated with states of being, one which is able to advise, dissuade, induce action."[36] If a vertigo effect can be produced, it is because vertigo itself is an effect that exposes the figure of the self projected by the suggestion of death. This suggestion is always *for others*, it holds the keys to intersubjectivity, and it produces *Dasein* and being-with: vertigo, as we have seen, is the temporal anticipation or life in the horizon of another's death and, at the same time, spatial determination. Once again, Klein explains that just as the artistic effect assumes that the others have been interiorized, so the encounter with the other will be internal to the vertiginous constitution or the opening of *Dasein*. For this reason, it is the common space (of the city) in its specific tonality (that of a necropolis) that guides and dictates actions, both uniting and individualizing (it is the dominion of the dead, in which "no one can take the Other's dying away from him"). And because a truly apotropaic function could not subsist here, that is, if it ever existed—at most, the secondary product of that very same suggestion, the vertigo of the absolute comic—the work itself cannot help but appear and reveal itself as the study of a passion, written in turn "so that those who read us may experience the presence and influence of the City."[37] All art can do is reveal, in its distinctive traits, the true character of those places, of those more or less busy streets, of the banks and canals.

When the pure effect is finally attained, when via a play of lenses and dollies spatiality itself is encountered, phenomenology—which once again shone brightly under the glimmering specter of anguish, which has endured the "subjection . . . of such an enemy as to posit itself as a necessary and constant vanishing point in the perspective of the living being"[38]—can finally be called a "philosophy of humor." But in transforming the vertigo of the city into a spectacle and in illuminating in the meantime the sober seriousness of technique, it is a political philosophy that thus designates itself with a doubly subtle joke. It has been written (Benjamin) that the correct tendency of politics corresponds to a correct tendency of technique.

60. Dressed as Madeleine, Judy is undressed and unmasked. But in the meantime, technique has transformed the person into an animated figurine. And because this technique is intersubjective, when it obtains the identification of the spectator (or the coinciding of real perception with the psychic mechanism of dreaming[39]), it separates every living being from itself; in other

words, by insinuating the effect and the fiction into the apperceptive relation with the alter ego, it disrupts the very structure of identity. Hence Husserl's initial perturbation at the waxworks, and Mary Pickford's tears before the screen. Such a deception cannot but enjoy easy success (and it rightly pretends to go back to the origin of every trick): coherent, as we now know, with the vertiginous nature of identity itself, onto which it will be able to successfully graft itself (the cinema-effect simulates the state of the subject, it is a subject-effect, as Baudry writes), and the tears and the perturbation are thus reabsorbed into a slow, crepuscular habit. But there is more: the question addressed by Hitchcock to Truffaut ("Did you notice the distortion . . . ?") is in fact typically Aristotelian, and insists on the poietic dimension itself. "All art concerns bringing into being [*génesis*] and using art means considering [*théorein*: to observe the spectacle (of)] how the genesis of things that may or may not exist is possible and whose principle lies in him who produces and not in the thing produced."[40] In art—which is not action, and does not concern that which has its *arché* in itself but the coming into being of things—it is not therefore praxis that coincides with *héxis* but *poíesis*.

For this reason, the artist's *habitus* can go beyond norms and routines and balance over the chasm of chance: if the origin of the thing lies within him, the thing puts him on the line, artifice concerns him intimately, and the arbitrariness of the product reveals to him the vertiginous impossibility of having one's own *habitus*. Technique will therefore be unhabitual as only *habitus* itself can be: it will be both the production of the thing and of oneself (and therefore of a thing which can only be called technique or *habitus*), until its true performance appears and all *poíesis* will fall silent and fade into *héxis*. Although for a long time limited, caged and, due to a misunderstanding, made to gaze at "our point of support," technique was in fact preparing the catalogue of artifices to "capture vertigos." And if that which cannot be had can be made, it is the very constitution of selfness (art as the disposition of the subject) that is technically transformed into generated vertigo.

What is therefore at play here is not a hallucination, that of the evening of Saint Silvester or of the Chelsea Arts Ball, that is finally tamed and depicted or reduced to an optical trick, but the vertigo of technique or *héxis*—the impossibility, which has since been recognized (the engram: "everything was going far away from me"), of possessing one's own *habitus*. Once again, but differently, we are dealing with a vertigo that is finally grasped and appears as such when technique (both trick and *héxis*) grasps and displays itself in a counter-effect. The artifice in question is an elementary and singular one, which being in itself intersubjective transforms and dissolves the very reciprocal and vertiginous implication of the self's alterity and selfness. In this case one neither remains serious (in one's own austere inviolability) nor does one laugh (at that which one no longer is); then there is well and truly only humor, or the seriousness of the effect. Just as the Chinese actor from the famous example "makes" the cloud and at the same time shows that he is making it, the director demonstrates the vertigo of the *poíesis* all while "making" vertigo (as an effect), and he shows and offers it not to an alter ego, to another *se ipse*, but above all to another "technician," that is, in the technique itself. It is in the conspicuous machination that the *Schwindel* of the self and of possession is finally exhibited as a product and consigned to disenchantment.

Let us reread Aristotle: "Production is different from action.... As a result, a *héxis* accompanied by a *lógos* that directs action is different from a *héxis* accompanied by a reasoning that directs production ... a *téchne* and a *héxis* accompanied by a *lógos* that directs production are identical. Every *téchne* concerns bringing into being [*génesis*] and using art [*technázein*: to invent, to makes use of artifices, tricks] means considering [*theoreín*: to observe the spectacle (of)] how [*ópos*] the genesis [*génetai*] of things that may or may not exist is possible and whose principle [*arché*] lies in him who produces and not in the thing produced.... Because production [*poíesis*] differs from action [*práxis*], it follows that *téchne* has *poíesis* and not *práxis* as its object."[41]

Production and action are distinct, as are their respective *héxeis*, and *téchne* is a *habitus*. Artifice is a theory of "how" and this theory is a *poíesis*. Art takes its starting point not from the thing itself but from him who produces it, from the artist-observer, since the factive habit is the production of the very thing that is observed. To produce what? "Mannering what? Clearly something that has already existed, and something of great value, at that. For this reason, there is no need to say that the first and most vibrant 'mannerists' of the sixteenth century belonged, already at the beginning of the century, to a group of Florentines who, as young lads, had worked on transcribing or 'polishing' (almost to the point of destroying them) the two cartoons of Michelangelo and Leonardo in the Palazzo Vecchio: the two famous war scenes of Anghiari and Càscina."[42] And who is "the one who makes"? Pontormo's Michelangelo and Pontormo in the *ékphrasis*, or better yet in Longhi's style or "transcription" (*trascrittura*), it is merely a copy, a mask or cartoon, which will be formed and "polished," theorizing and destroying, because destruction is production and the effect is never entirely unrealized but rather humorously exhibited. To manner what? Evidently, a "how," or a *habitus*. Aristotle—who in book 5 of the *Metaphysics* observes that it is "impossible to have a 'having' (*héxis, habitus*) in this sense, for there will be an infinite series if we can have the having of what we have"[43]—avoids the *regressio* in *poíesis*. There is then a break and the *héxis* of the *héxis* is replaced by *technázein*; instead of an infinite regression, something is produced, as impossibility is replaced by generation. Or rather: *héxis* as possession, *habitus*-property is replaced by a "factive habit"; the subject as the appropriation of the self, which bases and contemplates itself from its own absence and lives in a mossy light a life carved out of death, is replaced by one who theorizes and produces by orienting habituality toward observation-production; the dream of selfness is, in turn, replaced by the artifact that draws attention to its *ópos*. And if transcendental philosophy can "never become such a τέχνη,"[44] it is precisely artifice that supplants the centrality of the ego, which via a "new universal direction of interest" still turns to the "how" and only by virtue of a voluntary decision.[45]

"To conclude, *téchne* . . . is *héxis* accompanied by a true discourse [*lógos alethés*] which guides production, and the absence of *téchne*, or its opposite, is *héxis* that directs production accompanied by a false *lógos*."[46] If pseudo-reasoning confuses production with praxis and conceals the deception, the true *lógos* deals with vertigo, with *Schwindel*, that is with *habitus* as effect: this is therefore precisely what is theorized, destroyed and technically produced. The *lógos* itself is thereby disclosed because it coincides with the mode of its coming into being, concealing it neither in its subject matter nor in its manner. Here, truly, "truth is *essentially* linked to artifice."[47]

At this point, we can perhaps define the philosophical essay less as a *form* than as a *theory of machination*. The latter uncovers effectivity, it does not allow vertigo to take hold of us, constituting us as subjects, so that that which is in us may instead be made by us. *Héxis* accompanied by a false *lógos* concerns that which can be otherwise with respect to how it is, when disguised vertigo exchanges and confuses life with death. *Héxis* accompanied by a true *lógos* concerns that which can be otherwise with respect to how it is because it reveals its effect. In other words, thanks to it "a new need finally [becomes] perceptible."

Once again: if *habitus* implies the need for a transition to an intersubjective dimension it is because (as Klein's thesis implicitly seems to argue) the structure of the subject, master of itself, of consciousness and of selfness understood radically as the *identification et enchaînement à soi*, is vertiginous. For this reason, the ego cannot be the empty pole of thought's current, but is rather the substrate of its possessions. And for this same reason, furthermore, the centrality of the "I" is nothing but a *habitus* (the fundamental habit). Now, if the *arché* of art lies in the subject that creates it, the vertiginous effect produces and theorizes the very constitution or habit that identifies these subjects and makes them what they are. If its origin is in the subject, technique is the transformation of that which produces us in every one of our actions, both in product and in theory. It is therefore situated in a specific historical conjunction with *habitus* or the constitutive artifice of subjectivity. Hence its difficulty, or its eclipse. Precisely this conjunction, which conceals it, must however be studied and uncovered every time: only then will *téchne* once again bring to light its true political and ontological nature. If the *arché* lies in the subject ("one night at the Chelsea Arts Ball . . ."), then vertigo is production ("I thought about the problem for fifteen years"): in other words, it is always already the discovery of the constitutive lie, always already a second vertigo.

Explicit

The scene is well-known: The promise of safety and violence collaborate, and the rationality of the mechanism conspires with myth as both conceal themselves in vertiginous subjectivities. For three centuries that "enormous artificial man" reigned over the city,[1] when Leo Strauss could call the doctrine inaugurated by Hobbes Epicureanism or "political hedonism," adding that it "has revolutionized human life everywhere on a scale never yet approached by any other teaching."[2] This typical and subtle formula uncovers the most profound modern significance of the "political": it is precisely the tendency toward self-preservation and pleasure that establishes itself in the sphere of fear that Epicurus had disbanded, thus simultaneously both realizing and renewing this threat, making man into that being who of "all beings that have life, is the only one who voluntarily, with pleasure, goes to meet his death."[3] This undue and efficient conjunction of "edoné" and "thánatos" which—under the name of desire ("Begierde")— constitutes the subject and marks him in every way, attained its utmost transparency, or rather its most determined masking, before the Freudian theory of the alternation of impulses, in The Phenomenology of the Spirit, *in a definition that is both correct and beguiling, since it reveals within its history the fulfillment of the spirit and of history. In the meantime, suicidal exposure to peril makes an appearance as a principle of the State, whose essence—to employ the Hegelian formula that only seemingly contradicts Hobbes and which derives from the eighteenth-century development of the security model—does not consist in protection but lays claim to life itself. And if even the last remaining deceptions can thus disappear, it is because the system of political Epicureanism has by now formed and stabilized consciousness as such. When the lord wins out and the servant trembles and gives in to his rival, thus postponing his own end and that of his rival, power installs itself in place of the very death which, according to Epicurus, is not there when I am. It is in this empty space, in this "not there" that consciousness and recognition come to be, that the threat exercises its influence and acquires its characteristic force, which Alexandre Kojève accurately described with the term "prestige."*[4] *And concerning this power, the simple, frank statement of fact is still valid: "A conjurer [prestidigitateur], with his games of prestige, can make a snake appear where there is only a rope. Behind this prestige there is certainly something, but it is not what one thinks."*[5] *That "something" is not the "absolute master," death, the "eternal master," but the fearful object that appears when the latter is absent, that is, the threat that produces a servile consciousness. Behind the life that death spares, behind death itself, there is only power, which can disturb death's shadow, that old vertiginous mechanism, which by taking part in every desire animates every action. And behind absolute dominion there is only unmasked force and the deceit that it exercises, inducing others to live—in Hegelian terms—a deferred or "mediated" suicide, to realize that which one would wish to avoid and to follow someone who is actually coercing into working, serving, tyrannizing or fighting, and dying in search of salvation.*

It is true, however, that that which is merely feared is promised and will come about, when that which is feared is precisely that which does not exist. The Hegelian servant is indeed the one who cedes, or is shaken in the entirety of his being by his master, to thus "legitimate" ("anerkennen") his servitude and dominion. In other words, he trembles before that death which henceforth will constitute an actual, incarnate or recognized threat. And by working, by being formed under this sovereign, holding back or keeping desire as such, avoiding, as Hegel says, its dissolution (that is, avoiding pleasure, because desires, as the modern-day Epicurean explains, are "pleasures that have put on a few pounds"), lest nothingness should disappear into nothingness or "not-being-there" (Jesi: "ci non-è"; Plessner: "ohne 'da' zu sein") into pure nonbeing, he rids himself of the very anguish of death. But he could only liberate himself from a semblance, and so his freedom is therefore nothing but a semblance. Man therefore ceases to be afraid precisely when he should not, and realizes the lie, unduly transferring the dominion that terrifies him onto a servant who has never been one, projecting everywhere his anthropomorphism of death to tyrannize a being whom he calls nature but who has never recognized him. And therefore he rightly sees that "autonomous being" as himself, since in that being he actualizes the destruction of a "natural" and trembling life that is uniquely his. By now—while the sphere of pure pleasure remains isolated and intact—the fall has happened, and the vertiginous hallucination (the painful suffering) will only be able to manifest itself as its own sign, to explain itself as an anticipatory decision, until in a second vortex, which is nothing other than the first, the unconstrainable power of the planet will have to rise in its truly sovereign indifference (as is happening today) against the "consciousness that works" ("arbeitende Bewusstsein") or dominates natural life alone, and for which it becomes impossible to renounce itself or to seriously experience fear and to halt, finally, in a true tremor. Such is the vertiginous, enchanting and synthetic formula which encapsulates the unraveling of days toward a death worthy of a shadow of death, the formula of an existence that unfolds by precipitating toward its fulfillment or mythical totality. The "not-being-there" acts, forms life, and myth shapes history.

In such conditions, only a technique, by contrast, seems capable of escaping this grasp or self-deception: it is that which, in every gesture or word, fixates vertigo and in the meantime discloses itself; and if it is not afraid of the void it is because it does not fear the gaze capable of perceiving its "little deception" ("kleiner Betrug"):[6] it is familiar with an object even as it displays its way of knowing it, and it grasps and shows it only because, as has been said, it manages to call this operation "artistic."[7] "Only" does not designate a lack or a rarity here: in fact, technique (far from being work or action, as the false reasoning that accompanies it claims) is nothing but this, only and entirely this; just as the subject—or his, that is, our well-known scene—is nothing but the dark side of artifice.

Notes

Note: English editions are cited where possible, but translations are sometimes modified.—Trans.

Foreword

1. Andrea Cavalletti, *La Città biopolitica: Mitologie della sicurezza* (Milan: Bruno Mondadori, 2005).
2. Andrea Cavalletti, *Class*, trans. Elisa Fiaccadori, ed. with an afterword by Alberto Toscano (New York: Seagull Press, 2019); orig. published as *Classe* (Turin: Bollati Boringhieri, 2009).
3. Andrea Cavalletti, *Suggestione: Potenza e limiti del fascino politico* (Turin: Bollati Boringhieri, 2011), 155; my translation.
4. Cavalletti is now at work on the Italian edition of Robert Klein's dissertation, *Ars et Technè dans la tradition de Platon à Giordano Bruno*. The French edition is being prepared by Jérémie Koering, who has recently edited Klein's other dissertation, *L'Esthétique de la technè: L'Art selon Aristote et les théories des arts au XVIe siècle*, preface by Henri Zerner (Paris: Institut National d'Histoire de l'Art, 2017).
5. See Sergio Bettini, *Tempo e forma: Scritti 1935–1977*, ed. Andrea Cavalletti, 2nd ed. (Macerata: Quodlibet, 2020); Sergio Bettini, *Venezia: Nascita di una città*, ed. Andrea Cavalletti (Vicenza: Neri Pozza, 2006).
6. Alberto Toscano, afterword to *Class*, 154.
7. Andrea Cavalletti, *L'Immemorabile: Il soggetto e i suoi doppi* (Vicenza: Neri Pozza, 2020).

Incipit

1. Alain, *Mars, ou la guerre jugée* (Paris: Gallimard, 1936), 228.
2. Antonio De Giuliani, *La vertigine attuale dell'Europa* (Vienna: Alberti, 1790), 6.
3. Antonio De Giuliani, "Saggio politico sopra le vicissitudini inevitabili delle società civili," in *La cagione riposta delle decadenze e delle rivoluzioni: Due opuscoli politici del 1791 e del 1793*, ed. Benedetto Croce (Bari: Laterza, 1934), 24–25.
4. Friedrich Nietzsche, *The Genealogy of Morals*, trans. Horace B. Samuel (New York: Boni and Liveright, 1918), viii–ix.

1. Vertigo Effect

1. Michel de Montaigne, *The Complete Essays*, trans. M. A. Screech (London: Penguin Books, 1991), 672.
2. Edgar Allan Poe, "The Pit and the Pendulum," in *Collected Works of Edgar Allan Poe*, vol. 2, *Tales and Sketches 1831–1842*, ed. Thomas Ollive Mabbott (Cambridge, MA: Belknap Press, 1978), 697.
3. Pierre Boileau and Thomas Narcejac, *Vertigo*, trans. Geoffrey Sainsbury (London: Bloomsbury, 1997), 6–7.
4. Boileau and Narcejac, 7.
5. Edgar Allan Poe, "Morella," in *Collected Works of Edgar Allan Poe*, 2:231–232.
6. Boileau and Narcejac, *Vertigo*, 8–10. [Note: First two ellipses in the original.]
7. Boileau and Narcejac, 23.
8. Boileau and Narcejac, 37.
9. Boileau and Narcejac, 42–46. [Note: Ellipses in the original.]
10. Boileau and Narcejac, 74.
11. François Truffaut, *Hitchcock*, with the collaboration of Helen G. Scott (New York: Simon and Schuster, 1984), 246.
12. Gustave Flaubert, *Sentimental Education*, trans. Robert Baldick (London: Penguin Books, 2004), 132.
13. Gilbert Cohen-Séat, *Essai sur les principes d'une philosophie du cinéma: Notions fondamentales et vocabulaire de filmologie* (Paris: PUF, 1958), 172.
14. Erasmus Darwin, *Zoonomia or the Laws of Organic Life* (London: Johnson, 1796), 1:247.
15. Julien Offray de La Mettrie, *Traité du Vertige, avec la description d'une catalepsie hysterique & une lettre à Monsieur Astruc, dans laquelle on répond à la critique qu'il a faite d'une dissertation de l'auteur sur les maladies vénérienne* (Rennes: Garnier, 1737), 38.
16. Darwin, *Zoonomia*, 244–249.
17. Lazare Rivière, *Praxis medica* (Paris: Olivier de Varennes, 1640), 95.
18. La Mettrie, *Traité*, 66.
19. Gottfried Wilhelm Leibniz, *Leibniz's Monadology: A New Translation and Guide*, ed. and trans. Lloyd Strickland (Edinburgh: Edinburgh University Press, 2014), 18.

20. Leibniz, 16.
21. Jean Douchet, *Alfred Hitchcock* (Paris: Éditions de l'Herne, 1967), 30.
22. La Mettrie, *Traité*, 37.
23. Gilles Deleuze, *The Movement-Image*, trans. Hugh Tomlinson and Barbara Habberjam (Minneapolis: University of Minneapolis Press, 1986), 205.
24. Georges Poulet, *Les métamorphoses du cercle* (Paris: Flammarion, 1979), 387.
25. Victor Ieronim Stoichita, *The Pygmalion Effect: From Ovid to Hitchcock*, trans. Alison Anderson (Chicago: Chicago University Press, 2008), 189.
26. Károly Kerényi, "Agalma, Eikon, Eidolon," trans. Ornella Maria Nobile, *Archivio di Filosofia*, nos. 1–2 (1962): 92.
27. Truffaut, *Hitchcock*, 244.
28. Truffaut, 122.
29. Montaigne, *Essais*, 671.
30. Klaus Heinrich, *Versuch über die Schwierigkeit nein zu sagen* (Frankfurt: Suhrkamp, 1964), 137.
31. Henri Bergson, "The Perception of Change," in *The Creative Mind*, trans. Mabelle L. Andison (New York: Philosophical Library, 1946), 179–181; "La conscience et la vie," in *L'énergie spirituelle*, ed. Frédéric Worms (Paris: F. Alcan, 1920), 36–37.
32. Søren Kierkegaard, *The Concept of Anxiety*, ed. and trans. Reidar Thomte in collaboration with Albert B. Anderson (Princeton, NJ: Princeton University Press, 1980), 61.
33. Karl Jaspers, *Philosophie*, Band 2, *Existenzerhellung* (Berlin: Springer, 1956), 235–236.
34. Martin Heidegger, *Die Grundbegriffe der Metaphysik: Welt—Endlichkeit—Einsamkeit. Wintersemester 1929–30*, in *Gesamtausgabe*, Band 29/30, ed. Friedrich-Wilhelm von Herrmann (Frankfurt: Klostermann, 1983), 30:267.
35. Ernest Charles Lasègue, "Vertige mental," in *Études médicales*, ed. Albert Blum (Paris: Asselin, 1884), 1:768.
36. Johann Nepomuk von Raimann, *Handbuch der speciellen medicinischen Pathologie und Therapie* (Vienna: Volke, 1826), 2:646.
37. Maurice Krishaber, *De la névropathie cérébro-cardiaque* (Paris: Masson, 1873), 60.
38. David Hume, *A Treatise of Human Nature*, ed. David Fate Norton and Mary J. Norton (Oxford: Oxford University Press, 2014), 1:100–101.
39. Immanuel Kant, *Critique of Pure Reason*, trans. Paul Guyer and Allen W. Wood (Cambridge: Cambridge University Press, 1998), §§29, 32.
40. Charles Renouvier, *Traité de psychologie rationnelle d'après les principes du criticisme* (1859), in *Essais de critique générale* (Paris: Colin, 1912), 2.1:253.
41. Renouvier, 261.
42. Renouvier, 295–296.
43. Alain, *Histoire de mes pensées* (Paris: Gallimard, 1936), 137.
44. Alain, *Éléments de philosophie* (Paris: Gallimard, 1969), 48.
45. Alain, *Éléments de philosophie*, 49.

46. Edgar Allan Poe, "The Imp of the Perverse," in *Collected Works of Edgar Allan Poe*, vol. 3, *Tales and Sketches 1843–1849*, ed. Thomas Ollive Mabbott (Cambridge, MA: Belknap Press, 1978), 1223.

47. Joseph Frank, *Praxeos medicae universae praecepta*, vol. 2, issue 1.2, *Continens doctrinam de morbis systematis nervorum in genere et de iis encephali in specie* (Lipsiae: Kuehniani, 1832), 577.

48. Ludwig Ernst Borowski, *Darstellung des Lebens und Charakters Immanuel Kants: Von Kant selbst genau revidirt und gerichtig* (Königsberg: Nicolovius 1804), 65.

49. Peter Fenves, *Late Kant: Towards Another Law of the Earth* (New York: Routledge, 2003), 185.

50. Marcus Herz, Letter to Immanuel Kant, February 27, 1786, in *Immanuel Kant, Gesammelte Schriften*, Band 10, *Briefwechsel*, 1. Teil, 1747–1788 (Berlin: de Gruyter, 1922), 431.

51. Marcus Herz, *Versuch über den Schwindel* (Berlin: Vossische Buchandlung, 1791), 49.

52. Jan Evangelista Purkinje, "Beiträge zur näheren Kenntnis des Schwindels aus heautognostischen Daten," in *Medicinische Jahrbücher des kaiserlich-königlichen Österreichischen Staates* (1820), 6.2:80.

53. Herz, *Versuch*, 43.

54. Salomon Maimon, *Autobiography of Solomon Maimon*, ed. Yitzhak Y. Melamed and Abraham P. Socher, trans. Paul Reitter (Princeton, NJ: Princeton University Press, 2018), 195.

55. Maimon, 231.

56. Johann Wolfgang von Goethe, *Faust: Parts I and II*, trans. Bayard Taylor (Mineola, NY: Dover Publications, 2018). Orig. *Faust, eine Tragödie*, ed. Ernst Beutler (Zürich: Artemis, 1950), ll. 1946–1947; *Urfaust*, ll. 377–378.

57. Jason M. Peck, "Vertigo Ergo Sum: Kant, his Jewish 'Students' and the Origins of Romanticism," *European Romantic Review* 26 (2015): 38.

58. Herz, *Versuch*, 174.

59. Purkinje, "Beiträge," 117.

60. Herz, *Versuch*, 87.

61. Hume, *Treatise*, bk. 1, pt. 2, sec. 3.

62. Immanuel Kant, *Anthropologie in pragmatischer Hinsicht* (Königsberg: F. Nicolovius, 1789), §32.

63. Martin L. Davies, "Gedanken zu einem ambivalenten Verhältnis: Marcus Herz und Immanuel Kant," in *Kant und die Berliner Aufklärung: Akten des IX. Internationalen Kant-Kongress*, vol. 5, *Sektionen XV–XVIII*, ed. Gerhardt Volker, Rolf-Peter Horstmann, and Ralph Schumacher (Berlin-New York: de Gruyter, 2001), 143 and footnote.

64. Johann-Christoph Hoffbauer, *Die Psychologie in ihren Hauptanwendungen auf die Rechtspflege, nach den allgemeinen Gesichtspunkten der Gesetzgebung, oder die sogenannte gerichtliche Arzneywissenschaft nach ihrem psychologischen Theile* (Halle: Schimmelpfennig, 1823), 342–343.

65. Alfred Maury, *Le sommeil et les rêves: Études psychologiques sur ces phénomènes et les divers états qui s'y rattachent; suivies de Recherches sur le développement de l'instinct et de l'intelligence dans leurs rapports avec le phénomène du sommeil* (Paris: Didier, 1865), 422.

66. Jean-Étienne-Dominique Esquirol, *Des maladies mentales considérées sous les rapports médical, hygiénique et médico-légal* (Paris: Baillière, 1838), 727.

67. Simone Weil, *Oppression and Liberty*, trans. Arthur Wills and John Petrie (Amherst: University of Massachusetts Press, 1973), 124.

68. Weil, 108.

69. Roger Caillois, *La communion des forts: Études de sociologie contemporaine* (Mexico: Ediciones Quetzal, 1943), 53–54.

70. Salvatore Satta, *De profundis* (Milan: Adelphi, 1980), 100.

71. Charles Baudelaire, "On the Essence of Laughter," in *The Painter of Modern Life and Other Essays*, trans. and ed. Jonathan Mayne (London: Phaidon, 1964), 162.

72. Karl Marx, *Der achtzehnte Brumaire des Louis Bonaparte*, in *Werke*, vol. 8, *August 1851 bis März 1853* (Berlin: Dietz, 1960), 293.

73. Karl Marx, *Das Kapital: Kritik der politischen Ökonomie*, in *Werke*, Band 23–25 (Berlin: Dietz, 1948–1949).

74. Charles Coquelin and Gilbert-Urbain Guillaumin, eds., *Dictionnaire de l'économie politique* (Paris: Guillaumin, 1854), 2:636–637.

75. Max Friedmann, *Über Wahnideen im Völkerleben* (Wiesbaden: Bergmann, 1901), 253.

76. Christoph Hinteregger, *Der Judenschwindel* (Vienna: Wiener Volksbuchhandlung, 1923), 23.

77. Johann von Leers, *14 Jahre Judenrepublik: Die Geschichte eines Rassenkampfes* (Berlin: NS Druck und Verlag, 1933), 15.

78. Gustave Flaubert, *Le projet du "Sottisier": Le second volume de "Bouvard et Pécuchet"; Reconstruction conjecturale de la "copie" des deux bonshommes d'après le dossier de Rouen*, ed. Alberto Cento and Lea Caminiti Pennarola (Naples: Liguori, 1981), 328.

79. Roger Dragonetti, "Deux bâtons à la brèche du mur," in *Bouvard et Pécuchet centenaires*, ed. Dominique-Gilbert Laporte (Paris: Éditions du Seuil, 1981), 179–180.

80. Bernardino Ramazzini, *De morbis artificium diatriba* (Modena: Capponi, 1700), 134.

81. Étienne Trastour, *Des vertiges de cause nerveuse, ou vertiges nerveux* (Nantes: Velinet, 1858), 5.

82. Caillois, *La communion des forts*, 60.

83. German E. Berrios, *The History of Mental Symptoms: Descriptive Psychopathology Since the Nineteenth Century* (Cambridge: Cambridge University Press, 1996), 283n61.

84. Johann Jakob Wepfer, *Observationes medico-practicae de affectibus capitis internis et externis*, ed. Bernhard Wepfer and Georg Michael Wepfer (Scaphusii: Joh. Adami Ziegleri, 1727), 285.

85. Marcus Elieser Bloch, *Medizinische Bemerkungen: Nebst einer Abhandlung vom Pyrmonter-Augenbrunnen* (Berlin: Himburg, 1774), 105.

86. William Porterfield, *A Treatise on the Eye, the Manner and Phaenomena of Vision* (London-Edinburgh: Miller-Hamilton and Balfour, 1759), 2:425–426.

87. Nicholas J. Wade, *Perception and Illusion: Historical Perspectives* (New York: Springer, 2005), 92.

88. Jules Falret, *De l'état mental des épileptiques* (Paris: Asselin, 1861), 6.

89. Armand Trousseau, *Clinique médicale de l'Hôtel-Dieu de Paris* (Paris: Baillière et fils, 1868), 2:107.

90. Frank, *Praxeos medicae universae praecepta*, 389n73.

91. Georges-Gabriel Halternhoff, "Faits pour servir à l'histoire du vertige paralysant (maladie de Gerlier)," in *Progrès Médical* (1887), 15:515. Paul-Louis Ladame, "Quelques mots sur l'étiologie du vertige paralysant," *Revue Médicale de la Suisse Romande* 11, no. 6 (1891): 5.

92. Félix Gerlier, "Une épidémie de vertige paralysant: Nouvelle névrose de la motilité," *Revue Médicale de la Suisse Romande* 7 (1887): 5.

93. Max Simon, *Du vertige nerveux et de son traitement: Mémoire récompensé par l'Académie Impériale de Médecine* (Paris: Baillière et fils, 1858), 34.

94. Simon, 138.

95. Simon, 16.

96. Simon, 138.

97. Paul-Max Simon, *Le monde des rêves* (Paris: Baillière et fils, 1882), 246–247.

98. Maury, *Le sommeil et les rêves*, 295.

99. Edmond Weill, *Des vertiges* (Paris: Baillière et fils, 1886), 2–3.

100. Williams Gowers, *The Border-Land of Epilepsy: Faints, Vagal Attacks, Vertigo, Migraine, Sleep Symptoms, and their Treatment* (London: Churchill, 1907), 59–65.

101. Jean Epstein, *Jean Epstein: Critical Essays and New Translations*, ed. Sarah Keller and Jason N. Paul (Amsterdam: Amsterdam University Press, 2012), 342.

102. Jean Epstein, *Esprit de cinéma* (Genève-Paris: Jeheber, 1955), 169.

103. Jean Epstein, "The Delirium of a Machine," in *Critical Essays*, 372–380.

104. Jacques Rivette, "De l'abjection," *Cahiers du Cinéma*, no. 120 (1961): 54.

105. Luc Moullet, "Sam Fuller: In Marlowe's Footsteps," in *Cahiers du Cinéma: The 1950s—Neo-Realism, Hollywood, New Wave*, ed. Jim Hillier (Cambridge, MA: Harvard University Press, 1985), 148.

106. Jean Domarchi, Jacques Doniol-Valcroze, Jean-Luc Godard, Pierre Kast, Jacques Rivette, Eric Rohmer, "Hiroshima, notre amour," in Hillier, *Cahiers du Cinéma: The 1950s*, 62.

107. Serge Daney, "Le travelling de Kapo," in *Persévérance: Entretien avec Serge Toubiana* (Paris: POL, 1994), 16.

108. Nicolas-Philibert Adelon, *Dictionnaire de médecine, ou répertoire général des sciences médicales* (Paris: Béchet, 1836), 9:298.

109. Adelon, 9:298.

110. Simon, *Du vertige nerveux*, 48; Esquirol, *Des maladies mentales*, 1:156; 2:466.
111. Richard Hunter and Ida Macalpine, eds. *Three Hundred Years of Psychiatry 1535–1860: A History Presented in Selected English Texts* (Hartsdale, NY: Carlisle, 1982), 595.
112. Elvira Naselli, "Nel laboratorio dove si cura il capogiro," *La Repubblica*, November 2, 2010, 31.
113. Nicolas J. Wade and Benjamin W. Tatler, *The Moving Tablet of the Eye: The Origins of Modern Eye Movement Research* (Oxford: Oxford University Press, 2005), 110–113.
114. Eric Rohmer and Claude Chabrol, *Hitchcock: The First Forty-Four Films*, trans. Stanley Hochman (New York: F. Ungar, 1979), 151.
115. William Rothman, *Hitchcock: The Murderous Gaze* (Cambridge, MA: Cambridge University Press, 1984), 297.
116. Bernard Berenson, *Aesthetics and History in the Visual Arts* (New York: Pantheon, 1948), 73.
117. Jean Epstein, *Critical Essays*, 273.
118. Sergei M. Eisenstein, *Immoral Memories: An Autobiography by Sergei M. Eisenstein*, trans. Herbert Marshall (Boston, MA: Houghton Mifflin Company, 1983), 66.
119. Maurice Merleau-Ponty, "The Film and the New Psychology," in *Sense and Non-Sense*, trans. Hubert L. Dreyfus and Patricia Allen Dreyfus (Evanston, IL: Northwestern University Press, 1964), 53.
120. Sigmund Freud, "Fußnote," in Jean-Martin Charcot, *Poliklinische Vorträge*, vol. 1, *Schuljahr 1887–1888* (Leipzig-Wien: Deuticke, 1892), 157.
121. Michel Foucault, "Introduction," in Ludwig Binswanger, *Le rêve et l'existence*, translated into French by Jacqueline Verdeaux (Paris: Desclée de Bruower, 1954), 98.
122. Sigmund Freud and Joseph Breuer, *Studies on Hysteria*, trans. and ed. James Strachey (New York: Basic Books, 1957), 129.
123. Freud and Breuer, 112–114n2.
124. Sigmund Freud, "The Psychogenesis of a Case of Homosexuality in a Woman," in *The Standard Edition of the Complete Psychological Works of Sigmund Freud*, trans. and ed. James Strachey in collaboration with Anna Freud (London: Hogarth Press, 1953–1974), 18:162.
125. Freud, 213.
126. Sigmund Freud, *Inhibitions, Symptoms and Anxiety*, in *The Standard Edition of the Complete Psychological Works of Sigmund Freud*, 20:168n1.
127. Sigmund Freud, *The Psychopathology of Everyday Life*, in *The Standard Edition of the Complete Psychological Works of Sigmund Freud*, 6:3.
128. Freud, 6:66.
129. Freud, 6:9–10.
130. Foucault, "Introduction," 99.
131. Freud, "The Psychogenesis of a Case of Homosexuality in a Woman," 89.
132. Sebastiano Timpanaro, *Il lapsus freudiano: Psicoanalisi e critica testuale*, ed. Fabio Stok (Turin: Bollati Boringhieri, 2002), 19–29.

133. Jacques Lacan, *Speech and Language in Psychoanalysis*, trans. Anthony Wilden (Baltimore, MD: Johns Hopkins University Press, 1984), 32.

134. Jean-Claude Milner, "De la linguistique à la linguisterie," in *Lacan: L'écrit, l'image* (Paris: Flammarion, 2000), 24.

135. Lacan, *Speech and Language*, 31–32.

136. Sándor Ferenczi, "Sensations of Giddiness at the End of the Psycho-Analytic Session," in *Further Contributions to the Theory and Technique of Psychoanalysis*, ed. John Rickman, trans. Jane Isabel Suttie (New York: Boni and Liveright, 1927), 240.

137. Foucault, "Introduction," 22.

138. Walter Benjamin, "Aphorismen" in *Gesammelte Schriften*, ed. Rolf Tiedemann and Hermann Schweppenhäuser (Frankfurt: Suhrkamp, 1977), 2.2:199–200.

2. We Are Not Here

1. *Welt, Ich und Zeit nach unveröffenlichten Manuscripten Edmund Husserls*, 1955, which Klein occasionally reads in Enrico Filippini's version, conceived and with an introduction by Enzo Paci.

2. Edmund Husserl, *The Paris Lectures*, trans. Peter Koestenbaum (The Hague: M. Nijhoff, 1964), 29.

3. Edmund Husserl, *First Philosophy: Lectures 1923/1924*, trans. Sebastian Luft and Thane M. Naberhaus (Dordrecht: Springer, 2019), 292.

4. Edmund Husserl, *Cartesian Meditations: An Introduction to Phenomenology*, trans. Dorion Cairns (The Hague: Martinus Nijhoff Publishers, 1982), 67.

5. Jean Wahl, *Husserl* (Paris: Centre de Documentation Universitaire, 1958), 2:45.

6. Wilhelm Szilasi, *Einführung in die Phänomenologie Edmund Husserls* (Tübingen: Niemeyer, 1959), 83.

7. Edmund Husserl, *Ideas Pertaining to a Pure Phenomenology and to a Phenomenological Philosophy*, Second Book: *Studies in the Phenomenology of Constitution*, trans. Richard Rojcewicz and André Schuwer (Dordrecht: Kluwer Academic Publishers, 1989), 119.

8. Frédéric de Towarnicki, *À la rencontre de Heidegger: Souvenirs d'un messager de la Forêt- Noire* (Paris: Gallimard, 1993), 36.

9. Martin Heidegger, *Being and Time*, trans. Joan Stambaugh (Albany: State University of New York Press, 1996), §60, 276.

10. Martin Heidegger, *The Metaphysical Foundations of Logic*, trans. Michael Heim (Bloomington: Indiana University Press, 1984), 191.

11. Heidegger, *Metaphysical Foundations*, 192.

12. Jean Wahl, *Études Kiekegaardiennes* (Paris: Aubier, 1967).

13. Emmanuel Levinas, *Totality and Infinity: An Essay on Exteriority*, trans. Alphonso Lingis (Pittsburgh, PA: Duquesne University Press, 1969), 160.

14. Levinas, 143.

15. Emmanuel Levinas, *Otherwise Than Being or Beyond Essence*, trans. Alphonso Lingis (Dordrecht: Kluwer Academic Publishers, 1981), 164.

16. Emmanuel Levinas, *Existence and Existents*, trans. Alphonso Lingis (Pittsburgh, PA: Duquesne University Press, 2001), 1.

17. Robert Klein, *L'esthétique de la technè: L'art selon Aristote et les théories des arts visuels au XVIe siècle*, ed. Jérémie Joering (Paris: Institut National d'Histoire de l'Art, 2017), 134.

18. Robert Klein, "Le thème du fou dans l'ironie humaniste," in *La forme et l'intelligible. Écrits sur la Renaissance et l'arte moderne*, ed. André Chastel (Paris: Gallimard, 1970), 449. Edmund Husserl, *The Crisis of European Sciences and Transcendental Phenomenology*, trans. David Carr (Evanston, IL: Northwestern University Press, 1970), §26, 98.

19. Robert Klein, "Les limites de la morale transcendantale" (in collaboration with Ngô Tieng Hiên), in *La forme et l'intelligible: Écrits sur la Renaissance et l'arte moderne*, ed. André Chastel (Paris: Gallimard, 1970), 485.

20. Paul Ricoeur, *Soi-même comme un autre* (Paris: Éditions du Seuil, 1990), 78.

21. Robert Klein, "Le rire," in *L'umanesimo e la follia* (Rome: Abete, 1971), 195.

22. Reflection from December 31, 1931, in Edmund Husserl, *Zur Phänomenologie der Intersubjektivität: Texte aus dem Nachlass*, 2. Teil, in *Husserliana*, vol. 14, ed. Iso Kern (The Hague: Nijhoff, 1973), 369.

23. Robert Klein, "L'art et l'attention au technique," in *La forme et l'intelligible: Écrits sur la Renaissance et l'arte moderne*, ed. André Chastel (Paris: Gallimard, 1970), 390.

24. Robert Klein, "Thought, Confession, Fiction: On *A Season in Hell*," in *Form and Meaning: Essays on Renaissance and Modern Art*, trans. Madeline Jay and Leon Wieseltier (New York: Viking Press, 1979).

25. Klein, 204–207.

26. Robert Klein, "Nature et maniement du rire chez Georges Bataille," unpublished typescript and manuscript (BINHA 090, 079, 902, 07) and "Le rire."

27. Quoted in Gerd Brand, *Welt, Ich und Zeit nach unveröffenlichten Manuscripten Edmund Husserls* (The Hague: Nijhoff, 1955), 220–221.

28. Gerd Brand, *Mondo, io e tempo nei manoscritti inediti di Husserl*, introduction by Enzo Paci (Milan: Bompiani, 1960), 23.

29. Klein, "Les limites de la morale transcendantale," 474.

30. Robert Klein, "Appropriation et alienation," in *La forme et l'intelligible: Écrits sur la Renaissance et l'art moderne*, ed. André Chastel (Paris: Gallimard, 1970), 469n2. Brand, *Welt, Ich und Zeit*, 220–221.

31. Klein, "Appropriation et aliénation," 466.

32. Klein, 466.

33. Klein, 463.

34. Aristotle, *Metaphysics*, bk. 4, trans. Hugh Tredennick (Cambridge, MA: Harvard University Press, 1933), 1022b, 7–10.

35. Weill, *Des vertiges*, 266.

36. Henri-Paul-Hyacinthe Wallon, *La vie mentale*, ed. Émile Jalley (Paris: Éditions Sociales, 1982), 213.

37. Klein, "Appropriation et aliénation," 466n3.

38. Robert Klein, *L'esthétique de la technè*, 134.

39. François Truffaut, *Hitchcock*, with the collaboration of Helen G. Scott (New York: Simon and Schuster, 1984), 246.

40. Gaston Bachelard, *Air and Dreams*, trans. Edith Farell and Frederick Farell (Dallas, TX: Dallas Institute Publications, 1988), 111.

41. Caillois, *La communion des forts*, 61.

42. Caillois, 95.

43. Gerardus Van der Leeuw, *Phänomenologie der Religion* (Tübingen: Mohr, 1956), 222.

44. Charles Baudelaire, "On the Essence of Laughter," in *The Painter of Modern Life and Other Essays*, trans. and ed. by Jonathan Mayne (London: Phaidon, 1964), 159–162.

45. Pierre Boileau and Thomas Narcejac, *Vertigo*, trans. Geoffrey Sainsbury (London: Bloomsbury, 1997), 116.

46. Boileau and Narcejac, 131.

47. Georges Rodenbach, *Bruges-la-Morte: A novel*, trans. Philip Mosley (Paisley, Scotland: Wilfion Books, 1986), 58.

48. Jean-Louis Schefer, "Vertigo, vert tilleul," *Trafic* 15 (1995): 51–56.

49. Boileau and Narcejac, *Vertigo*, 26.

50. Boileau and Narcejac, 33.

51. Boileau and Narcejac, 34.

52. Henri Maldiney, *Regard, parole, espace* (Lausanne: L'Age d'Homme, 1973), 74.

53. Boileau and Narcejac, *Vertigo*, 34.

54. Boileau and Narcejac, 46. [Note: Ellipses in the original.]

55. Maurice Merleau-Ponty, *The Prose of the World*, trans. John O'Neill (Evanston, IL: Northwestern University Press, 1973), 134.

56. Merleau-Ponty, 134.

57. Boileau and Narcejac, *Vertigo*, 58. [Note: The last two ellipses in the original.]

58. Boileau and Narcejac, 75–76.

59. François Truffaut, *Hitchcock*, with the collaboration of Helen G. Scott (New York: Simon and Schuster, 1984), 247.

60. Boileau and Narcejac, *Vertigo*, 15.

61. Boileau and Narcejac, 15.

62. Klein, "Les limites de la moral transcendatale," 474–475.

63. Gilbert Cohen-Séat, *Essai sur les principes d'une philosophie du cinema: Notions fondamentales et vocabulaire de filmologie* (Paris: PUF, 1958), 156.

64. Ernest Charles Lasègue, "Vertige mental," in *Études médicales*, ed. Albert Blum (Paris: Asselin, 1884), 1:781.

65. Serge Daney, "Vertigo: Sueurs froides," in *Ciné journal*, vol. 2, 1983–1986 (Paris: Cahiers du cinéma, 1998), 95.

66. Rodenbach, *Bruges-la-Morte*, 46.
67. Klein, "Le rire," 195.
68. Klein, "L'art et l'attention au technique," 390.
69. Bin Kimura, "Temporalité de la schizophrénie," translated into French by Joël Bouderlique, in Bin Kimura, *Écrits de psychopathologie phénoménologique* (Paris: PUF, 1992), 65.
70. Klein, "Appropriation et aliénation," 467.
71. Robert Klein, "Essai sur la responsabilité" (post-1953), unpublished typescript and manuscript (BINHA, 090, 081 bis).
72. Emmanuel Levinas, *De l'évasion*, ed. Jacques Rolland (Montpellier: Morgana, 1982), 33.
73. Klein, "Essai sur la responsabilité," 21.
74. Klein, 20.
75. Klein, 22.
76. Jean-Paul Sartre, *Being and Nothingness: An Essay on Phenomenological Ontology*, trans. Hazel E. Barnes (New York: Philosophical Library, 1956), 270.
77. Sartre, 270.
78. Klein, "Essai sur la responsabilité," 23.
79. Klein, 23.
80. Klein, "Appropriation et aliénation," 467.
81. Husserl, *Paris Lectures*, 15.
82. Sartre, *Being and Nothingness*, 260.
83. Sartre, 261.
84. Sartre, 291.
85. Sartre, 260.
86. Husserl, *Cartesian Meditations*, §§53–54.
87. Husserl, §43, 91.
88. Edmund Husserl, *Méditations cartésiennes: Introduction à la phénoménologie*, trans. Gabrielle Peiffer and Emmanuel Levinas (Paris: Colin, 1931), 76.
89. Husserl, *Cartesian Meditations*, §50.
90. Husserl, §53, 116.
91. Husserl, §53.
92. Husserl, §54, 117–118.
93. Husserl, §53.
94. Husserl, §54.
95. Husserl, §54, 118–119.
96. Husserl, §56, 129.
97. Ludwig Feuerbach, *Principles of the Philosophy of the Future*, trans. Manfred H. Vogel (Indianapolis: Hackett, 1986), 61.
98. Maurice Merleau-Ponty, "On the Phenomenology of Language," in *Phenomenology, Language and Sociology: Selected Essays of Maurice Merleau-Ponty*, ed. John O'Neill (London: Heinemann, 1974), 90–91.
99. Husserl, *Cartesian Meditations*, §§43, 50, 51.

100. Merleau-Ponty, "On the Phenomenology of Language," 91.
101. Maurice Merleau-Ponty, *The Structure of Behavior*, trans. Alden L. Fisher (Boston, MA: Beacon Press, 1963), 224.
102. Maurice Merleau-Ponty, *Phenomenology of Perception*, trans. Donald A. Landes (New York: Routledge, 2012), 433.
103. Merleau-Ponty, *Prose of the World*, 135.
104. Merleau-Ponty, "On the Phenomenology of Language," 94.
105. Merleau-Ponty, *Phenomenology of Perception*, 353.
106. Merleau-Ponty, 358.
107. Merleau-Ponty, *Structure of Behavior*, 222.
108. Merleau-Ponty, *Phenomenology of Perception*, 353.
109. Merleau-Ponty, "On the Phenomenology of Language," 91.
110. Merleau-Ponty, *Structure of Behavior*, 222.
111. Klein, "Appropriation et aliénation," 469.
112. Klein, 466–469; Brand *Welt, Ich und Zeit*, 64–65.
113. Husserl, *Cartesian Meditations*, §32, 66.
114. Vladimir Jankélévitch, *L'innocence et la méchanceté. Traité des vertus* (Paris: Flammarion, 1986), 3:230.
115. Paul Ricoeur, *Husserl: An Analysis of His Phenomenology*, trans. Edward G. Ballard and Lester E. Embree (Evanston, IL: Northwestern University Press, 1967), 55.
116. Klein, "Appropriation et aliénation," 466.
117. Klein, *L'esthétique de la technè*, 134.
118. Maurice Merleau-Ponty, "The Film and the New Psychology," in *Sense and Non-Sense*, trans. Hubert L. Dreyfus and Patricia Allen Dreyfus (Evanston, IL: Northwestern University Press, 1964), 59.
119. Merleau-Ponty, *Phenomenology of Perception*.
120. Blaise Pascal, *Pensées*, trans. A. J. Krailsheimer (London: Penguin Books, 1995), 10.
121. Claude Pichois and Jean Ziegler, *Baudelaire*, trans. Graham Robb (London: H. Hamilton, 1989), 341.
122. Ernest Charles Lasègue, "De Stahl, et sa doctrine médicale," MD diss., February 25, 1846 (Paris: Rignoux, 1846), 57.
123. Ernest Charles Lasègue, "L'école psychique allemande" (1845), in *Études médicales*, vol. 1, ed. Albert Blum (Paris: Asselin, 1884), 59.
124. Ernest Charles Lasègue, "Questions de thérapeutique mentale," in *Études médicales*, 1:599.
125. Lasègue, "Vertige mental," 765.
126. Ernest Charles Lasègue, "Des Vertiges, leçon recueillie et redigée par le Dr. Frémy," in *Études médicales*, 1:776.
127. Lasègue, "Vertige mental," 1:771.
128. Lasègue, 1:772.
129. Lasègue, "Questions de thérapeutique mentale," 1:610.
130. Husserl, *First Philosophy*, 169.

131. Husserl, *Cartesian Meditations*, §44, 94.
132. Giovanni Piana, *Esistenza e storia negli inediti di Husserl* (Milan: Lampugnani Nigri, 1965), 32n7.
133. Husserl, *Cartesian Meditations*, §44, 94.
134. Enzo Melandri, *Logica e esperienza in Husserl* (Bologna: Il Mulino), 207.
135. Jacques Derrida, "Violence and Metaphysics," in *Writing and Difference*, trans. Alan Bass (Chicago: University of Chicago Press, 1978), 125.
136. Husserl, *Cartesian Meditations*, §52, 115.
137. Edith Stein, *Letters to Roman Ingarden: Self-Portrait in Letters*, trans. Hugh Candler Hunt (Washington, DC: ICS Publications, 2014), 55.
138. Edith Stein, *On the Problem of Empathy*, trans. Waltraut Stein (Washington, DC: ICS Publications, 1989), 8.
139. Stein, 11.
140. Edmund Husserl, *Zur Phänomenologie der Intersubjektivität: Texte aus dem Nachlass, Teil 1, 1905–1920*, in *Husserliana*, vol. 13, ed. Iso Kern (The Hague: Nijhoff, 1973), 319–320.
141. Husserl, *Crisis of the European Sciences*, 185.
142. Husserl, *Cartesian Meditations*, §52, 115.
143. Hans-Georg Gadamer, *Philosophische Lehrjahre: Eine Ruckschau* (Frankfurt: Klostermann, 1977), 27.
144. Edmund Husserl, *Phantasy, Image Consciousness, and Memory*, trans. John B. Brough (Dordrecht: Springer, 2005), 497–498.
145. Husserl, 43–44.
146. Marc Richir, *Phénoménologie en esquisses: Nouvelles fondations* (Grenoble: Millon, 2000), 68.
147. Edmund Husserl, *Logical Investigations*, trans. J. N. Findlay (London: Routledge and K. Paul, 1970), Investigation 5, §27.
148. Husserl, 609–611.
149. Edmund Husserl, *Experience and Judgment: Investigations in a Genealogy of Logic*, trans. James S. Churchill and Karl Ameriks (Evanston, IL: Northwestern University Press, 1973), 95.
150. Husserl, 96.
151. Husserl, 229.
152. Husserl, 217.
153. Husserl, *Phantasy, Image Consciousness, and Memory*, 44.
154. Hans Blumenberg, *Höhlenausgänge* (Frankfurt: Suhrkamp, 1989), 549.
155. Husserl, *Cartesian Meditations*, §18.
156. Brand, *Welt, Ich und Zeit*, 134–135.
157. Emmanuel Levinas, *En découvrant l'existence avec Husserl et Heidegger* (Paris: Vrin, 2006), 44.
158. Edmund Husserl, *Zur Phänomenologie der Intersubjektivität: Texte aus dem Nachlass, Teil 3, 1929–1935*, in *Husserliana*, vol. 15, ed. Iso Kern (The Hague: Nijhoff, 1973), 254.

159. Husserl, *Cartesian Meditations*, §44, 119.
160. Emmanuel Levinas, *Quelques réflexions sur la philosophie de l'hitlérisme*, with an essay by Miguel Abensour (Paris: Rivages, 1997), 31.
161. Husserl, *Cartesian Meditations*, §50, 131.
162. Ricoeur, *Husserl*, 248.
163. Richir, *Phénoménologie en esquisses*, 144.
164. Husserl, *Texte aus dem Nachlass*, 1:311.
165. Richir, *Phénoménologie en esquisses*, 154.
166. Husserl, *Texte aus dem Nachlass*, 1:311–312.
167. Roman Ingarden, "Kritische Bemerkungen von Professor Dr. Roman Ingarden, Krakau," in *Cartesianische Meditationen und Pariser Vorträge*, in *Husserliana*, vol. 1, ed. Stephan Strasser (The Hague: Nijhoff, 1973), 213.
168. Jan Patočka, *Phänomenologische Schriften*, vol. 2, *Die Bewegung der menschlichen Existenz*, ed. Klaus Nellen, Jiri Nemen, and Ilja Srubar (Stuttgart: Klett-Cotta, 1991), 280.
169. Didier Franck, *Chair et corps: Sur la phénoménologie de Husserl* (Paris: Éditions de Minuit, 1981), 108.
170. Husserl, *Texte aus dem Nachlass*, 1:256.
171. Brand, *Welt, Ich und Zeit*.
172. Husserl, *Cartesian Meditations*, §58, 136.
173. Ricoeur, *Husserl*, 238.
174. Husserl, *Cartesian Meditations*, §44, 94.
175. Klein, "Appropriation et aliénation," 467.
176. Husserl, *Cartesian Meditations*, 128.
177. Husserl, 129–130.
178. Husserl, *Texte aus dem Nachlass*, 3:77.
179. Husserl, *Cartesian Meditations*, §55, 128.
180. Eugen Fink, *VI Cartesianische Meditation: Texte aus dem Nachlass Eugen Finks (1932) mit Ammerkungen und Beilagen aus dem Nachlass Edmund Husserls*, in *Husserliana: Dokumente*, vol. 2.2, ed. Guy Van Kerckhoven (Dordrecht: Kluwer, 1988), 254.
181. Fink, 260.
182. Heidegger, *Being and Time*, §26, 113.
183. Fink, *VI Cartesianische Meditation*, 264.
184. Sartre, *Being and Nothingness*, 392.
185. Husserl, *Cartesian Meditations*, 94.
186. Theodor W. Adorno, *Against Epistemology: A Metacritique. Studies in Husserl and the Phenomenological Antinomies*, trans. Willis Domingo (Cambridge, MA: MIT Press, 1983), 230.
187. Jacques Derrida, *Voice and Phenomenon: Introduction to the Problem of the Sign in Husserl's Phenomenology*, trans. Leonard Lawlor (Evanston, IL: Northwestern University Press, 2011), 78–79.

188. Maurice Merleau-Ponty, *The Visible and the Invisible*, ed. Claude Lefort, trans. Alphonso Lingis (Evanston, IL: Northwestern University Press, 1968), 138.
189. Merleau-Ponty, 148.
190. Fink, *VI Cartesianische Meditation*, 266.
191. Fink, 267.
192. Helmut Plessner, *Grenzen der Gemeinschaft: Eine Kritik des sozialen Radikalismus*, in *Gesammelte Schriften*, Band 5, *Macht und menschliche Natur*, ed. Günther Dux, Odo Marquard, and Elisabeth Ströke (Frankfurt: Suhrkamp, 1981), 76.

3. Habit, Mask

1. Eric Rohmer, "Alfred Hitchcock's Vertigo," in *The Taste for Beauty*, trans. Carol Volk (Cambridge: Cambridge University Press, 1989), 136.
2. Georges Rodenbach, *Bruges-la-Morte: A novel*, trans. Philip Mosley (Chester Springs, PA: Dufour Editions, 1986), 2.
3. Rodenbach, 11–19.
4. Walter Benjamin, "Johann Jakob Bachofen," in *Selected Writings*, trans. Edmund Jephcott et al. (Cambridge, MA: Belknap Press, 2002), 3:19.
5. Gaston Bachelard, *L'eau et les rêves: Essai sur l'imagination de la matière* (Paris: Corti, 1942), 121.
6. Rodenbach, *Bruges-la-Morte*, 47.
7. Robert Louis Stevenson, *Weir of Hermiston*, in *The New Edinburgh Edition of the Collected Works of Robert Louis Stevenson*, ed. Gillian Hughes (Edinburgh: Edinburgh University Press, 1995), 70.
8. Pierre Boileau and Thomas Narcejac, *Vertigo*, trans. Geoffrey Sainsbury (London: Bloomsbury, 1997), 169. [Note: Ellipses in brackets indicate omission.]
9. Rodenbach, *Bruges-la-Morte*, 76.
10. Rodenbach, 76.
11. Rodenbach, 76.
12. Boileau and Narcejac, *Vertigo*, 169.
13. Jean-Paul Sartre, *The Transcendence of the Ego*, trans. Forrest Williams and Robert Kirkpatrick (New York: Hill and Wang, 1957), 40–53.
14. Martin Heidegger, Letter to Edmund Husserl, October 22, 1927, in *Edmund Husserl: Phänomenologische Psychologie; Vorlesungen Sommersemester 1925*, in *Husserliana*, vol. 9, ed. Walter Biemel (The Hague: Nijhoff, 1968), 602.
15. Roman Ingarden, "Kritische Bemerkungen von Professor Dr. Roman Ingarden, Krakau," in *Cartesianische Meditationen und Pariser Vorträge*, in *Husserliana*, vol. 1, ed. Stephan Strasser (The Hague: Nijhoff, 1973), 213.
16. Ingarden, 214.
17. Ingarden, 213.
18. Husserl, *Cartesian Meditations: An Introduction to Phenomenology*, trans. Dorion Cairns (The Hague: Martinus Nijhoff Publishers, 1982), §15, 35.

19. Edmund Husserl, *First Philosophy: Lectures 1923/1924*, trans. Sebastian Luft and Thane M. Naberhaus (Dordrecht: Springer, 2019), 311.

20. Charles Féré, *La pathologie des émotions: Études physiologiques et cliniques* (Paris: Alcan, 1892), 156.

21. Georges Poulet, "Bergson: Le thème de la vision panoramique des mourants et la juxtaposition," in *L'espace proustien* (Paris: Gallimard, 1982), 112–113.

22. Arthur Schnitzler, *Beatrice and her son*, trans. Shaun Whiteside (New York: Penguin, 1999), 41.

23. Henri Bergson, "The Perception of Change," in *The Creative Mind*, trans. Mabelle L. Andison (New York: Philosophical Library, 1946), 177.

24. Bergson, 170.

25. Henri Bergson, *Matière et mémoire: Essai sur la relation du corps à l'esprit*, ed. Frédéric Worms (Paris: PUF, 2012), 126.

26. Henri Bergson, *Creative Evolution*, trans. Arthur Mitchell (Mineola, NY: Dover, 1998), 346–347.

27. Gilles Deleuze, *The Movement-Image*, trans. Hugh Tomlinson and Barbara Habberjam (Minneapolis: University of Minnesota Press, 1986), 204.

28. Gilles Deleuze, *Time-Image*, trans. Hugh Tomlinson and Robert Galeta (London: Athlone, 1989), 82.

29. Melandri, *Logica e esperienza in Husserl* (Bologna: Il Mulino, 1960), 192.

30. Edmund Husserl, *Ideas Pertaining to a Pure Phenomenology and to a Phenomenological Philosophy*, Second Book: *Studies in the Phenomenology of Constitution*, trans. Richard Rojcewicz and André Schuwer (Dordrecht: Kluwer Academic Publishers, 1989), 117.

31. Sartre, *Transcendence of the Ego*, 82.

32. Sartre, 53.

33. Sartre, 48.

34. Jean-Paul Sartre, *Being and Nothingness: An Essay on Phenomenological Ontology*, trans. Hazel E. Barnes (New York: Philosophical Library, 1956), 103.

35. Sartre, 103.

36. Jean-Paul Sartre, *L'imaginaire: Psychologie phénoménologique de l'imagination*, ed. Arlette Elkaïm-Sartre (Paris: Gallimard, 1986), 195.

37. Husserl, *Cartesian Meditations*, §56, 128.

38. Husserl, §60, 139.

39. Charles Renouvier, *Nouvelle monadologie* (Paris: Colin, 1899), 3.

40. Charles Renouvier, *Traité de psychologie rationnelle d'après les principes du criticisme* (1859), in *Essais de critique générale* (Paris: Colin, 1912), 2.1:253.

41. Renouvier, 261–263.

42. Jan Evangelista Purkinje, "Beiträge zur näheren Kenntnis des Schwindels aus heautognostischen Daten," *Medicinische Jahrbücher des kaiserlich-königlichen Österreichischen Staates* 6, no. 2 (1820): 33.

43. Jean Wahl, *La philosophie de Heidegger* (Paris: Centre de Documentation Universitaire, 1952), 1:94n1.

44. Melandri, *Logica e esperienza*, 142.
45. Derrida, *Voice and Phenomenon: Introduction to the Problem of the Sign in Husserl's Phenomenology*, trans. Leonard Lawlor (Evanston, IL: Northwestern University Press, 2011), 71.
46. Derrida, 46.
47. Melandri, *Logica e esperienza*, 197.
48. Derrida, *Voice and Phenomenon*, 82–83.
49. Ernesto De Martino, *Morte e pianto rituale: Dal lamento pagano al pianto di Maria* (Turin: Bollati Boringhieri, 2000), 35.
50. Alfred Jarry, *Days and Nights: Novel of a Deserter*, trans. Alexis Lykiard (London: Atlas, 1989), 58.
51. Giovanni Pascoli, "La vertigine," in "Nuovi poemetti," in *Poesie*, vol. 2, *Primi poemetti—Nuovi poemetti*, ed. Francesca Latini (Turin: UTET, 2008), 510.
52. Charles Féré, *La pathologie des émotions: Études physiologiques et cliniques* (Paris: Alcan, 1892), 378–380.
53. Elvio Fachinelli, "Il magistrato e la tarantola," in *Il bambino dalle uova d'oro* (Milan: Adelphi, 2010), 102–108.
54. Siegfried Kracauer, *Theory of Film: The Redemption of Physical Reality* (New York: Oxford University Press, 1960), 157.
55. Sartre, *Transcendence of the Ego*, 68.
56. Sartre, 58.
57. Derrida, *Voice and Phenomenon*, 72.
58. Edmund Husserl, *On the Phenomenology of the Consciousness of Internal Time*, trans. John Barnett Brough (Dordrecht: Kluwer Academic Publishers, 1991), 123.
59. Derrida, *The Problem of Genesis in Husserl's Philosophy*, trans. Marian Hobson (Chicago: University of Chicago Press, 2003), 96.
60. Melandri, *Logica e esperienza*, xi.
61. Melandri, 197.
62. Melandri, 197.
63. Aristotle, *The Metaphysics*, trans. Hugh Tredennick (Cambridge, MA: Harvard University Press, 1936), 1022b, 7–10.
64. Ingarden, "Kritische Bemerkungen," 216.
65. Husserl, *Cartesian Meditations*, §31, 92.
66. Roman Ingarden, "Über die Gefahr einer Petitio Principii in der Erkenntistheorie," in *Jahrbuch für Philosophie und phänomenologische Forschung* 4 (1921).
67. Ingarden, "Kritische Bemerkungen," 216.
68. Husserl, *Cartesian Meditations*, 66.
69. Eugen Fink, *VI Cartesianische Meditation: Texte aus dem Nachlass Eugen Finks (1932) mit Ammerkungen und Beilagen aus dem Nachlass Edmund Husserls (1933/34)*, in *Husserliana: Dokumente*, ed. Guy Van Kerckhoven (Dordrecht: Kluwer, 1988), 2.2:235.

70. Husserl, *Cartesian Meditations*, §32, 67.
71. Husserl, §32, 67.
72. Fink, *VI Cartesianische Meditation*, 236.
73. Gilles Deleuze and Félix Guattari, *What is Philosophy?* (New York: Columbia University Press, 1994), 48.
74. Paul Ricoeur, *Husserl: An Analysis of His Phenomenology*, trans. Edward G. Ballard and Lester E. Embree (Evanston, IL: Northwestern University Press, 1967), 120.
75. Gerhard Funke, "Gewohnheit als philosophisches Problem," in *Philosophisches Jahrbuch*, vol. 57 (1958), 525.
76. Gerhard Funke, "Transzendental-phänomenologische Untersuchung über 'universalen Idealismus,' 'Intentionalanalyse' und 'Habitusgenese,'" in *Archivio di Filosofia* (1957), 1:123.
77. Funke, "Gewohnheit," 542.
78. Oskar Becker, "Transzendenz und Paratranszendenz," in *Travaux du IXe Congrès international de philosophie. Congrès Descartes*, vol. 8, *Analyse réflexive et transcendance* (Paris: Hermann, 1937); "Para-Existenz: Menschliches Dasein und Dawesen," in *Blätter für deutsche Philosophie*, vol. 17 (1943).
79. Becker, "Transzendenz und Paratranszendenz," 102.
80. Funke, "Transzendental-phänomenologische Untersuchung," 135.
81. Funke, 136.
82. Husserl, *Cartesian Meditations*, §32, 67.
83. Gerhard Funke, *Zur transzendentalen Phänomenologie* (Bonn: Bouvier, 1957), 11.
84. Funke, "Transzendental-phänomenologische Untersuchung," 136.
85. Funke, 136.
86. Gerd Brand, "Husserl-Literatur und Husserl," *Philosophische Rundschau* 8, no. 4 (1960): 263.
87. Robert Klein, "Appropriation et aliénation," in *La forme et l'intelligible: Écrits sur la Renaissance et l'art moderne*, ed. André Chastel (Paris: Gallimard, 1970), 463n2.
88. Klein, 462.
89. Klein, 462.
90. Klein, 463n2.
91. Edmund Husserl, *Ideas Pertaining to a Pure Phenomenology and to a Phenomenological Philosophy, Second Book: Studies in the Phenomenology of Constitution*, trans. Richard Rojcewicz and André Schuwer (Dordrecht: Kluwer Academic Publishers, 1989), 263–265.
92. Husserl, *Cartesian Meditations*, §32, 67.
93. Husserl, §44, 94.
94. Simone Weil, *Oppression and Liberty*, trans. Arthur Wills and John Petrie (Amherst: University of Massachusetts Press, 1973), 130.
95. Sartre, *Transcendence of the Ego*, 40.

96. Derrida, *Voice and Phenomenon*, 71.
97. Michel Foucault, *The Archeology of Knowledge*, trans. A. M. Sheridan Smith (New York: Pantheon Books, 1972), 117.
98. Foucault, 130.
99. Robert Klein, Letter to André Chastel, August 31, 1966 (partially published in *L'esthétique de la technè*, 41n66): typescript with corrections and signature (BINHA, 090, 079, 902, 07).
100. Robert Klein, Letter without addressee, September 3, 1966 (partially published in *L'esthétique de la technè*, 41n66): typescript transcription (BINHA 090, 079, 902, 07).
101. Foucault, 130–131.
102. Derrida, *Voice and Phenomenon*, 73.
103. Foucault, 12.
104. Foucault, 12.
105. Boileau and Narcejac, *Vertigo*, 131.
106. Boris Sidis, *Philistine and Genius* (New York: Moffat, Yard and Co., 1911), 60.

4. A Singular Rapture

1. Vladimir Jankélévitch, *La mort* (Paris: Flammarion, 1977), 272.
2. Vladimir Jankélévitch, *Traité des vertus*, vol. 3, *L'innocence et la méchanceté* (Paris: Flammarion, 1986), 229.
3. Jankélévitch, 229–230.
4. Jankélévitch, 231–232.
5. Jankélévitch, *The Bad Conscience*, trans. Andrew Kelley (Chicago: University of Chicago Press, 2015), 83.
6. Jankélévitch, 84.
7. Jankélévitch, 47.
8. Jankélévitch, 49.
9. Pierre Boileau and Thomas Narcejac, *Vertigo*, trans. Geoffrey Sainsbury (London: Bloomsbury, 1997), 46. [Note: Ellipses in the original.]
10. Jean-Paul Sartre, *The Transcendence of the Ego*, trans. Forrest Williams and Robert Kirkpatrick (New York: Hill and Wang, 1957), 80.
11. Robert Klein, "Appropriation et aliénation," in *La forme et l'intelligible: Écrits sur la Renaissance et l'art moderne*, ed. André Chastel (Paris: Gallimard, 1970), 466.
12. Robert Klein, "Appropriation et alienation," in *La forme et l'intelligible: Écrits sur la Renaissance et l'art moderne*, ed. André Chastel (Paris: Gallimard, 1970), 467.
13. Edmund Husserl, *Cartesian Meditations: An Introduction to Phenomenology*, trans. Dorion Cairns (The Hague: Martinus Nijhoff Publishers, 1982), §56.
14. Edmund Husserl, *The Paris Lectures*, trans. Peter Koestenbaum (The Hague: M. Nijhoff, 1964), 35.
15. Michel Foucault, *The Archeology of Knowledge*, trans. A. M. Sheridan Smith (New York: Pantheon Books, 1972), 131.

16. Rachilde, *Les romans* [Edmond Cazal, *Le vertige de la volupté et de la mort*], *Mercure de France*, December 15, 1922, 731.

17. Thomas Hobbes, *Elements of Law: Natural and Politic* (Charlottesville, VA: InteLex Corporation, 1995), part 1, chap. 12, §3.

18. Aristotle, *Nicomachean Ethics*, trans. H. Rackham (Cambridge, MA: Harvard University Press, 2014), 1.1.10–17.

19. Jacques Derrida, *Voice and Phenomenon: Introduction to the Problem of the Sign in Husserl's Phenomenology*, trans. Leonard Lawlor (Evanston, IL: Northwestern University Press, 2011), 82–83.

20. François Cuzin, "Notes sur la mort d'autrui," in *Revue de Métaphysique et de Morale* 58, no. 4 (1953): 391.

21. Husserl, *Cartesian Meditations*, §44, 94.

22. Maurice Merleau-Ponty, "On the Phenomenology of Language," in *Phenomenology, Language and Sociology: Selected Essays of Maurice Merleau-Ponty*, ed. John O'Neill (London: Heinemann, 1974), 90–91.

23. Cuzin, "Notes sur la mort d'autrui," 391.

24. Cuzin, 394.

25. Cuzin, 394.

26. Epstein, *Esprit de cinéma*, 26.

5. Chasm

1. Martin Heidegger, *Kant and the Problem of Metaphysics*, trans. Richard Taft (Bloomington: Indiana University Press, 1990), §41, 154.

2. Martin Heidegger, *History of the Concept of Time: Prolegomena*, trans. Theodore Kisiel (Bloomington: Indiana University Press, 2010), 91.

3. Heidegger, 123.

4. Kant, *Critique of Pure Reason*, trans. Paul Guyer and Allen W. Wood (Cambridge: Cambridge University Press, 1998), 615.

5. Heidegger, *Being and Time*, trans. Joan Stambaugh (Albany: State University of New York Press, 1996), §27, 122.

6. Heidegger, §9, 67.

7. Edmund Husserl, "Randbemerkungen Husserls zu Heideggers 'Sein und Zeit' und 'Kant und das Problem der Metaphysik,'" *Husserl Studies* 11, nos. 1–2 (1994): 64.

8. Edith Stein, *Martin Heideggers Existenzphilosophie*, in *Gesamtausgabe*, Band 11/12, *Phänomenologie und Ontologie*, 3/4. Teil, *Endliches und ewiges Sein; Versuch eines Aufstiegs zum Sinn des Seins*, ed. Andreas Uwe Müller (Freiburg: Herder, 2006), 60.

9. Edmund Husserl, *Ideas Pertaining to a Pure Phenomenology and to a Phenomenological Philosophy*, Second Book, *Studies in the Phenomenology of Constitution*, trans. Richard Rojcewicz and André Schuwer (Dordrecht: Kluwer Academic Publishers, 1989), 118.

10. Christian Wolff, *Philosophia prima sive ontologia*, 3rd ed., in *Gesammelte Werke*, ed. Jean Ècole (Hildesheim: Olms, 1962), 2.3:§768, 574.

11. Edith Stein, *On the Problem of Empathy*, trans. Waltraut Stein (Washington, DC: ICS Publications, 1989), 102.

12. Robert Klein, "Appropriation et aliénation," in *La forme et l'intelligible: Écrits sur la Renaissance et l'art moderne*, ed. André Chastel (Paris: Gallimard, 1970), 459.

13. Martin Heidegger, *The Metaphysical Foundations of Logic*, trans. Michael Heim (Bloomington: Indiana University Press, 1984), 206.

14. Heidegger, *Being and Time*, §65.

15. Günther Anders, *Über Heidegger*, ed. Gerhard Oberschlick and Werner Reimann (München: Beck, 2001), 175.

16. Edmund Husserl, *Ideas Pertaining to a Pure Phenomenology and to a Phenomenological Philosophy*, First Book, *General Introduction to a Pure Phenomenology*, trans. F. Kersten (The Hague: Nijhoff, 1983), 112.

17. Martin Heidegger, *The Basic Problems of Phenomenology*, trans. Albert Hofstadter (Bloomington: Indiana University Press, 1982), §15, 161.

18. Heidegger, 162.

19. Edmund Husserl, *Phenomenological Interpretation of Kant's Critique of Pure Reason*, trans. Parvis Emad and Kenneth Maly (Bloomington: Indiana University Press, 1997), §§35–36.

20. Jean Wahl, *La philosophie de Heidegger* (Paris: Centre de Documentation Universitaire, 1952), 1:96.

21. Martin Heidegger, *Die Grundprobleme der Phänomenologie*, in *Gesamtausgabe*, vol. 24, *Marburger Vorlesung Sommersemester 1927*, ed. Friedrich-Wilhelm von Herrmann (Frankfurt: Klostermann, 1975), §15, 170.

22. Martin Heidegger, *Being and Time*, trans. Joan Stambaugh (Albany: State University of New York Press, 1996), §9.

23. Heidegger, §64, 369.

24. Martin Heidegger, *The Essence of Reasons*, trans. Terrence Malick (Evanston, IL: Northwestern University Press, 1969), 129.

25. Heidegger, *Being and Time*, §63, 288.

26. Heidegger, *History of the Concept of Time*, §33, 307.

27. Heidegger, *Being and Time*, §48, 225.

28. Heidegger, §47, 221.

29. Heidegger, *History of the Concept of Time*, §34, 313.

30. Heidegger, 317.

31. Heidegger, *Kant and the Problem of Metaphysics*, §34, 131.

32. Heidegger, *Essence of Reasons*, 93.

33. Heidegger, §34, 132.

34. Heidegger, *Phenomenological Interpretation of Kant's Critique of Pure Reason*, §25, 267–268.

35. Heidegger, *History of the Concept of Time*, §34, 313.

36. Jean Fallot, *Le plaisir et la mort dans la philosophie d'Épicure* (Paris: Juillard, 1951), 78.

37. Heidegger, *History of the Concept of Time*, §34, 313.

38. Heidegger, *Being and Time*, §50, 232.

39. Husserl, *Randbemerkungen*, 85.

40. Heidegger, *Being and Time*, 117.

41. Heidegger, §47, 221.

42. Heidegger, 283.

43. Heidegger, 223.

44. Heidegger, 223.

45. Heidegger, 232.

46. Emmanuel Levinas, *Time and the Other and Additional Essays*, trans. Richard A. Cohen (Pittsburgh, PA: Duquesne University Press, 1987), 70n43.

47. Heidegger, *Being and Time*, §47, 222.

48. Anders, *Über Heidegger*, ed. Gerhard Oberschlick and Werner Reimann (Munich: Beck, 2001), 93.

49. Levinas, *Time and the Other*, 77.

50. Heidegger, *Being and Time*, 225.

51. Heidegger, 221.

52. Maurice Merleau-Ponty, *Les relations avec autrui chez l'enfant* (Paris: Centre de Documentation Universitaire, 1969), 91.

53. Heidegger, *Being and Time*, §63, 288.

54. Heidegger, §52, 239.

55. Marcel Mauss, "The Physical Effect on the Individual of the Idea of Death Suggested by the Collectivity (Australia, New Zealand)," in *Sociology and Psychology: Essays*, trans. Ben Brewster (London: Routledge and Kegan Paul, 1979), 44.

56. Mauss, 53.

57. Heidegger, *Being and Time*, §52, 239.

58. Anders, *Über Heidegger*, 94.

59. Heidegger, *Being and Time*, §63, 291.

60. Hannah Arendt, "Einleitung," in Hermann Broch, *Dichten und Erkennen: Essays*, ed. Hannah Arendt (Zürich: Rhein-Verlag, 1955), 19.

61. Heidegger, *Being and Time*, §74, 352.

62. Heidegger, *History of the Concept of Time*, §33, 310; Heidegger, *Being and Time*, §47, 223.

63. Heidegger, *Being and Time*, §30, 133.

64. Heidegger, §74, 351.

65. Heidegger, §63, 289.

66. Wahl, *La philosophie de Heidegger*, 160 and footnote.

67. Martin Heidegger, "The Self-Assertion of the German University: Address, Delivered on the Solemn Assumption of the Rectorate of the University Freiburg the Rectorate 1933/34: Facts and Thoughts," trans. Karsten Harries, *Review of Metaphysics* 38, no. 3 (March, 1985): 476.

68. Heidegger, *Being and Time*, §74, 351.
69. Heidegger, §64, 296.
70. Heidegger, "Self-Assertion of the German University," 28.
71. Edmund Husserl, *Cartesian Meditations: An Introduction to Phenomenology*, trans. Dorion Cairns (The Hague: Martinus Nijhoff, 1982), §64, 157.
72. Heidegger, "Self-Assertion of the German University," 29.
73. Heidegger, *Being and Time*, §74, 352–353.
74. Arendt, "Einleitung," 20.
75. Martin Heidegger, *On Time and Being*, trans. Joan Stambaugh (New York: Harper and Row, 1972), 23.
76. Heidegger, *Kant and the Problem of Metaphysics*, §34, 129.
77. Heidegger, *Being and Time*, 103.
78. Heidegger, 337.
79. Heidegger, §70, orig. ed. 369 and 338.
80. Heidegger, §26, 116.
81. Heidegger, 112.
82. Heidegger, §47, 222.
83. Heidegger, §26, 115.
84. Heidegger, §60, 275.
85. Heidegger, §23, 97–98.
86. Heidegger, §23, 100.
87. Heidegger, §74.
88. Heidegger, *Essence of Reasons*, 131; Heidegger, *Metaphysical Foundations of Logic*, 221.
89. Heidegger, *Essence of Reasons*, 125.
90. Heidegger, *Being and Time*, §38, 167.
91. Heidegger, §38, 167.
92. Heidegger, §60.
93. Furio Jesi, *Spartakus: The Symbology of Revolt*, ed. Andrea Cavalletti, trans. Alberto Toscano (London: Seagull Books, 2014), 46.
94. Henri Maldiney, *Regard, parole, espace* (Lausanne: L'Age d'Homme, 1973), 150.
95. Rohmer, "Alfred Hitchcock's *Vertigo*," in *The Taste for Beauty*, trans. Carol Volk (Cambridge: Cambridge University Press, 1989), 171.

6. Surface

1. Klein, "Appropriation et aliénation," in *La forme et l'intelligible: Écrits sur la Renaissance et l'art moderne*, ed. André Chastel (Paris: Gallimard, 1970), 466n2.
2. Henri Maldiney, "Sur le vertige" in *Henri Maldiney: penser plus avant . . . Acts of the Lyon Conference, November 12–14, 2010*, ed. Jean-Pierre Charcosset (Chatou: Éditions de la Transparence, 2012), 14.
3. Henri Maldiney, *Regard, parole, espace* (Lausanne: L'Age d'Homme, 1973), 150.

4. Maldiney, "Sur le vertige," 14.

5. Maldiney, 14.

6. Henri Maldiney, "Notes sur le rythme," in *Henri Maldiney: penser plus avant . . .* , ed. Jean-Pierre Charcosset (Chatou: Éditions de la Transparence, 2012), 21.

7. Maldiney, "Sur le vertige," 15.

8. Wilhelm Worringer, *Griechentum und Gotik: Vom Weltreich des Hellenismus* (Munich: Piper, 1928), 29.

9. Sergio Bettini, *Venezia* (Novara: De Agostini, 1953), 12–13.

10. Sergio Bettini, *Pittura delle origini cristiane* (Novara: De Agostini, 1942), xv.

11. Sergio Bettini, *L'arte alla fine del mondo antico* (Padova: Liviana, 1948), 93–94.

12. Bettini, 17.

13. Martin Heidegger, *Being and Time*, trans. Joan Stambaugh (Albany: State University of New York Press, 1996), §23, 100.

14. Daney, "Vertigo: Sueurs froides," (1984), in *Ciné journal*, vol. 2, 1983–1986 (Paris: Cahiers du cinéma, 1998), 95.

15. Rodenbach, *Bruges-la-Morte: A Novel*, trans. Philip Mosley (Chester Springs, PA: Dufour Editions, 1986), 1.

16. André Breton, *L'amour fou* (Paris: Gallimard, 1937), 28. [Note: Ellipses in the original.]

17. Henri Bergson, ""Fantômes de vivants" et "Recherche psychique": Conférence faite à la Society for Psychical Research de Londres le 28 mai 1913," in *L'énergie spirituelle* (1919), ed. Frédéric Worms (Paris: F. Alcan, 1920), 62.

18. Robert Klein, "Ars et Technè dans la tradition de Platon à Giordano Bruno," unpublished *mémoire de thèse*, typescript with handwritten notes, held at the library of the Institut National d'Histoire de l'Art de Paris (BINHA, 090, 079, 03), 340.

19. Michel Foucault, *The Hermeneutics of the Subject. Lectures at the Collège de France, 1981–1982*, ed. Fédéric Gros, trans. Graham Burchell (New York: Palgrave Macmillan, 2005), 533.

20. Jean Wahl, *Études kierkegaardiennes* (Paris: Aubier, 1967), 433.

21. Jean-Paul Sartre, *Being and Nothingness: An Essay on Phenomenological Ontology*, trans. Hazel E. Barnes (New York: Philosophical Library, 1956), 30.

22. Sartre, 32.

23. Jean-Paul Sartre, *Saint Genet: Actor and Martyr*, trans. Bernard Frechtman (New York: G. Braziller, 1963), 17.

24. Sartre, 18.

25. Sartre, 41.

26. Sartre, *Being and Nothingness*, 67.

27. Sartre, lxii.

28. Robert Klein, *L'esthétique de la technè: L'art selon Aristote et les théories des arts visuels au XVIe siècle*, ed. Jérémie Joering (Paris: Institut National d'Histoire de l'Art, 2017), 131.

29. Klein, 133.

30. Robert Klein, "L'art et l'attention au technique" (1964), in *La forme et l'intelligible: Écrits sur la Renaissance et l'arte moderne*, ed. André Chastel (Paris: Gallimard, 1970), 383–386, 390.

31. Roberto Longhi, "Ricordo dei manieristi," in *Da Cimabue a Morandi: Saggi di storia della pittura italiana*, ed. Gianfranco Contini (Milan: Mondadori, 2001), 728.

32. Lotte H. Eisner, *The Haunted Screen: Expressionism in the German Cinema and the Influence of Max Reinhardt*, trans. Roger Greaves (Berkeley: University of California Press, 1969), 217.

33. Henri-Paul-Hyacinthe Wallon, "L'acte perceptif et le cinéma," *Revue Internationale de Filmologie* 4, no. 13 (1953): 110.

34. Robert Klein, "Discussione" (on *Les limites de la morale transcendantale*, with Paul Ricœur, Karl Kerényi, Jean Brun, Odette Laffoucrière, Antoine Vergote, and Adolphe de Waelhens), in *Archivio di Filosofia*, nos. 1–2 (1965): 308.

35. Boileau and Narcejac, *Vertigo*, trans. Geoffrey Sainsbury (London: Bloomsbury, 1997), 48.

36. Rodenbach, *Bruges-la-Morte*, 1.

37. Rodenbach, 1.

38. Furio Jesi, "Károly Kérényi 2. L'esperienza dell'isola," in *Materiali mitologici: Mito e antropologia nella cultura mitteleuropea*, ed. Andrea Cavalletti (Turin: Einaudi, 2001), 60.

39. Jean-Louis Baudry, "Le dispositif: Approches métapsychologiques de l'impression de réalité," *Communications* 23 (1975): 71.

40. Aristotle, *Nich. Eth.*, 6.4.1140a, 10–14. [Trans. note: my translation].

41. Aristotle, *Nic. Eth.* 6.4.1140a, 3–17 [Trans. note: my translation].

42. Roberto Longhi, "Ricordo dei manieristi," in *Da Cimabue a Morandi: Saggi di storia della pittura italiana*, ed. Gianfranco Contini (Milan: Mondadori, 2001), 728.

43. Aristotle, *Metaphysics*, 1022b, 7–10.

44. Edmund Husserl, *The Crisis of European Sciences and Transcendental Phenomenology*, trans. David Carr (Evanston, IL: Northwestern University Press, 1970), §57, 200.

45. Husserl, §38, 144.

46. Aristotle, *Nich. Eth.*, 6.4.1140a, 20–23 [Trans. note: my translation].

47. Robert Klein, "Thought, Confession, Fiction: On *A Season in Hell*," in *Form and Meaning: Essays on Renaissance and Modern Art*, trans. Madeline Jay and Leon Wieseltier (New York: Viking Press, 1979), 207.

Explicit

1. Michel Foucault, *Society Must be Defended: Lectures at the Collège de France, 1975–1976*, trans. David Macey (New York: Picador, 2003), 98.

2. Leo Strauss, *Natural Right and History* (Chicago: University of Chicago Press, 1965), 169.

3. Antonio De Giuliani, "Saggio politico sopra le vicissitudini inevitabili delle società civili," in *La cagione riposta delle decadenze e delle rivoluzioni: Due opuscoli politici del 1791 e del 1793*, ed. Benedetto Croce (Bari: Laterza, 1934), 11.

4. Alexandre Kojève, *Introduction à la lecture de Hegel* (Paris: Gallimard, 1947).

5. Jean Fallot, *Prestiges de la science* (Neuchâtel: Éditions de la Baconnière, 1960), 11.

6. Friedrich Nietzsche, *Morgenröte*, in *Werke: Kritische Studienausgabe*, Band 3, *Morgenröte—Idyllen aus Messina—Die fröhliche Wissenschaft*, ed. Giorgio Colli and Mazzino Montinari (Berlin-New York: de Gruyter, 1967), 163.

7. Furio Jesi, "Prefazione," in *Materiali mitologici*, ed. Andrea Cavalletti (Turin: Einaudi, 2001), 347.

Bibliography

Adelon, Nicolas-Philibert. *Dictionnaire de médecine, ou répertoire général des sciences médicales*. Vol. 9. Paris: Béchet, 1836.

Adorno, Theodor W. *Against Epistemology: A Metacritique; Studies in Husserl and the Phenomenological Antinomies*. Translated by Willis Domingo. Cambridge, MA: MIT Press, 1983. Orig. *Zur Metakritik der Erkenntnistheorie: Studien über Husserl und die phänomenologischen Antinomien*. Stuttgart: Kolhammer, 1956.

Agamben, Giorgio. *The Use of Bodies: Homo sacer*. IV.2. Translated by Adam Kotsko. Stanford, CA: Stanford University Press, 2016. Orig. *L'uso dei corpi: Homo sacer IV.2*. Vicenza: Neri Pozza, 2014.

Alain. *Éléments de philosophie* (1916–41). Paris: Gallimard, 1969.

———. *Histoire de mes pensées*. Paris: Gallimard, 1936.

———. *Mars, ou la guerre jugée*. Paris: Gallimard, 1936.

Anders, Günther. *Über Heidegger*. Edited by Gerhard Oberschlick and Werner Reimann. Munich: Beck, 2001.

Arendt, Hannah. "Einleitung." In Hermann Broch, *Dichten und Erkennen: Essays*. Edited by Hannah Arendt. Zurich: Rhein-Verlag, 1955.

Aristotle. *Metaphysics*. Vol. 1, Bks. 1–9. Translated by Hugh Tredennick. Cambridge, MA: Harvard University Press, 1933.

———. *Nicomachean Ethics*. Translated by H. Rackham. Cambridge, MA: Harvard University Press, 2014.

Auiler, Dan. *The Making of a Hitchcock Classic*. New York: St. Martin's Press, 1998.

Bachelard, Gaston. *Air and Dreams*. Translated by Edith Farell and Frederick Farell. Dallas, TX: Dallas Institute Publications, 1988. Orig. *L'air et les songes: Essai sur l'imagination du mouvement*. Paris: Corti, 1943.

———. *L'eau et les rêves: Essai sur l'imagination de la matière*. Paris: Corti, 1942.

———. *La terre et les rêveries de la volonté*. Paris: Corti, 1947.

Ball, Benjamin. *Du délire des persecutions, ou Maladie de Lasègue*. Paris: Asselin et Houzeau, 1890.
———. *Leçons sur les maladies mentales*. Paris: Asselin et Hozeau, 1890.
Baudelaire, Charles. "On the Essence of Laughter." In *The Painter of Modern Life and Other Essays*. Translated and edited by Jonathan Mayne. London: Phaidon, 1964. Orig. "De l'essence du rire et généralement du comique dans les arts plastiques" (1855). In *Curiosités esthétiques: L'art romantique et autres œuvres critiques*. Edited by Henri Lemaître. Paris: Garnier, 1962.
Baudry, Jean Louis. "Le dispositif: Approches métapsychologiques de l'impression de réalité." *Communications*, no. 23 (1975): 56–72.
Becker, Oskar. "Para-Existenz: Menschliches Dasein und Dawesen." In *Blätter für deutsche Philosophie* 17 (1943): 62–95.
———. "Transzendenz und Paratranszendenz." In *Travaux du IXe Congrès international de philosophie: Congrès Descartes*. Vol. 8, *Analyse réflexive et transcendance*. 97–104. Paris: Hermann, 1937.
Bellini, Lorenzo. *De urinis et pulsibus: De missione sanguinis, de febribus, de morbis capitis, et pectoris*. Bologna: Pisarii, 1683.
Benjamin, Walter. "Aphorismen." In *Gesammelte Schriften*. Vol. 2.2, edited by Rolf Tiedemann and Hermann Schweppenhäuser. Frankfurt: Suhrkamp, 1977.
———. "Johann Jakob Bachofen." In *Selected Writings*. Vol. 3, 1935–1938. Translated by Edmund Jephcott, Howard Eiland, and others. Cambridge, MA: Belknap Press, 2002.
———. "The Work of Art in the Age of Mechanical Reproduction." In *Illuminations: Essays and Reflections*, edited by Hannah Arendt and translated by Harry Zohn. Orig. "Das Kunstwerk im Zeitalter seiner technischen Reproduziertbarkeit [Zweite Fassung]" (1936), in *Gesammelte Schriften*. Vol. 7.1–2. Frankfurt: Suhrkamp, 1989.
Berenson, Bernard. *Aesthetics and History in the Visual Arts*. New York: Pantheon, 1948.
———. *Central Italian Painters*. New York: Putnam's Sons, 1897.
———. *Florentine Painters of the Renaissance*. New York: Putnam's Sons, 1896.
Bergson, Henri. *Creative Evolution*. Translated by Arthur Mitchell. Mineola, NY: Dover, 1998.
———. "'Fantômes de vivants' et 'Recherche psychique': Conférence faite à la Society for Psychical Research de Londres le 28 mai 1913." In *L'énergie spirituelle* (1919), edited by Frédéric Worms. Paris: F. Alcan, 1920.
———. "La conscience et la vie." In *L'énergie spirituelle*, edited by Frédéric Worms. Paris: F. Alcan, 1920.
———. "L'âme et le corps" (1912), in *L'énergie spirituelle* (1919), edited by Frédéric Worms. Paris: F. Alcan, 1920.
———. *Matière et mémoire: Essai sur la relation du corps à l'esprit* (1896). Edited by Frédéric Worms. Paris: PUF, 2012.
———. "The Perception of Change." In *The Creative Mind*, translated by Mabelle L. Andison. New York: Philosophical Library, 1946. Orig. "La perception du

changement" (1911). In *La pensée et le mouvant: Essais et conférences* (1938). Paris: PUF, 2003.
Berrios, German E. *The History of Mental Symptoms: Descriptive Psychopathology Since the Nineteenth Century*. Cambridge: Cambridge University Press, 1996.
Bettini, Sergio. *L'arte alla fine del mondo antico*. Padova: Liviana, 1948.
———. *Pittura delle origini cristiane*. Novara: De Agostini, 1942.
———. *Venezia*. Novara: De Agostini, 1953.
Bloch, Marcus Elieser. *Medizinische Bemerkungen: Nebst einer Abhandlung vom Pyrmonter-Augenbrunnen*. Berlin: Himburg, 1774.
Blumenberg, Hans. *Höhlenausgänge*. Frankfurt: Suhrkamp, 1989.
Boileau, Pierre, and Thomas Narcejac. *Vertigo*. Translated by Geoffrey Sainsbury. London: Bloomsbury, 1997. Orig. *D'entre les morts*. Paris: Denoël, 1954.
Borowski, Ludwig Ernst. *Darstellung des Lebens und Charakters Immanuel Kants: Von Kant selbst genau revidirt und gerichtig*. Königsberg: Nicolovius, 1804.
Brand, Gerd. "Husserl-Literatur und Husserl." *Philosophische Rundschau* 8, no. 4 (1960): 261–289.
———. *Welt, Ich und Zeit nach unveröffenlichten Manuscripten Edmund Husserls*. The Hague: Nijhoff, 1955.
Breton, André. "Lâchez tout!" In *Les pas perdus*. Paris: Gallimard, 1924.
———. *L'amour fou*. Paris: Gallimard, 1937.
Caillois, Roger. *La communion des forts: Études de sociologie contemporaine*. México: Ediciones Quetzal, 1943.
Catucci, Stefano. *Imparare dalla Luna*. Macerata: Quodlibet, 2013.
Cazal, Edmond. *Voluptés de guerre*. Paris: L'Édition Française Illustrée, 1918.
Clément, Paul. *Étiologie du vertige*. Paris: Parent, 1873.
Cohen-Séat, Gilbert. *Essai sur les principes d'une philosophie du cinema: Notions fondamentales et vocabulaire de filmologie*. Paris: PUF, 1958.
Coquelin, Charles. *Du crédit des banques*. Guillaumin: Paris, 1848.
Coquelin, Charles, and Gilbert-Urbain Guillaumin, eds. *Dictionnaire de l'économie politique*. Vol. 2. Paris: Guillaumin, 1854.
Cortellessa, Andrea. "Bruges-la-morte, Naja, Vertigo." In *Dal nulla al sogno. Dada e Surrealismo dalla Collezione del Museo Boijmans Van Beuningen*. Exhibit catalogue. Edited by Marco Vallora. Cinisello Balsamo, Milano: Silvana editoriale, 2018.
Cuzin, François. "Notes sur la mort d'autrui." *Revue de Métaphysique et de Morale* 58, no. 4 (1953): 376–395.
Daney, Serge. "Le travelling de *Kapo*." In *Persévérance: Entretien avec Serge Toubiana*, 13–39. Paris: POL, 1994.
———. "Vertigo: Sueurs froides" (1984). In *Ciné journal*. Vol. 2, 1983–1986. Paris: Cahiers du cinéma, 1998.
Darwin, Erasmus. *Zoonomia or the Laws of Organic Life*. Vol. 1. London: Johnson, 1796.
Davies, Martin L. "Gedanken zu einem ambivalenten Verältnis: Marcus Herz und Immanuel Kant." In *Kant und die Berliner Aufklärung: Akten des IX.*

Internationalen Kant-Kongress, vol. 5, *Sektionen XV–XVIII*, edited by Gerhardt Volker, Rolf-Peter Horstmann, and Ralph Schumacher, 140–147. Berlin/New York: de Gruyter, 2001.

De Giuliani, Antonio. *La vertigine attuale dell'Europa*. Vienna: Alberti, 1790.

———. "Saggio politico sopra le vicissitudini inevitabili delle società civili." In *La cagione riposta delle decadenze e delle rivoluzioni: Due opuscoli politici del 1791 e del 1793*, edited by Benedetto Croce (Bari: Laterza, 1934).

De Martino, Ernesto. *Morte e pianto rituale: Dal lamento pagano al pianto di Maria*. Turin: Bollati Boringhieri, 2000.

Deleuze, Gilles. *The Movement-Image*. Translated by Hugh Tomlinson and Barbara Habberjam. Minneapolis: University of Minnesota Press, 1986. Orig. *L'image-mouvement: Cinéma 1*. Paris: Éditions de Minuit, 1983.

———. *The Time-Image*. Translated by Hugh Tomlinson and Robert Galeta. London: Athlone, 1989. Orig. *L'image-temps: Cinéma 2*. Paris: Éditions de Minuit, 1985.

Deleuze, Gilles, and Félix Guattari. *What is Philosophy?* Translated by Hugh Tomlinson and Graham Burchell. New York: Columbia University Press, 1994. Orig. *Qu'est-ce que la philosophie?* Paris: Éditions de Minuit, 1991.

Depraz, Nathalie. *Transcendance et incarnation: Le statut de l'intersubjectivité comme altérité à soi chez Husserl*. Paris: Vrin, 1995.

Derrida, Jacques. *Le toucher, Jean-Luc Nancy: Accompagné de travaux de lecture de Simon Hantaï*. Paris: Galilée, 2000.

———. *The Problem of Genesis in Husserl's Philosophy*. Translated by Marian Hobson. Chicago: University of Chicago Press, 2003. Orig. *Le problème de la genèse dans la philosophie de Husserl*. Paris: PUF, 1990.

———. "Violence and Metaphysics." In *Writing and Difference*. Translated by Alan Bass, 97–192. Chicago: University of Chicago Press, 1978. Orig. "Violence et métaphysique." In *L'écriture et la différence*. Paris: Éditions du Seuil, 1967.

———. *Voice and Phenomenon: Introduction to the Problem of the Sign in Husserl's Phenomenology*. Translated by Leonard Lawlor. Evanston, IL: Northwestern University Press, 2011. Orig. *La voix et le phénomène* (1967). Paris: PUF, 1993.

Di Cesare, Donatella. *Heidegger e gli ebrei*. Vol. 1, "*Quaderni neri*." Turin: Bollati Boringhieri, 2016.

Domarchi, Jean and Jean Douchet. "Entretien avec Alfred Hitchcock." *Cahiers du Cinéma*, no. 102 (1959): 17–29.

Domarchi, Jean, Jean Douchet, Jacques Doniol-Valcroze, Pierre Kast, Jean-Luc Godard, Jacques Rivette, and Éric Rohmer. "'Hiroshima, notre amour' (discussion on Alain Resnais's Hiroshima mon amour)." In Hillier, *Cahiers du Cinéma: The 1950s*, 59–70. Orig. "Table ronde sur *Hiroshima, mon amour* d'Alain Resnais." In *La Nouvelle Vague: Textes et entretiens parus dans les cahiers du cinéma*, edited by Antoine de Baecque and Charles Tesson, 36–62. Paris: Cahiers du Cinéma, 1999.

Douchet, Jean. *Alfred Hitchcock*. Paris: Éditions de l'Herne, 1967.

Dragonetti, Roger. "Deux bâtons à la brèche du mur." In *Bouvard et Pécuchet centenaires*, edited by Dominique-Gilbert Laporte, 97–124. Paris: Éditions du Seuil, 1981.
Egger, Victor. "La durée apparente des rêves." In *Revue Philosophique de la France et de l'Étranger* 40 (1895): 41–59.
———. "Le moi des mourants." In *Revue Philosophique de la France et de l'Étranger* 41, (1896) : 26–38.
———. "Le moi des mourants: Nouveaux faits." *Revue Philosophique de la France et de l'Étranger* 42 (1896) : 337–368.
Eisenstein, Sergei M. *Immoral Memories: An Autobiography by Sergei M. Eisenstein*. Translated by Herbert Marshall. Boston, MA: Houghton Mifflin Company, 1983. Orig. Избранные произведения в шести томах. Moscow: Iskustvo, 1964.
Eisner, Lotte H. *The Haunted Screen: Expressionism in the German Cinema and the Influence of Max Reinhardt*. Translated by Roger Greaves. Berkeley: University of California Press, 1969. Orig. *L'Écran démoniaque: Les influences de Max Reinhardt et de l'expressionisme*. Paris: Losfeld, 1981.
Epstein, Jean. *Esprit de cinéma*. Genève-Paris: Jeheber, 1955.
———. *Jean Epstein: Critical Essays and New Translations*. Edited by Sarah Keller and Jason N. Paul. Amsterdam: Amsterdam University Press, 2012.
———. *La poésie d'aujourd'hui: Un nouvel état de l'intelligence*. Paris: Éditions de la Sirène, 1921.
Esquirol, Jean-Étienne-Dominique. *Des maladies mentales considérées sous les rapports médical, hygiénique et médico-légal*. Paris: Baillière, 1838.
Fachinelli, Elvio. "Il magistrato e la tarantola." In *Il bambino dalle uova d'oro*. Milan: Adelphi, 2010.
Fallot, Jean. *Le plaisir et la mort dans la philosophie d'Épicure*. Paris: Juillard, 1951.
———. *Prestiges de la science*. Neuchâtel: Éditions de la Baconnière, 1960.
Falret, Jules. *De l'état mental des épileptiques*. Asselin: Paris, 1861.
Fenves, Peter. *Late Kant: Towards Another Law of the Earth*. New York: Routledge 2003.
Féré, Charles. *La pathologie des émotions: Études physiologiques et cliniques*. Paris: Alcan, 1892.
Ferenczi, Sándor. "Sensations of Giddiness at the End of the Psycho-Analytic Session." In *Further Contributions to the Theory and Technique of Psychoanalysis*. Compiled by John Rickman, translated by Jane Isabel Suttie, 239–241. New York: Boni and Liveright, 1927. Orig. "Szédülés érzete az analízis-óra végén." In *A pszichoanalízis haladása*. Budapest: Neumann Kht., 2005.
Feuerbach, Ludwig. *Principles of the Philosophy of the Future*. Translated by Manfred H. Vogel. Indianapolis, IN: Hackett, 1986. Orig. *Grundsätze der Philosophie der Zukunft* (1843). In *Gesammelte Werke*, Band 9, *Kleinere Schriften*, 2. Teil, 1839–1846, edited by Werner Schuffenhauer and Wolfgang Harich. Berlin: Akademie-Verlag, 1970.
Fink, Eugen. *VI Cartesianische Meditation: Texte aus dem Nachlass Eugen Finks (1932) mit Ammerkungen und Beilagen aus dem Nachlass Edmund Husserls*

(1933/34). In *Husserliana: Dokumente*, vol. 2/2, edited by Guy Van Kerchoven. Dordrecht: Kluwer, 1988.

———. "Die Phänomenologische Philosophie Edmund Husserls in der Gegenwärtigen Kritik" (1933). In *Studien zur Phänomenologie 1930–1939*, 79–156. The Hague: Nijhoff, 1966.

Flaubert, Gustave. *Le projet du "Sottisier": Le second volume de "Bouvard et Pécuchet"; Reconstruction conjecturale de la "copie" des deux bonshommes d'après le dossier de Rouen*. Edited by Alberto Cento and Lea Caminiti Pennarola. Napoli: Liguori, 1981.

———. *Sentimental Education*. Translated by Robert Baldick. London: Penguin Books, 2004. Orig. *L'éducation sentimentale*. Paris: Garnier-Flammarion, 1985.

Foucault, Michel. *The Archeology of Knowledge*. Translated by A. M. Sheridan Smith. New York: Pantheon Books, 1972. Orig. *L'archéologie du savoir*. Paris: Gallimard, 1969.

———. *The Hermeneutics of the Subject: Lectures at the Collège de France, 1981–1982*. Edited by Fédéric Gros, translated by Graham Burchell. New York: Palgrave Macmillan, 2005. Orig. *L'herméneutique du sujet: Cours au Collège de France, 1981–1982*. Edited by Frédéric Gros. Paris: Éditions du Seuil, 2001.

———. "Introduction." In Ludwig Binswanger, *Le rêve et l'éxistence*. Translated into French by Jacqueline Verdeaux. Paris: Desclée de Bruower, 1954.

———. *Society Must be Defended: Lectures at the Collège de France, 1975–1976*. Translated by David Macey. New York: Picador, 2003.

Franck, Didier. *Flesh and Body: On the Phenomenology of Husserl*. Translated by Joseph River and Scott Davidson. New York: Bloomsbury Academic, 2014. Orig. *Chair et corps: Sur la phénoménologie de Husserl*. Paris: Éditions de Minuit, 1981.

———. *Heidegger et le problème de l'espace*. Paris: Éditions de Minuit, 1986.

Frank, Joseph. *Praxeos medicae universae praecepta*, II.1.2, *Continens doctrinam de morbis systematis nervorum in genere et de iis encephali in specie*. Lipsiae: Kuehniani, 1832.

Freud, Sigmund. "Fußnote." In Jean-Martin Charcot, *Poliklinische Vorträge*, Band 1, *Schuljahr 1887–1888*. Leipzig/Wien: Deuticke, 1892.

———. *Inhibitions, Symptoms and Anxiety*. In *The Standard Edition of the Complete Psychological Works of Sigmund Freud*, vol. 20, translated and edited by James Strachey in collaboration with Anna Freud. London: Hogarth Press, 1953–1974. Orig. *Hemmung, Symptom und Angst*. Leipzig/Wien/Zürich: Internationaler Psychoanalytischer Verlag, 1926.

———. *Massenpsychologie und Ich-Analyse*. Leipzig/Wien/Zürich: Internationaler Psychoanalytischer Verlag, 1921.

———. "The Psychogenesis of a Case of Homosexuality in a Woman." In *The Standard Edition of the Complete Psychological Works of Sigmund Freud*, vol. 18, translated and edited by James Strachey in collaboration with Anna Freud, 145–172. London: Hogarth Press, 1953–1974. Orig. "Über die Psychogenese eines

Falles von weiblicher Homosexualität." *Internationale Zeitschrift für Psychoanalyse*, 6, no. 1 (1920): 1–24.

———. *The Psychopathology of Everyday Life*. In *The Standard Edition of the Complete Psychological Works of Sigmund Freud*, vol. 6, translated and edited by James Strachey in collaboration with Anna Freud. London: Hogarth Press, 1953–1974. Orig. "Zur Psychopathologie des Alltagslebens (Über Vergessen, Versprechen, Vergreifen, Aberglaube und Irrtum)." *Monatsschrift für Psychiatrie und Neurologie* 10, nos. 1–2 (1901): 1–32.

———. "Traum und Telepathie." *Imago* 8, no. 1 (1922): 1–22.

———. "Zum psychischen Mechanismus der Vergessenheit," in *Monatsschrift für Psychiatrie und Neurologie* 4, no. 6 (1898): 436–443.

Freud, Sigmund, and Joseph Breuer. *Studies on Hysteria*. Translated and edited by James Strachey. New York: Basic Books, 1957. Orig. *Studien über Hysterie*. Leipzig/Wien: Deuticke, 1895.

Friedmann, Max. *Über Wahnideen im Völkerleben*. Wiesbaden: Bergmann, 1901.

Funke, Gerhard. "Ethos: Gewohnheit, Sitte, Sittlichkeit." In *Archiv für Rechts- und Sozialphilosophie* 47 (1961).

———. "Gewohnheit als philosophisches Problem." In *Philosophisches Jahrbuch* 57 (1958).

———. "Transzendental-phänomenologische Untersuchung über 'universalen Idealismus,' 'Intentionalanalyse' und 'Habitusgenese.'" In *Archivio di Filosofia* 1 (1957).

———. *Zur transzendentalen Phänomenologie*. Bonn: Bouvier, 1957.

Gadamer, Hans-Georg. *Philosophische Lehrjahre: Eine Ruckschau*. Frankfurt: Klostermann, 1977.

Gallois, Nicolas. "L'analyse des économistes français du XIXe siècle." *L'Économie Politique*, no. 55 (2012–2013): 14–26.

Gerlier, Félix. "Une épidémie de vertige paralysant: Nouvelle névrose de la motilité." *Revue Médicale de la Suisse Romande*, no. 7 (1887): 5–29.

Gethmann, Carl Friedrich. *Dasein: Erkennen und Handeln; Heidegger im phänomenologischen Kontext*. Berlin: de Gruyter, 1993.

Glagau, Otto. *Der Börsen- und Gründungsschwindel in Berlin: Gesammelte und stark vermehrte Artikel der "Gartenlaube."* Leipzig: Frohberg, 1876.

Goethe, Johann Wolfgang von. *Faust: Parts I and II*. Translated by Bayard Taylor. Mineola, NY: Dover Publications, 2018. Orig. *Faust: eine Tragödie* (1808). Edited by Ernst Beutler. Zürich: Artemis, 1950.

Gorter, Johannes de. *Medicina dogmatica tres morbos particulares, delirium, vertiginem, et tussim aphoristice conscriptos, et coram auditoribus suis ante aliquot annos commentariis illustratos, pro specimine exhibens*. Harderovici: Brinkink, 1741.

Gowers, William. *The Border-Land of Epilepsy: Faints, Vagal Attacks, Vertigo, Migraine, Sleep Symptoms, and their Treatment*. London: Churchill, 1907.

Grasset, Joseph. "Le vertige: Étude physiopathologique de la fonction de l'orientation et de l'équilibre." *Revue Philosophique de la France et de l'Étranger* 51 (1901): 225–251.

Haltenhoff, Georges-Gabriel. "Du vertige paralysant. Note lue à l'Academie de Médicine de Paris le 10 mai 1887." *Semaine Médicale*, May 11, 1887.

———. "Faits pour servir à l'histoire du vertige paralysant (maladie de Gerlier)." In *Progrès Médical*, 15 (1887).

Hegel, Georg Wilhelm Friedrich. *Grundlinien der Philosophie des Rechts* (1821–1833). In *Gesammelte Werke*, vol. 14, edited by Klaus Grotsch and Elisabeth Weisser-Lohmann. Hamburg: Meiner, 2009.

———. *Phänomenologie des Geistes*. In *Gesammelte Werke*, vol. 9, edited by Wolfgang Bonsiepen and Reinhard Heede. Hamburg: Meiner, 1980.

Heidegger, Martin. *Being and Time*. Translated by Joan Stambaugh. Albany: State University of New York Press, 1996. Orig. *Sein und Zeit (1927), Unveränderter Nachdruck der fünfzehnten, an Hand der Gesamtausgabe durchgesehene Auflage mit den Randbemerkungen aus dem Handexemplar des Autors im Anhang*. Tübingen: Niemeyer, 1993.

———. *Die Grundbegriffe der Metaphysik. Welt—Endlichkeit—Einsamkeit. Wintersemester 1929–30*. In *Gesamtausgabe*, Band 29/30, edited by Friedrich-Wilhelm von Herrmann. Frankfurt: Klostermann, 1983.

———. *The Basic Problems of Phenomenology*. Translated by Albert Hofstadter. Bloomington: Indiana University Press, 1982. Orig. *Die Grundprobleme der Phänomenologie*. In *Gesamtausgabe*, Band 24, *Marburger Vorlesung Sommersemester 1927*, edited by Friedrich-Wilhelm von Herrmann. Frankfurt: Klostermann, 1975.

———. *The Essence of Reasons*. Translated by Terrence Malick. Evanston, IL: Northwest University Press, 1969. Orig. *Vom Wesen des Grundes* (1929). In *Gesamtausgabe*, Band 9, *Wegmarken*, edited by Friedrich-Wilhelm von Herrmann. Frankfurt: Klostermann, 1976.

———. *History of the Concept of Time: Prolegomena*. Translated by Theodore Kisiel. Bloomington: Indiana University Press, 2010. Orig. *Prolegomena zur Geschichte des Zeitbegriffs*. In *Gesamtausgabe*, Band 20, *Marburger Vorlesung, Sommersemester 1925*, edited by Petra Jaeger. Frankfurt: Klostermann, 1975.

———. *Kant and the Problem of Metaphysics*. Translated by Richard Taft. Bloomington: Indiana University Press, 1990. Orig. *Kant und das Problem der Metaphysik* (1929). In *Gesamtausgabe*, Band 3, edited by Friedrich-Wilhelm von Herrmann. Frankfurt: Klostermann, 1991.

———. Letter to Edmund Husserl, October 22, 1927. In *Phänomenologische Psychologie: Vorlesungen Sommersemester 1925*, in *Husserliana*, vol. 9, edited by Walter Biemel. The Hague: Nijhoff, 1968.

———. *The Metaphysical Foundations of Logic*. Translated by Michael Heim. Bloomington: Indiana University Press, 1984. Orig. *Metaphysische Anfangsgründe der Logik im Ausgang von Leibniz*. In *Gesamtausgabe*, Band 26,

Marburger Vorlesung Sommersemester 1928, edited by Klaus Held. Frankfurt: Klostermann, 1978.

———. *On Time and Being*. Translated by Joan Stambaugh. New York: Harper and Row, 1972. Orig. *Zeit und Sein* (1962). In *Gesamtausgabe*, Band 14, *Zur Sache des Denkens*, edited by Friedrich-Wilhelm von Herrmann. Frankfurt: Klostermann, 2007.

———. *Phenomenological Interpretation of Kant's Critique of Pure Reason*. Translated by Parvis Emad and Kenneth Maly. Bloomington: Indiana University Press, 1997. Orig. *Phänomenologische Interpretation von Kants "Kritik der reinen Vernuft."* In *Gesamtausgabe*, Band 25, *Marburger Vorlesung Wintersemester 1927–28*, edited by Ingtraud Görland. Frankfurt: Klostermann, 1977.

———. "The Self-Assertion of the German University: Address, Delivered on the Solemn Assumption of the Rectorate of the University Freiburg the Rectorate 1933/34: Facts and Thoughts." In *The Review of Metaphysics* 38, no. 3 (March 1985): 467–502. Translated by Karsten Harries. Orig. *Die Selbstbehauptung der deutschen Universität* (1933). In *Gesamtausgabe*, Band 16, *Reden und andere Zeugnisse eines Lebensweges*, 1. Teil, *Veröffentliche Schriften 1910–1976*, edited by Hermann Heidegger. Frankfurt: Klostermann, 2000.

———. *Überlegungen II–VI (Schwarze Hefte 1931–1938)*. Edited by Peter Trawny. Frankfurt: Klostermann, 2014.

Heinrich, Klaus. *Versuch über die Schwierigkeit nein zu sagen*. Frankfurt: Suhrkamp, 1964.

Herz, Marcus. Letter to Immanuel Kant, February 27, 1786. In *Immanuel Kant, Gesammelte Schriften*, Band 10, *Briefwechsel*, 1. Teil, 1747–1788. Berlin: De Gruyter, 1922.

———. *Versuch über den Schwindel*. Berlin: Vossische Buchhandlung, 1791.

Hillier, Jim. *Cahiers du Cinéma: The 1950s—Neo-Realism, Hollywood, New Wave*. Cambridge, MA: Harvard University Press, 1985.

Hinteregger, Christoph. *Der Judenschwindel*. Vienna: Wiener Volksbuchhandlung, 1923.

Hoffbauer, Johann-Christoph. *Die Psychologie in ihren Hauptanwendungen auf die Rechtspflege, nach den allgemeinen Gesichtspunkten der Gesetzgebung, oder die sogenannte gerichtliche Arzneywissenschaft nach ihrem psychologischen Theile*. Halle: Schimmelpfennig, 1823.

Hume, David. *A Treatise of Human Nature*. Vol. 1. Edited by David Fate Norton and Mary J. Norton. Oxford: Oxford University Press, 2014.

Hunter, Richard, and Ida Macalpine, eds. *Three Hundred Years of Psychiatry 1535–1860. A History Presented in Selected English Texts*. Hartsdale: Carlisle, 1982.

Husserl, Edmund. *Analysen zur passiven Synthesis: Aus Vorlesungs-und Forschungsmanuskripten 1918–1926*. In *Husserliana*, vol. 11, edited by Margot Fleischer. The Hague: Nijhoff, 1966.

———. *Cartesian Meditations: An Introduction to Phenomenology*. Translated by Dorion Cairns. The Hague: Martinus Nijhoff Publishers, 1982. Orig. *Cartesianische*

Meditationen und Pariser Vorträge. In *Husserliana*, vol. 1, edited by Stephan Strasser. The Hague: Nijhoff, 1973.
———. *The Crisis of European Sciences and Transcendental Phenomenology.* Translated by David Carr. Evanston, IL: Northwestern University Press, 1970. Orig. *Die Krisis der europäischen Wissenschaften und die transzendentale Phänomenologie: Eine Einleitung in die phänomenologische Philosophie.* In *Husserliana*, vol. 6, edited by Walter Biemel. The Hague: Nijhoff, 1954.
———. *Experience and Judgment. Investigations in a Genealogy of Logic.* Translated by James S. Churchill and Karl Ameriks. Evanston, IL: Northwestern University Press, 1973. Orig. *Erfahrung und Urteil: Untersuchungen zur Genealogie der Logik.* Edited by Ludwig Landgrebe. Hamburg: Meiner, 1999.
———. *First Philosophy: Lectures 1923/1924.* Translated by Sebastian Luft and Thane M. Naberhaus. Dordrecht: Springer, 2019. Orig. *Erste Philosophie (1923–24).* Zweiter Teil: *Theorie der phänomenologischen Reduktion.* In *Husserliana*, vol. 8, edited by Rudolf Boehm. The Hague: Nijhoff, 1973.
———. *Ideas Pertaining to a Pure Phenomenology and to a Phenomenological Philosophy.* First Book: *General Introduction to a Pure Phenomenology.* Translated by F. Kersten. The Hague: Nijhoff, 1983. Orig. *Ideen zu einer reinen Phänomenologie und phänomenologischen Philosophie.* Erstes Buch: *Allgemeine Einführung in die reine Phänomenologie.* In *Husserliana*, vol. 3.1–2, edited by Karl Schuhmann. The Hague: Nijhoff, 1976.
———. *Ideas Pertaining to a Pure Phenomenology and to a Phenomenological Philosophy.* Second Book: *Studies in the Phenomenology of Constitution.* Translated by Richard Rojcewicz and André Schuwer. Dordrecht: Kluwer Academic Publishers, 1989. Orig. *Ideen zu einer reinen Phänomenologie und phänomenologischen Philosophie.* Zweites Buch: *Phänomenologische Untersuchungen zur Konstitution.* In *Husserliana*, vol. 4, edited by Walter Biemel. The Hague: Nijhoff, 1952.
———. *Ideas Pertaining to a Pure Phenomenology and to a Phenomenological Philosophy.* Third Book: *Phenomenology and the Foundation of the Sciences.* Translated by Ted E. Klein and William E. Pohl. The Hague: Nijhoff, 1980. Orig. *Ideen zu einer reinen Phänomenologie und phänomenologischen Philosophie.* Drittes Buch: *Die Phänomenologie und die Fundamente der Wissenschaften* in *Husserliana*, vol. 5, edited by Walter Biemel. The Hague: Nijhoff, 1952.
———. *Logical Investigations.* Translated by J. N. Findlay. London: Routledge and K. Paul, 1970. Orig. *Logische Untersuchungen: Untersuchungen zur Phänomenologie und Theorie der Erkenntnis*, Band 2.1. In *Husserliana*, vol. 19, edited by Ursula Panzer. The Hague: Nijhoff, 1984.
———. *Méditations cartésiennes: Introduction à la phénoménologie.* Translated into French by Gabrielle Peiffer and Emmanuel Levinas. Paris: Colin, 1931.
———. "Ms. D 17. Grundlegende Untersuchungen zum phänomenologischen Ursprung der Räumlichkeit der Natur. Umsturz der kopernikanischen Lehre in

der gewölichen weltanschauulichen Interpretation. Die Ur-Arche Erde bewegt sich nicht. Grundlegende Untersuchungen zum phänomenologischen Ursprung der Körperlichkeit, der Räumlichkeit der Natur im ersten naturwissenschaftlichen Sinne. Alles notwendige Anfangs-untersuchungen (7–9 March, 1934)." In *Philosophical Essays in Memory of Edmund Husserl*, edited by Marvin Faber, 307–325. Cambridge, MA: Harvard University Press, 1940.

———. *On the Phenomenology of the Consciousness of Internal Time (1893–1917)*. Translated by John Barnett Brough. Dordrecht: Kluwer Academic Publishers, 1991. Orig. *Zur Phänomenologie des inneren Zeitbewusstsein (1893–1917)*. In *Husserliana*, vol. 10, edited by Rudolf Boehm. The Hague: Nijhof, 1966.

———. *The Paris Lectures*. Translated by Peter Koestenbaum. The Hague: M. Nijhoff, 1964.

———. *Phantasy, Image Consciousness, and Memory (1898–1925)*. Translated by John B. Brough. Dordrecht: Springer, 2005. Orig. *Phantasie, Bildbewusstsein, Erinnerung: Zur Phänomenologie der anschaulichen Vergegenwärtigungen. Texte aus dem Nachlass (1898–1925)*. In *Husserliana*, vol. 23, edited by Eduard Marbach. The Hague: Nijhoff, 1980.

———. *Phenomenological Interpretation of Kant's* Critique of Pure Reason. Translated by Parvis Emad and Kenneth Maly. Bloomington: Indiana University Press, 1997.

———. "Randbemerkungen Husserls zu Heideggers Kant und das Problem der Metaphysik." *Husserl Studies* 11, nos. 1–2, (1994): 49–63.

———. "Randbemerkungen Husserls zu Heideggers Sein und Zeit." *Husserl Studies* 11, nos. 1–2, (1994): 3–48.

———. *Zur Phänomenologie der Intersubjektivität: Texte aus dem Nachlass*, 1. Teil, 1905–1920. In *Husserliana*, vol. 13, edited by Iso Kern. The Hague: Nijhoff, 1973.

———. *Zur Phänomenologie der Intersubjektivität. Texte aus dem Nachlass*, 2. Teil, 1921–1928. In *Husserliana*, vol. 14, edited by Iso Kern. The Hague: Nijhoff, 1973.

———. *Zur Phänomenologie der Intersubjektivität: Texte aus dem Nachlass*, 3. Teil, 1929–1935. In *Husserliana*, vol. 15, edited by Iso Kern. The Hague: Nijhoff, 1973.

Ingarden, Roman. "Kritische Bemerkungen von Professor Dr. Roman Ingarden, Krakau." In *Cartesianische Meditationen und Pariser Vorträge*. In *Husserliana*, vol. 1. Edited by Stephan Strasser. The Hague: Nijhoff, 1973.

———. "Über die Gefahr einer Petitio Principii in der Erkenntnistheorie." In *Jahrbuch für Philosophie und phänomenologische Forschung* 4 (1921): 545–568.

Jankélévitch, Vladimir. *The Bad Conscience*. Translated by Andrew Kelley. Chicago: University of Chicago Press, 2015. Orig. *La mauvaise conscience* (1939). Paris: Aubier-Montaigne, 1981.

———. *L'innocence et la méchanceté: Traité des vertus*. Vol. 3. Paris: Flammarion, 1986.

———. *La mort*. Paris: Flammarion, 1977.

———. *Le sérieux de l'intention: Traité des vertus*. Vol. 1. Paris: Flammarion, 1983.

Jarry, Alfred. *Days and Nights: Novel of a Deserter*. Translated by Alexis Lykiard. London: Atlas, 1989. Orig. *Les jours et les nuits: Roman d'un déserteur*. Paris: Gallimard, 1981.

Jaspers, Karl. *Philosophie*. Band 2, *Existenzerhellung*. Berlin: Springer, 1956.
Jesi, Furio. "Károly Kérényi 2. L'esperienza dell'isola." In *Materiali mitologici: Mito e antropologia nella cultura mitteleuropea*, edited by Andrea Cavalletti, 54–66. Turin: Einaudi, 2001.
———."Prefazione." In *Materiali mitologici*, edited by Andrea Cavalletti, 346–348. Turin: Einaudi, 2001.
———. *Spartakus: The Symbology of Revolt* (2000). Edited by Andrea Cavalletti, translated by Alberto Toscano. London: Seagull Books, 2014. Orig. *Spartakus: Simbologia della rivolta*. Edited by Andrea Cavalletti. Turin: Bollati Boringhieri, 2000.
Kant, Immanuel. *Anthropologie in pragmatischer Hinsicht*. In *Werkausgabe*, Band 12.2, *Schriften zur Anthropologie, Geschichtsphilosophie, Politik und Pädagogik*. Frankfurt: Suhrkamp, 1977.
———. *Critique of Pure Reason*. Translated by Paul Guyer and Allen W. Wood. Cambridge: Cambridge University Press, 1998. Orig. *Kritik der reinen Vernunft*. In *Werkausgabe* 3–4, edited by Wilhelm Weischedel. Frankfurt: Suhrkamp, 1974.
———. Letter to Marcus Herz, April 7, 1786. In Immanuel Kant, *Gesammelte Schriften*, Band 10, *Briefwechsel*, 1. Teil, 1747–1788. Berlin: De Gruyter, 1922.
Kerényi, Károly. "Agalma, Eikon, Eidolon." Translated by Ornella Maria Nobile. In *Archivio di Filosofia* 1–2 (1962), later in Károly Kerényi, *Scritti italiani (1955–1971)*, edited by Giampiero Moretti. Napoli: Guida, 1993.
Kierkegaard, Søren. *The Concept of Anxiety*. Edited and translated by Reidar Thomte in collaboration with Albert B. Anderson. Princeton, NJ: Princeton University Press, 1980. Orig. *Begrebet angest*. In *Semlede Voerker* 4, edited by Anders Bjørn Drachman, Johan Ludvig Heiberg and Hans Ostenfeldt Lange. Copenhagen: Gyldendal, 1962–1964.
Kimura, Bin. "Temporalité de la schizophrénie." In Bin Kimura, *Écrits de psychopathologie phénoménologique*, translated into French by Joël Bouderlique. Paris: PUF, 1992.
Klein, Robert. "Appropriation et aliénation." In *La forme et l'intelligible: Écrits sur la Renaissance et l'art moderne*, edited by André Chastel, 459–472. Paris: Gallimard, 1970.
———. Ars et Technè dans la tradition de Platon à Giordano Bruno. Unpublished *mémoire de thèse*. Typescript with handwritten notes, held at the library of the Institut National d'Histoire de l'Art de Paris (BINHA, 090, 079, 03).
———. "Discussione" (on *Les limites de la morale transcendantale*, with Paul Ricœur, Karl Kerényi, Jean Brun, Odette Laffoucrière, Antoine Vergote e Adolphe de Waelhens). *Archivio di Filosofia*, nos. 1–2 (1965): 305–310.
———. Essai sur la responsabilité. Unpublished typescript and manuscript (BINHA, 090, 081 bis).
———. "L'art et l'attention au technique" (1964). In *La forme et l'intelligible: Écrits sur la Renaissance et l'arte moderne*, edited by André Chastel, 382–393. Paris: Gallimard, 1970.

———. *L'esthétique de la technè: L'art selon Aristote et les théories des arts visuels au XVIe siècle* (1962). Edited by Jérémie Joering. Paris: Institut National d'Histoire de l'Art, 2017.

———. "Le rire." In *L'umanesimo e la follia*, 177–195. Rome: Abete, 1971.

———. "Le thème du fou dans l'ironie humaniste." In *La forme et l'intelligible. Écrits sur la Renaissance et l'arte modern*, edited by André Chastel, 433–450. Paris: Gallimard, 1970.

———. "Les limites de la morale transcendantale" [in collaboration with Ngô Tieng Hiên]. In *La forme et l'intelligible: Écrits sur la Renaissance et l'arte moderne*, edited by André Chastel, 473–485. Paris: Gallimard, 1970.

———. Letter to André Chastel, August 31, 1966. Partially published in *L'esthétique de la technè*, 41n66. Typescript with corrections and signature (BINHA, 090, 079, 902, 07).

———. Letter without addressee, September 3, 1966. Partially published in *L'esthétique de la technè*, 41n66. Typescript transcription (BINHA 090, 079, 902, 07).

———. "Modern Painting and Phenomenology." In *Form and Meaning: Essays on Renaissance and Modern Art*, translated by Madeline Jay and Leon Wieseltier, 184–199. New York: Viking Press, 1979. Orig. "Peinture modern et phénoménologie." In *La forme et l'intelligible: Écrits sur la Renaissance et l'arte moderne*, edited by André Chastel, 411–429. Paris: Gallimard, 1970.

———. "Nature et maniement du rire chez Georges Bataille" (1966). Unpublished typescript and manuscript (BINHA 090, 079, 902, 07).

———. "Thought, Confession, Fiction: On *A Season in Hell*." In *Form and Meaning: Essays on Renaissance and Modern Art*, translated by Madeline Jay and Leon Wieseltier, 200–207. New York: Viking Press, 1979. Orig. "Pensée, confession, fiction. À propos de la 'Saison en enfer.'" (1959) In *La forme et l'intelligible: Écrits sur la Renaissance et l'arte moderne*, edited by André Chastel, 451–458. Paris: Gallimard, 1970.

Kojève, Alexandre. *Introduction à la lecture de Hegel: Leçons sur la "Phénoménologie de l'Esprit," professées de 1933 à 1939 à l'École Pratique des Hautes Études, réunies et publiées par Raymond Queneau*. Paris: Gallimard, 1947.

Kracauer, Siegfried. *Theory of Film: The Redemption of Physical Reality*. New York: Oxford University Press, 1960.

Krishaber, Maurice. *De la névropathie cérébro-cardiaque*. Paris: Masson, 1873.

La Mettrie, Julien Offray de. *Traité du Vertige, avec la description d'une catalepsie hysterique & une lettre à Monsieur Astruc, dans laquelle on répond à la critique qu'il a faite d'une dissertation de l'auteur sur les maladies vénérienne*. Rennes: Garnier, 1737.

Lacan, Jacques. *Speech and Language in Psychoanalysis*. Translated by Anthony Wilden. Baltimore, MD: Johns Hopkins University Press, 1984. Orig. *Fonction et champ de la parole et du langage en psychanalyse*. In *Écrits*. Paris: Éditions du Seuil, 1966.

Ladame, Paul-Louis. "Quelques mots sur l'étiologie du vertige paralysant." *Revue Médicale de la Suisse Romande* 11, no. 6 (1891): 351–354.
Ladewig, Rebekka. *Schwindel: Eine Epistemologie der Orientierung*. Tübingen: Mohr, 2016.
Lasègue, Ernest Charles. "De Stahl, et sa doctrine médicale." MD dissertation, February 25, 1846. Paris: Rignoux, 1846.
———. "Des Vertiges: Leçon recueillie et redigée par le Dr. Frémy." In *Études médicales*, vol. 1, edited by Albert Blum, 775–796. Paris: Asselin, 1884.
———. "L'école psychique allemande." In *Études médicales*, vol. 1, edited by Albert Blum, 1–59. Paris: Asselin, 1884.
———. "Questions de thérapeutique mentale." In *Études médicales*, vol. 1, edited by Albert Blum, 585–615. Paris: Asselin, 1884.
———. "Vertige mental." In *Études médicales*, vol. 1, edited by Albert Blum, 765–774. Paris: Asselin, 1884.
Leder, Christoph Maria. *Die Grenzgänge des Marcus Herz: Beruf, Haltung und Identität eines jüdischen Arztes gegen Ende des 18. Jahrhunderts*. Münster: Waxmann, 2007.
Leers, Johann von. *14 Jahre Judenrepublik: Die Geschichte eines Rassenkampfes*. Berlin: NS Druck und Verlag, 1933.
Leibniz, Gottfried Wilhelm. *Leibniz's Monadology: A New Translation and Guide*. Edited and translated by Lloyd Strickland. Edinburgh: Edinburgh University Press, 2014. Orig. *Monadologie* (1714). In *Principes de la nature et de la grâce fondés en raison—Principes de la philosophie ou Monadologie*. Edited by André Robinet. Paris: PUF, 1986.
Leroux, Henri. "Vertige." In Amédée Dechambre and Léon Lereboullet, *Dictionnaire encyclopédique des sciences médicales*, vol. 3, Ver-Zyt. Paris: Masson, Asselin et Hozeau, 1889.
Levinas, Emmanuel. *De l'évasion*. Edited by Jacques Rolland. Montpellier: Morgana, 1982.
———. *En découvrant l'existence avec Husserl et Heidegger*. Paris: Vrin, 2006.
———. *Existence and Existents*. Translated by Alphonso Lingis. Pittsburgh, PA: Duquesne University Press, 2001. Orig. *De l'existence à l'existant*. Paris: Vrin, 1947.
———. *La mort et le temps*. Edited by Jacques Rolland. Paris: Éditions de l'Herne, 1992.
———. *Otherwise Than Being or Beyond Essence*. Translated by Alphonso Lingis. Dordrecht: Kluwer Academic Publishers, 1981. Orig. *Autrement qu'être, ou au-delà de l'essence*. The Hague: Nijhoff, 1971.
———. *Quelques réflexions sur la philosophie de l'hitlérisme*. Paris: Rivages, 1997.
———. *Théorie de l'intuition dans la phénoménologie de Husserl*. Paris: Vrin, 1994.
———. *Time and the Other and Additional Essays*. Translated by Richard A. Cohen. Pittsburgh, PA: Duquesne University Press, 1987.
———. *Totality and Infinity: An Essay on Exteriority*. Translated by Alphonso Lingis. Pittsburgh (PA): Duquesne University Press, 1969. Orig. *Totalité et infini: Essai sur l'extériorité*. The Hague: Nijhoff, 1971.

Longhi, Roberto. "Ricordo dei manieristi." In *Da Cimabue a Morandi: Saggi di storia della pittura italiana*, edited by Gianfranco Contini, 722–734. Milan: Mondadori, 2001.

Mach, Ernst. *Grundlinien der Lehre von den Bewegungsempfindungen*. Leipzig: Engelmann, 1875.

Maimon, Salomon. *Autobiography of Solomon Maimon*. Edited by Yitzhak Y. Melamed and Abraham P. Socher, translated by Paul Reitter. Princeton, NJ: Princeton University Press, 2018. Orig. *Lebensgeschichte*. Edited by Karl Philipp Moritz. Berlin: F. Vieweg dem älteren, 1793.

Maldiney, Henri. "Notes sur le rythme." In *Henri Maldiney: penser plus avant . . . : Acts of the Lyon Conference, November 12–14, 2010*, edited by Jean-Pierre Charcosset, 17–22. Chatou: Éditions de la Transparence, 2012.

———. *Regard, parole, espace*. Lausanne: L'Age d'Homme, 1973.

———. "Sur le vertige." In *Henri Maldiney: penser plus avant . . . : Acts of the Lyon Conference, November 12–14, 2010*, edited by Jean-Pierre Charcosset, 13–15. Chatou: Éditions de la Transparence, 2012.

Marx, Karl. *Der achtzehnte Brumaire des Louis Bonaparte*. In *Werke*, Band 8, *August 1851 bis Marz 1853*. Berlin: Dietz, 1960.

———. *Das Kapital: Kritik der politischen Ökonomie*. In *Werke*, Band 13–25. Berlin: Dietz, 1948–1949.

Marx, Karl, and Friedrich Engels, *Manifest der Kommunistischen Partei*. In *Werk*, Band 4: *Mai 1846 bis Marz 1848*. Berlin: Dietz, 1959.

Maury, Alfred. *Le sommeil et les rêves: Études psychologiques sur ces phénomènes et les divers états qui s'y rattachent; suivies de Recherches sur le développement de l'instinct et de l'intelligence dans leurs rapports avec le phénomène du sommeil*. Paris: Didier, 1865.

Mauss, Marcel. "The Physical Effect on the Individual of the Idea of Death Suggested by the Collectivity (Australia, New Zealand)." In *Sociology and Psychology: Essays*, translated by Ben Brewster, 79–96. London: Routledge and Kegan Paul, 1979. Orig. "Effet physique chez l'individu de l'idée de mort suggerée par la collectivité (Australie, Nouvelle-Zélande)," in *Sociologie et anthropologie*, 312–330. Paris: PUF, 2009.

Melandri, Enzo. *Logica e esperienza in Husserl*. Bologna: Il Mulino, 1960.

Merleau-Ponty, Maurice. "The Film and the New Psychology." In *Sense and Non-Sense*, translated by Hubert L. Dreyfus and Patricia Allen Dreyfus, 48–60. Evanston, IL: Northwestern University Press, 1964. Orig. "Le cinéma et la nouvelle psychologie." In *Sens et non-sens* (1966), 85–73. Paris: Gallimard, 1996.

———. *Les relations avec autrui chez l'enfant*. Paris: Centre de Documentation Universitaire, 1969.

———. "On the Phenomenology of Language." In *Phenomenology, Language and Sociology: Selected Essays of Maurice Merleau-Ponty*, edited by John O'Neill, 84–97. London: Heinemann, 1974. Orig. "Sur la phénoménologie du langage." In *Signes*, 83–96. Paris: Gallimard, 1960.

———. *Phenomenology of Perception*. Translated by Donald A. Landes. New York: Routledge, 2012. Orig. *Phénoménologie de la perception* (1945). Paris: Gallimard, 2003.
———. *The Prose of the World*. Translated by John O'Neill. Evanston, IL: Northwestern University Press, 1973. Orig. *La prose du monde*. Edited by Claude Lefort. Paris: Gallimard, 1969.
———. *The Structure of Behavior*. Translated by Alden L. Fisher. Boston, MA: Beacon Press, 1963. Orig. *La structure du comportement*. Paris: PUF, 1977.
———. *The Visible and the Invisible*. Edited by Claude Lefort, translated by Alphonso Lingis. Evanston, IL: Northwestern University Press, 1968. Orig. *Le visible et l'invisible: Suivi de notes de travail*. Edited by Claude Lefort. Paris: Gallimard, 1964.
Milner, Jean-Claude. "De la linguistique à la linguisterie." In *Lacan: L'écrit, l'image*, 7–25. Paris: Flammarion, 2000.
Montaigne, Michel de. *The Complete Essays*. Translated by M. A. Screech. London: Penguin Books, 1991. Orig. *Les essais*. Edited by André Tournon. Paris: Imprimerie Nationale, 1998.
Moullet, Luc. "Sam Fuller: In Marlowe's Footsteps." In Hillier, *Cahiers du Cinema: The 1950s*, 145–156. Orig. "Sam Fuller: Sur les brisées de Marlowe." *Cahiers du Cinéma*, no. 93 (1959): 11–19.
Naselli, Elvira, "Nel laboratorio dove si cura il capogiro." *La Repubblica*, November 2, 2010.
Negrelli, Giorgio. *L'illuminista diffidente: Giuseppinismo e Restaurazione nel pensiero politico di Antonio de Giuliani*. Bologna: il Mulino, 1974.
Nietzsche, Friedrich. *The Genealogy of Morals*. Translated by Horace B. Samuel. New York: Boni and Liveright, 1918. Orig. *Zur Genealogie der Moral: Eine Streitschrift*. In *Werke*, Band 6.2, *Jenseits von Gut und Böse—Zur Genealogie der Moral*. Berlin: De Gruyter, 1968.
———. *Morgenröte* (1881). In *Werke: Kritische Studienausgabe*, Band 3, *Morgenröte—Idyllen aus Messina—Die fröliche Wissenschaft*. Edited by Giorgio Colli and Mazzino Montinari. Berlin: De Gruyter, 1967.
Novak, Kim. "The Making of a Perfect Hitchcock Heroine." Interview. BFI Film Forever. 2012. https://www2.bfi.org.uk/films-tv-people/39steps/#/?item=12.
Pascal, Blaise. *Pensées*. Translated by A. J. Krailsheimer. London: Penguin Books, 1995. Orig. *Pensées* (1669). Edited by Michel Le Guern. Paris: Gallimard, 1977.
Pascoli, Giovanni. "Nuovi poemetti" (1909). In *Poesie*, vol. 2, *Primi poemetti—Nuovi poemetti*. Edited by Francesca Latini. Turin: UTET, 2008.
Patočka, Jan. *Phänomenologische Schriften*, Band 2, *Die Bewegung der menschlichen Existenz*, edited by Klaus Nellen, Jiri Nemen e Ilja Srubar. Stuttgart: Klett-Cotta, 1991.
Peck, Jason M. "*Vertigo Ergo Sum*: Kant, his Jewish 'Students' and the Origins of Romanticism." *European Romantic Review* 26, no. 1 (2015): 29–41.
Piana, Giovanni. *Esistenza e storia negli inediti di Husserl*. Milan: Lampugnani Nigri, 1965.
Pichois, Claude, and Jean Ziegler. *Baudelaire*. Translated by Graham Robb. London: H. Hamilton, 1989. Orig. *Baudelaire*. Paris: Julliard, 1987.

Plessner, Helmut. *Grenzen der Gemeinschaft. Eine Kritik des sozialen Radikalismus.* In *Gesammelte Schriften,* Band 5, *Macht und menschliche Natur.* Edited by Günther Dux, Odo Marquard and Elisabeth Ströke. Frankfurt: Suhrkamp, 1981.
Poe, Edgar Allan. "The Imp of the Perverse." In *Collected Works of Edgar Allan Poe,* vol. 3, *Tales and Sketches 1843–1849,* edited by Thomas Ollive Mabbott, 1217–1227. Cambridge, MA: Belknap Press, 1978.
——. "Morella." In *Collected Works of Edgar Allan Poe,* vol. 2, *Tales and Sketches 1831–1842,* edited by Thomas Ollive Mabbott, 221–237. Cambridge, MA: Belknap Press, 1978.
——. "The Pit and the Pendulum." In *Collected Works of Edgar Allan Poe,* vol. 2, *Tales and Sketches 1831–1842,* edited by Thomas Ollive Mabbott, 678–699. Cambridge, MA: Belknap Press, 1978.
Porterfield, William. *A Treatise on the Eye, the Manner and Phaenomena of Vision.* Vol. 2. London-Edinburgh: Miller-Hamilton and Balfour, 1759.
Postel, Jacques. "Naissance et décadence du traitement moral pendant la première moitié du XIXe siècle." *L'Évolition Psychiatrique* 44, no. 3 (1979): 585–616.
Poulet, Georges. "Bergson: Le thème de la vision panoramique des mourants et la juxtaposition." In *L'espace proustien.* 186–190. Paris: Gallimard, 1982.
——. *Les métamorphoses du cercle.* Paris: Flammarion, 1979.
Purkinje, Jan Evangelista. "Beiträge zur näheren Kenntnis des Schwindels aus heautognostischen Daten." In *Medicinische Jahrbücher des kaiserlich-königlichen Österreichischen Staates* 6, no. 2 (1820): 79–125.
——. "Über die physiologische Bedeutung des Schwindels und die Beziehung desselben zu den neusten Versuchen über die Hirnfunctionen." In *Rust: Magazin für die gesammte Heilkunde,* no. 23 (1827): 284–310.
Quinodoz, Danielle. *Le vertige: Entre angoisse et plaisir.* Paris: PUF, 1994.
Rachilde (Marguerite Eyméry). "Les romans [Edmond Cazal, *Le vertige de la volupté et de la mort*]." *Mercure de France,* December 15, 1922.
Raimann, Johann Nepomuk von. *Handbuch der speciellen medicinischen Pathologie und Therapie.* Band 2. Vienna: Volke, 1826.
Ramazzini, Bernardino. *De morbis artificium diatriba.* Modena: Capponi, 1700.
Ravaisson, Félix. *De l'habitude.* Paris: Fayard, 1984.
Reik, Theodor. *Geständniszwang and Strafbedürfnis: Probleme der Psychoanalyse und der Kriminologie.* Lepizig: Internationaler Psychoanalytischer Verlag, 1925.
Renouvier, Charles. *Nouvelle monadologie.* Paris: Colin, 1899.
——. *Traité de psychologie rationnelle d'après les principes du criticisme* (1859). In *Essais de critique générale,* vol. 2.1. Paris: Colin, 1912.
Ribot, Théodule. *Les maladies de la mémoire.* Paris: Baillière et fils, 1881.
Richir, Marc. *Phénoménologie en esquisses: Nouvelles fondations.* Grenoble: Millon, 2000.
Richter, Emil (Germanicus). *Der neueste Raub am deutschen Nationalwohlstand: Zweiter Anhang zu "Die Frankfurter Juden und die Aufsaugung des Volkswohlstandes."* Frankfurt: Germanicus Verlag, 1881.

———. *Die Frankfurter Juden und die Aufsaugung des Volkswohlstandes: Eine Anklage wider die Agiotage und wider den Wucher.* Leipzig: Glaser and Garte, 1880.

Ricoeur, Paul. *Husserl: An Analysis of His Phenomenology.* Translated by Edward G. Ballard and Lester E. Embree. Evanston, IL: Northwestern University Press, 1967. Orig. *À l'école de la phénoménologie.* Paris: Vrin, 2004.

———. *Soi-même comme un autre.* Paris: Éditions du Seuil, 1990.

Riegl, Alois. *Spätrömische Kunstindustrie.* Vienna: Österreichische Staatsdruckerei, 1927.

Rivette, Jacques. "De l'abjection." *Cahiers du Cinéma,* no. 120 (1961): 54–55.

Rivière, Lazare. *Praxis medica.* Paris: Olivier de Varennes, 1640.

Rodenbach, Georges. *Bruges-la-Morte: A Novel.* Translated by Philip Mosley. Orig. *Bruges-la-morte. Le Figaro,* February 4–14, 1892.

Rohmer, Éric. "Alfred Hitchcock's *Vertigo.*" In *The Taste for Beauty,* translated by Carol Volk, 167–172. Cambridge: Cambridge University Press, 1989. Orig. "L'hélice et l'idée." In *Le goût de la beauté,* edited by Jean Narboni. Paris: Éditions de l'Étoile, 1984.

Rohmer, Éric, and Claude Chabrol. *Hitchcock: The First Forty-Four Films.* Translated by Stanley Hochman. New York: F. Ungar, 1979. Orig. *Hitchcock.* Paris: Éditions Universitaires, 1957.

Rothman, William. *Hitchcock. The Murderous Gaze.* Cambridge, MA: Cambridge University Press, 1984.

Sartre, Jean Paul. *Being and Nothingness: An Essay on Phenomenological Ontology.* Translated by Hazel E. Barnes. New York: Philosophical Library, 1956. Orig. *L'être et le néant: Essai d'ontologie phénoménologique.* Edited by Arlette Elkaïm-Sartre. Paris: Gallimard, 1976.

———. *L'imaginaire: Psychologie phénoménologique de l'imagination.* Edited by Arlette Elkaïm-Sartre. Paris: Gallimard, 1986.

———. *Saint Genet: Actor and Martyr.* Translated by Bernard Frechtman. New York: G. Braziller, 1963. Orig. *Saint Genet, comédien et martyr.* Paris: Gallimard, 2011.

———. *The Transcendence of the Ego.* Translated by Forrest Williams and Robert Kirkpatrick. New York: Hill and Wang, 1957. Orig. "La transcendance de l'ego" (1937). In *La transcendance de l'ego et Conscience de soi et connaissance de soi, précédés de Une idée fondamentale de la phénoménologie de Husserl: l'intentionnalité.* Edited by Vincent de Coorebyter, 91–131. Paris: Vrin, 2003.

Satta, Salvatore. *De profundis* (1948). Milan: Adelphi, 1980.

Schefer, Jean-Louis. "Vertigo, vert tilleul" in *Trafic,* no. 15 (1995): 51–56.

Schellhammer, Günther Christoph. "Vertigo nocturna." In *Miscellanea curiosa, sive Ephemeridum medico-physicarum Germanicarum Academiae Naturae Curiosorum.* Decuria 2, vol. 5 (1686).

Schnitzler, Arthur. *Beatrice and her son.* Translated by Shaun Whiteside. New York: Penguin, 1999. Orig. *Frau Beate und ihr Sohn.* Berlin: Fischer, 1913.

Schürmann, Reiner. *Heidegger on Being and Acting: From Principles to Anarchy.* Bloomington: Indiana University Press, 1986.
Sidis, Boris. *Philistine and Genius.* New York: Moffat, Yard and Co., 1911.
Simon, Max. *Du vertige nerveux et de son traitement: Mémoire récompensé par l'Académie Impériale de Médecine.* Paris: Baillière et fils, 1858.
Simon, Paul-Max. *Le monde des rêves.* Paris: Baillière et fils, 1882.
Solla, Gianluca. "Elogio della vertigine o guerra senza fine." In Roger Caillois, *La vertigine della guerra.* Translated into Italian by Marco Tabacchini, Silvia Uberti and Elia Verzegnassi. Gussago: Casa di Marrani, 2014.
Spitzer, Leo. "Unkehrbare Lyrik" (1927). In *Stilstudien.* Band 2, *Stilsprachen.* Munich: Hueber, 1928.
Stein, Edith. *Beiträge zur philosophischen Begründung der Psychologie und der Geisteswissenschaften.* In *Gesamtausgabe*, Band 6, *Frühe Phänomenologie*, 2. Teil, edited by Beate Beckmann-Zöller. Freiburg: Herder, 2010.
———. *Einführung in die Philosophie.* In *Gesamtausgabe*, Band 8, *Frühe Phänomenologie*, 4. Teil, edited by Claudia Mariéle Wulf. Freiburg: Herder, 2004.
———. *Letters to Roman Ingarden: Self-Portrait in Letters.* Translated by Hugh Candler Hunt. Washington, DC: ICS Publications, 2014. Orig. *Gesamtausgabe*, Band 4, *Selbstbildnis in Briefen*, 2. Teil, *Briefe an Roman Ingarden.* Freiburg: Herder, 2000.
———. *Martin Heideggers Existenzphilosophie.* In *Gesamtausgabe*, Band 11/12, *Phänomenologie und Ontologie*, 3/4. Teil, *Endliches und ewiges Sein: Versuch eines Aufstiegs zum Sinn des Seins*, edited by Andreas Uwe Müller. Freiburg: Herder, 2006.
———. *On the Problem of Empathy.* Translated by Waltraut Stein. Washington, DC: ICS Publications, 1989. Orig. *Zum Problem der Einfühlung* (1917). In *Gesamtausgabe*, Band 5, *Frühe Phänomenologie*, 1. Teil, edited by Michael Linssen. Freiburg: Herder, 2008.
Stevenson, Robert Louis. *Weir of Hermiston.* In *The New Edinburgh Edition of the Collected Works of Robert Louis Stevenson*, edited by Gillian Hughes. Edinburgh: Edinburgh University Press, 1995.
Stoichita, Victor Ieronim. *The Pygmalion Effect: From Ovid to Hitchcock.* Translated by Alison Anderson. Chicago: Chicago University Press, 2008.
Strauss, Leo. *Natural Right and History* (1953). Chicago: University of Chicago Press, 1965.
Szilasi, Wilhelm. *Einführung in die Phänomenologie Edmund Husserls.* Tübingen: Niemeyer, 1959.
Tarde, Gabriel. *Monadologie et sociologie* (1893). In *Essais et mélanges sociologiques.* Lyon-Paris: Storck-Masson, 1895
———. "Qu'est-ce qu'une société?" *Revue Philosophique* 18 (1884): 489–510.
Timpanaro, Sebastiano. *Il lapsus freudiano: Psicoanalisi e critica testuale* (1974). Edited by Fabio Stok. Turin: Bollati Boringhieri, 2002.

Towarnicki, Frédéric de. À *la rencontre de Heidegger: Souvenirs d'un messager de la Forêt-Noire*. Paris: Gallimard, 1993.
Trastour, Étienne. *Des vertiges de cause nerveuse, ou vertiges nerveux*. Nantes: Velinet, 1858.
Trousseau, Armand. *Clinique médicale de l'Hôtel-Dieu de Paris*. Vol. 2. Paris: Baillière et fils, 1868.
Truffaut, François. *Hitchcock*. With the collaboration of Helen G. Scott. New York: Simon and Schuster, 1984.
Van der Leeuw, Gerardus. *Religion in Essence and Manifestation*. Translated by J. E. Turner. Princeton, NJ: Princeton University Press, 1986. Orig. *Phänomenologie der Religion*. Tübingen: Mohr, 1956.
Van Kerckhoven, Guy. *Mondanisation et individuation* (1995). Translated into Italian and edited by Massimo Mezzanzanica. *Mondanizzazione e individuazione. La posta in gioco nella Sesta meditazione cartesiana di Husserl e Fink*. Genoa: Il Melangolo, 1998.
Wade, Nicolas J. *Perception and Illusion: Historical Perspectives*. New York: Springer, 2005.
Wade, Nicolas J., and Benjamin W. Tatler. *The Moving Tablet of the Eye: The Origins of Modern Eye Movement Research*. Oxford: Oxford University Press, 2005.
Wahl, Jean. *Études kierkegaardiennes*. Paris: Aubier, 1967.
———. *Husserl*. Vol. 2. Paris: Centre de Documentation Universitaire, 1958.
———. *La philosophie de Heidegger*. Vol. 1. Paris: Centre de Documentation Universitaire, 1952.
Wallon, Henri. "L'acte perceptif et le cinéma." *Revue Internationale de Filmologie* 4, no. 13 (1953): 97–110.
———. *La vie mentale* (1938). Edited by Émile Jalley. Paris: Éditions Sociales, 1982.
Weil, Simone. *Oppression and Liberty*. Translated by Arthur Wills and John Petrie. Amherst: University of Massachusetts Press, 1973. Orig. *Réflexions sur les causes de la liberté et de l'oppression sociale* (1934). Paris: Gallimard, 1980.
Weill, Edmond. *Des vertiges*. Paris: Baillière et fils, 1886.
Wepfer, Johann Jakob. *Observationes medico-practicae de affectibus capitis internis et externis*. Edited by Bernhard Wepfer and Georg Michael Wepfer. Scaphusii: Joh. Adami Ziegleri, 1727.
Wolff, Christian. *Philosophia prima sive ontologia*. 3rd ed. In *Gesammelte Werke*. Band 2.3. Edited by Jean Ècole. Hildesheim: Olms, 1962.
Worringer, Wilhelm. *Griechentum und Gotik: Vom Weltreich des Hellenismus*. Munich: Piper, 1928.
Yang, Pao-San. *La psychologie de l'intelligence chez Renouvier: Étude spéciale de la théorie du vertige mental*. Paris: Presses Modernes, 1930.

Index

Abadie, Jean, 19
Adelon, Nicolas-Philibert, 156nn108–109
Adorno, Theodor Wiesengrund, 69, 77, 84, 99, 164n186
Alain (Émile-Auguste Chartier), 1, 11, 12, 90, 152n1, 153nn43–45
Ancelle, Narcisse, 60
Anders, Günther (Günther Stern), 115, 119, 121, 171n15, 172nn48,58
Andrews, Julie (Julia Elizabeth Wells), 108
Antonioni, Michelangelo, 5
Arcimboldo, Giuseppe, 138
Arendt, Hannah, 122, 128, 172n60, 173n74
Aristotle, 35, 41, 94, 97, 109, 138, 143, 159n34, 167n63, 170n18, 175nn40, 41, 43, 46
Auber, Brigitte, 9
Avicenna, 18

Bachelard, Gaston, 6, 42, 43, 80, 93, 133, 160n40, 165n5
Ball, Benjamin, 60
Bárány, Robert, 19, 25
Barthez, Paul-Joseph, 20
Bass, Saul, 26
Bataille, Georges, 38
Baudelaire, Charles, ix, 9, 60, 133, 155n71, 160n44
Baudry, Jean-Louis, 142, 175n39
Bauer, Ida (Dora), 33
Bauer, Otto, 17
Becker, Oskar, 97, 98, 99, 123, 168nn78,79
Bellini, Lorenzo, 6, 7, 9, 18, 20, 21

Benjamin, Walter, vii, 23, 33, 78, 86, 122, 123, 141, 158n138, 165n4
Berenson, Bernard, 26, 157n116
Bergson, Henri, 26, 85–86, 134, 153n31, 166nn21, 23–26, 174n17
Bernard, Claude, 60
Berrios, German E., 155n83
Bespaloff, Rachel, 36
Bettini, Sergio, xi–xii, 132, 151n5, 174nn9–12
Binswanger, Ludwig, 33
Bloch, Marcus Elieser, 156n85
Blumenberg, Hans, 6, 163n154
Boerhaave, Hermannus, 19, 20
Boileau, Pierre, 4, 6, 9, 46, 49, 80, 83, 110, 141, 152nn3–10, 160nn45–46,49–51,53–54, 57–58,60–61, 165nn8,12, 169nn105, 9, 175n35
Boltraffio, Giovanni Antonio, 29, 30, 31
Borowski, Ludwig Ernst, 15, 154n48
Böttiger, Karl August, 15
Brand, Gerd, 34, 35, 40, 58, 66, 96, 99, 159nn27, 28, 30, 162n112, 163n156, 164n171, 168n86
Breton, André, 174n16
Breuer, Joseph, 28, 157nn122–123
Burrows, George Man, 25
Butler, Samuel, 35

Cabanis, Pierre-Jean-Georges, 35
Caillois, Roger, 16, 43, 129, 155nn69,82, 160nn41–42
Canguilhem, Georges, 89

Castelli, Enrico, 39, 40
Cazal, Edmond (Adolphe d'Espie), 109, 129, 170n16
Chabrol, Claude, 9, 79, 157n114
Charcot, Jean-Martin, 20–21, 27, 28, 92
Chastel, André, 39, 103
Clausewitz, Carl von, 124
Cohen-Séat, Gilbert, 27, 93, 152n13, 160n63
Condillac, Étienne Bonnot de, 35
Coquelin, Charles, 16, 155n74
Cousin, Victor, 60
Cox, Joseph Mason, 24, 93
Cuignet, Ferdinand, 19
Cuzin, François, 110–111, 170nn20,23–25

Daguerre, Louis, 21
Daney, Serge, 23, 26, 48, 156n107, 160n65, 174n14
Darwin, Erasmus, 6, 18, 24, 25, 89, 152nn14,16
Davies, Martin L., 154n63
Dechambre, Amédée, 18
De Giuliani, Antonio, 2, 152nn2–3, 176n3
Deleuze, Gilles, vii, 8, 86, 102, 153n23, 166nn27–28, 168n73
De Martino, Ernesto, 40, 91, 93, 167n49
Derrida, Jacques, x, 77, 90–91, 93, 103, 163n135, 164n187, 167nn45–46, 48, 57, 59, 169nn96, 102, 170n19
Descartes, René, x, 88
Dilthey, Wilhelm, 113
Dodge, Raymond, 25
Douchet, Jean, 153n21
Dragonetti, Roger, 17, 155n79
Duchamp, Marcel, 22, 26
Dumas, Georges, 91
Dupont, Ewald André, 27

Egger, Victor, 85
Eisenstein, Sergei M., 157n118
Eisner, Lotte, 175n32
Engels, Friedrich, 16
Epicurus, 117, 118, 147, 148
Epstein, Jean, 22, 27, 50, 111, 134, 156nn101–103, 157n117, 170n26
Esquirol, Jean-Étienne-Dominique, 16, 24, 60, 155n66, 157n110

Fachinelli, Elvio, 93, 167n53
Fallot, Jean, 172n36, 176n5
Falret, Jean-Pierre, 60
Falret, Jules, 19, 60, 156n88

Fenves, Peter, 12, 154n49
Féré, Charles, 92, 101, 166n20, 167n52
Ferenczi, Sándor, 30, 32, 93, 158n136
Feuerbach, Ludwig, 54, 161n97
Filippini, Enrico, 158n1
Fink, Eugen, x, 74–75, 78, 95–97, 99, 109, 111, 121, 164nn180–181, 183, 165nn190–191, 167n69, 168n72
Flaubert, Gustave, viii, 5, 17, 152n12, 155n78
Flourens, Marie-Jean-Pierre, 19
Fonda, Henry, 25, 79
Fontaine, Joan (Joan de Beauvoir de Havilland), 5
Foucault, Michel, vii, 28, 30, 33, 102–104, 157nn121,130, 158n137, 169nn97–98, 101, 103–104,15, 174n19, 175n1
Fozio, 130
Franck, Didier, 69, 164n169
Frank, Johann Peter, 20, 24
Frank, Joseph, 12, 17, 19, 20, 93, 156n90
Freud, Sigmund, 20, 21, 27–33, 157nn120, 122–129, 130
Friedmann, Max, 16, 155n75
Funke, Gerhard, 96–99, 168nn75–77, 80–85

Gadamer, Hans-Georg, 64, 163n143
Genet, Jean, 137
Genovesi, Antonio, vii, 1
Gerlier, Félix, 19, 20, 156n92
Glagau, Otto, 17
Godard, Jean-Luc, 23, 156n106
Goethe, Johann Wolfang von, 154n56
Gorter, Johannes de, 18
Gowers, William, 21, 156n100
Grant, Cary (Archibald Alexander Leach), 10, 47
Griffith, Coleman, 25
Gris, Juan (José Victoriano González), 138
Guattari, Félix, 168n73
Guéneau de Mussy, Nöel-François-Odon, 19
Guillaumin, Gilbert-Urbain, 155n74

Hallaran, William Sauders, 24
Haltenhoff, Georges-Gabriel, 19
Haufniensis, Vigilius. *See* Kierkegaard, Søren
Hegel, Georg Wilhelm Friedrich, 148
Heidegger, Martin, x, 10, 36–37, 53, 56, 69, 74, 84, 88, 97, 110, 113–116, 118–123, 125–127, 129, 132, 135–137, 153n34, 158nn9–10, 164n182, 165n14, 170nn1–5, 171nn13–14, 17–18,21–35, 172nn37–38, 40–45, 47, 50–51,

INDEX

53–54, 57, 59, 61–65, 67, 173nn68–70, 72–73, 75–92, 174n13
Heine, Heinrich, 16
Heinrich, Klaus, 10, 153n30
Hermann, Bernard, 25
Herz, Marcus, ix, 10, 12–15, 19, 27, 41, 108, 129, 154nn50–51, 53, 58, 60
Hinteregger, Christoph, 17, 155n76
Hitchcock, Alfred, vii, viii, x, xii, 4–6, 8–9, 15, 24–26, 42, 43, 46–50, 59, 79, 86, 108, 139, 142
Hobbes, Thomas, vii, 1, 2, 110, 147, 170n16
Hoffbauer, Johann-Christoph, 15, 154n64
Horn, Anton Ludwig Ernst, 24
Horner, William G., 21, 24
Hufeland, Christoph Wilhelm, 24
Hume, David, 11, 14, 153n38, 154n61
Hunter, Richard, 157n111
Husserl, Edmund, ix–xi, xii, 33, 34–42, 53–59, 61–68, 70–78, 84, 87–88, 90–102, 104, 106, 108, 109, 112, 113–115, 118, 121, 124, 132, 142, 158nn2–3,7, 159nn18,22, 161nn81, 86–96, 99, 162nn113,130, 163nn131, 133, 136, 140–142, 144–145, 147–153, 155, 158, 164nn159, 161, 164, 166, 170, 172, 174, 176–179, 185, 165nn14, 18, 166nn19, 30, 37–38, 167nn58, 65, 68, 168nn70–71, 82, 91–93, 169nn13–14, 170n21, 7, 9, 171nn16, 19, 172n39, 173n71, 175nn44–45

Ingarden, Roman, x, 69, 84, 94–100, 164n167, 165nn15–17, 167nn64, 66–67

Janet, Pierre, 47
Jankélévitch, Vladimir, 40, 51, 58, 106–109, 162n114, 169nn1–8
Jarry, Alfred, 167n50
Jaspers, Karl, 10, 72, 153n33
Jenkins, Charles F., 21
Jesi, Furio, 129, 148, 173n93, 175n38, 176n7
Jung, Carl Gustav, 30

Kant, Immanuel, ix, 10–15, 108, 113, 129, 153n39, 154nn50,62, 170n4
Kautsky, Karl, 17
Kerényi, Károly, 9, 153n26
Khnopff, Fernand, 79
Kienböck, Viktor, 17
Kierkegaard, Søren, 10, 36, 153n32
Kimura, Bin, 50–52, 123, 161n69
Klein, Robert, x–xii, 34, 37–41, 50–55, 57–59, 71, 73, 90, 94, 99–100, 103, 107, 108, 126,

130, 134, 135, 138–141, 144, 151n4, 158n1, 159nn17–19, 21, 23–26, 29–33, 160nn37–38, 62, 161nn67–68,70–71,73–75,78–80, 162nn111–112, 116–117, 164n175, 168nn87–90, 169nn99–100, 11–12, 171n12, 173n1, 174nn18, 28, 175nn29–30, 34, 47
Koering, Jérémie, 39, 151n4
Kojève, Alexandre, 148, 176n4
Kracauer, Sigfried, 93, 167n54
Krishaber, Maurice, 6, 10, 153n37

La Boétie, Étienne de, 36
Lacan, Jacques, 158nn133, 135
Ladame, Paul-Louis, 156n91
Ladewig, Rebekka, 18
La Mettrie, Julien Offroy de, 6–8, 15, 20, 152nn15, 18, 153n22
Lasègue, Ernest-Charles, 47, 60–61, 90, 153n35, 160n64, 162nn122–129
Laughton, Charles, 9
Leers, Johann von, 17, 155n77
Legrand du Saulle, Henri, 20
Leibniz, Gottfried Wilhelm, 7, 40, 88, 152n19, 153n20
Leonardo da Vinci, 139, 143
Le Prince, Louis-Aimé-Augustin, 21
Lequier, Jules, 11
Leroux, Henri, 18, 21
Leroux, Pierre, 16
Levinas, Emmanuel, x, 36, 37, 51, 53, 68, 113, 119, 120, 158nn13–14, 159nn15–16, 161n72, 163n157, 164n160, 172nn46, 49
L'Herbier, Marcel, 4
Lipps, Theodor, 55, 62, 101
Locke, John, 13, 14
Longhi, Roberto, 139, 143, 175nn31, 42
Lumière, Auguste, 6, 26
Lumière, Louis, 6, 26

Macalpine, Ida, 157n111
Mach, Ernst, 19
Maimon, Salomon, 13, 154nn54–55
Maine de Biran, François-Pierre, 11, 35, 89, 96
Maldiney, Henri, xi, 129, 130, 160n52, 173nn94, 2–3, 174nn4–7
Mallarmé, Stéphane, 138
Marinetti, Filippo, 27
Martin, Pierre-Étienne (Martin-le-Jeune), 24
Marx, Karl, vii, 16, 87, 155nn72–73
Maury, Alfred, 155n65, 156n98
Mauss, Marcel, 121, 172nn55–56

Melandri, Enzo, 87, 91, 163n134, 166n29, 167nn44, 47, 60–62
Méliès, Georges, 22
Mendelssohn, Moses, ix, 13
Menière, Prosper, 19
Merleau-Ponty, Maurice, 53, 55–56, 59, 69, 72, 77, 97–98, 106, 108, 121, 157n119, 160nn55–56, 161n98, 162nn100–110, 118–119, 165nn188–189, 170n22, 172n52
Michelangelo, 138,139, 143
Milner, Jean-Claude, 158n134
Minkowski, Eugène, 50
Montaigne, Michel Eyquem de, ix, 3, 6, 10, 11, 47, 59, 152n1, 153n29
Morel, Bénédict, 60
Moullet, Luc, 23, 24, 156n105
Murnau, Friedrich W., 25, 80, 139

Narcejac, Thomas, ix, 4, 6, 9, 46, 49, 80, 83, 110, 141, 152nn4,6–10, 160nn45–46,49–51, 53–54, 57–58, 60–61, 165nn8,12, 169nn105, 9, 175n35
Naselli, Elvira, 157n112
Newman, Paul, 101
Nietzsche, Friedrich, 152n4, 176n6
Novak, Kim (Marylin Pauline Novak), 3, 25, 80, 81

Odier, Louis, 24

Paci, Enzo, 39, 40, 158n1
Pascal, Blaise, 59, 162n120
Pascoli, Giovanni, 167n51
Patočka, Jan, x, 69, 164n168
Peck, Jason M., 154n57
Pfeiffer, Gabrielle, 53
Piana, Giovanni, 163n132
Pichois, Claude, 162n121
Pickford, Mary (Gladys Louise Smith), 111, 112, 142
Pinel, Philippe, 60
Plateau, Joseph, 21, 22
Plessner, Helmut, 78, 148, 165n192
Poe, Edgar Allan, ix, 3–4, 6, 8, 10, 12, 32, 91, 152nn2,5, 154n46
Pontecorvo, Gillo, 23, 24
Pontormo (Iacopo Carucci), 143
Porterfield, William, 18, 156n86
Poulet, Georges, 9, 85–86, 153n24, 166n21
Purkinje, Jan Evangelista, ix, 13, 14, 19, 25, 61, 89, 154nn52,59, 166n42

Quincey, Thomas de, 43

Rachilde (Marguerite Eyméry), 109, 170n16
Raimann, Johann Nepomuk von, 10, 153n36
Ramazzini, Bernardino, 17, 155n80
Ramskill, Jabez Spence, 19
Ravaisson, Félix, 35, 36, 138
Reik, Theodor, 16
Renouvier, Charles, 11–12, 88–90, 93, 101, 106, 129, 134, 153nn40–42, 166nn39–41
Reynaud, Charles-Émile, 21
Richir, Marc, 64, 68, 75, 163n146, 164nn163, 165
Richter, Emil (Germanicus), 17
Ricoeur, Paul, 37, 40, 58, 68, 71, 103, 140, 159n20, 162n115, 164nn162,173, 168n74
Riegl, Alois, xi, 131–133
Rimbaud, Arthur, ix, xiii, 27, 39
Riva, Emmanuelle, 23
Rivette, Jacques, 23, 156nn104,106
Rivière, Lazare, 6, 152n17
Rodenbach, Georges, 4, 9, 44, 79, 80, 81, 141, 160n47, 161n66, 165nn2–3, 6, 9–11, 174n15, 175nn36–37
Rohmer, Éric, 4, 9, 26, 79, 133, 156n106, 157n114, 165n1, 173n95
Rothacker, Erich, 96
Rothman, William, 157n115

Sandras, Claude-Marie-Stanislaus, 20
Sartre, Jean-Paul, 10, 51–53, 74, 84, 87, 93, 102, 103, 108, 136–138, 161nn76–77, 82–85, 164n184, 165n13, 166nn31–36, 167nn55–56, 168n95, 169n10, 174nn21–27
Satta, Salvatore, 16, 155n70
Schefer, Jean-Louis, 160n48
Scheler, Max, 56, 74, 99, 113
Schellhammer, Günther Christoph, 18
Schnitzler, Arthur, 166n22
Schürmann, Reiner, 121, 123
Sidis, Boris, 104, 169n106
Signorelli, Luca (Luca d'Egidio di Ventura), 29–31
Simon, Max, 17, 19, 21, 24, 156nn93–96, 157n110
Simon, Paul-Max, 21, 156n97
Sonnenfels, Joseph von, 1–2
Souriau, Étienne, 37
Spitzer, Leo, xiii
Stahl, Georg Ernst, 60

Stein, Edith, x, 62, 114, 115, 165nn136–139, 170n8, 171n11
Stevenson, Robert L., 81, 165n7
Stewart, James, 3, 5, 6, 10, 25, 46, 48
Stewart, Thomas Grainger, 20
Stoichita, Victor Ieronim, 153n25
Strauss, Leo, 147, 176n2
Szilasi, Wilhelm, 35, 158n6

Tarde, Gabriel, 11, 88–90
Tatler, Benjamin W., 157n113
Timpanaro, Sebastiano, 157n132
Tissot, Samuel-Auguste, 20
Towarnicki, Frédéric de, 36, 158n8
Trastour, Étienne, 18, 155n81
Trousseau, Armand, 19, 60, 156n89
Truffaut, François, 5, 8, 46, 49, 142, 152n11, 153nn27–28, 160nn39,59

Valéry, Paul, 138
Van der Leeuw, Gerardus, 160n43
Van Helmont, Jan Baptist, 19

Varchi, Benedetto, 138
Verlaine, Paul, 39
Virgil, 30, 31

Wade, Nicolas J., 156n87, 157n113
Waelhens, Adolphe de, 140
Wahl, Jean, 35, 36, 90, 119, 121, 123, 158nn5,12, 166n43, 171n20, 172n66, 174n20
Wallon, Henri-Paul-Hyacinthe, 92, 101, 160n36, 175n33
Weil, Simone, 16, 26, 155nn67–68, 168n94
Weill, Edmond, 20–21, 156n99, 159n35
Wells, William Charles, 18
Wepfer, Johann Jakob, 18, 155n84
Westphal, Karl Friedrich, 20
Wittgenstein, Ludwig, 37
Wolff, Christian, 114, 171n10
Worringer, Wilhelm, xi, 131, 132, 174n8

Zellenka, Hans (K.), 33
Ziegler, Jean, 162n121

ANDREA CAVALLETTI teaches philosophy at the University of Verona. He is the author of five books in Italian, translated into several languages, including *Class* (Seagull Books, 2019).

MAX MATUKHIN is a doctoral student in comparative literature at Princeton University.

DANIEL HELLER-ROAZEN is Arthur W. Marks '19 Professor of Comparative Literature and the Council of the Humanities at Princeton University. His books include *Absentees: On Variously Missing Persons* (2021) and *The Inner Touch: Archaeology of a Sensation* (2007), winner, the Aldo and Jeanne Scaglione Prize for Comparative Literary Studies.

www.ingramcontent.com/pod-product-compliance
Lightning Source LLC
Chambersburg PA
CBHW032035290426
44110CB00012B/812